Global Health
and
Social
Murder
JULY 4, 2026

CHRIS SIMMS PhD

Global Health

and

Social

Murder

JULY 4, 2026

Chris Simms, PhD

Global Health and Social Murder
July 4, 2026
1st edition, September 2025 © 2025 Christopher Simms.

Mill Cove Publishing
Halifax, NS Canada
Global Health & Social Murder: July 4 2026
ISBN 978-1-7388626-4-1 (paperback)
ISBN 978-1-7388626-5-8 (e-book)

Table of Contents

Part Two: Social Murder in the Time of Pandemic

Part Three: Social Murder: Inequalities and Human Rights

Part Four: Lessons

"A phenomenon noticeable throughout history regardless of place or period is the pursuit by governments of policies contrary to their own interests.
—**Barbara Tuchman, March of Folly**

Acknowledgements

The author wishes to acknowledge the input of Rebecca Visser, Mary Myketyn-Driscoll, and Cameron Yetman in the preparation of this reader. Without their contributions it is uncertain whether this work would have seen the light of day. Any errors or omissions remain the responsibility of the author.

PREFACE

This collection is about "social murder" and "crimes against humanity". It's also about dehumanization, the mental loophole that enables us to ignore or harm others. I've appended the subtitle "*July 4, 2026*" to an already evocative title to underscore a grim reality: as Americans prepare for the 250th anniversary of the Declaration of Independence, they are sleepwalking through full-on state oppression and authoritarianism.

Throughout 2025, President Donald Trump "flooded the zone" with orders and utterances that upended Washington and the world order, increasing—not decreasing—the reach of government. Although many of these actions reflect ideas from the MAGA movement and Project 2025, recognizing the influence of the neo-reactionary movement (NRx) that permeates his administration may provide a better understanding of Trump's agenda and its dangers around the world. Far-right neo-reactionaries are antidemocratic and antiegalitarian and intent on dismantling what they perceive as collusion among progressive elements in society: academia, mainstream media, the justice system, the administrative state, and the scientific community.

Over the last two decades, the far-right has spread globally. It emerged from disillusionment with traditional conservatism during the George W. Bush era, fueled by the Iraq War, the Great Recession, the decline of neo-liberalism, the collapse of globalization, and backlash against environmentalism, COVID-19 mandates, and so-called "woke" culture.

I have chronicled these crises over the past 20 years as they unfolded – and am now publishing some of these observations in the hope they provide insight into how we got here and where we may be headed.

This reader is dedicated to my parents, brothers and sisters, and extended family - especially to my children, James and Samantha, my inspiration. I also wish to acknowledge the influence of Herman Newman, [1] David E. Bell,[2] and Reginald H. Green,[3] who opened my eyes and offered direction. Their stories are about the dark days of 1930s Europe, displacement and exile, McCarthyism, the Vietnam War, apartheid, financial crises, and terrorism.

As I wind down these days, time feels compressed. On my desk sits a photo of me with my grandfather (born in 1864) and another with my children (born in 2001 and 2004). Together, their lifespans will likely exceed 225 years—spanning from pre-Confederation Canada, before the end of U.S. slavery and the "Scramble for Africa," to today's nihilism, and an unknowable future for both the planet and its inhabitants.

---

[1] Herman Newman was a survivor of Auschwitz and Dachau, rehabilitated in British hospitals, he then came to Halifax, Canada in 19

[2] https://news.harvard.edu/gazette/story/2000/09/economist-david-bell-dies-at-81/

[3] https://opendocs.ids.ac.uk/opendocs/handle/20.500.12413/4256

PROLOGUE:
From Past to Present

Neither bacteria, viruses nor pandemics have 'intelligence', nevertheless, they seem clever, crafty, and often deceitful. Likewise, the climate crisis, immigration crisis, terrorism, genocide, trade wars, and far-right extremism appear to have a life of their own. They exhibit distinct structures, functions, histories and above all, are exquisitely opportunistic. And nothing creates opportunity better than bad leadership and inequalities.

Decades of predatory and weak leadership in both the public and private sectors, combined with economic and social disparities have contributed to what is sometimes called, a "polycrisis" – a dense network of causally interconnected crises, that in 2025 has humankind in chaos and the planet hurtling towards a tipping point.

Three ideologies, neoliberalism, neoconservatism, and the neo-reactionary movement (NRx) are relevant to a discussion of social murder and crimes against humanity - the failures of the first two helping to set the stage for the rise of the third.[4]

---

[4] For a discussion of relationship between MAGA and the tech-elites see https://www.washingtonpost.com/technology/2025/06/08/trump-musk-tech-industry-profitable/

***

Neoliberal Hawks Former World Bank economics guru, US Treasury Secretary, President of Harvard, and OpenAI's "man-to-the-rescue", Lawrence Summers said of the polycrisis, "This is the most complex, disparate and cross-cutting set of challenges that I can remember in the 40 years that I have been paying attention to such things.[5]"

Summers would know. A neoliberal hawk he is somewhat of a cult figure (cited in an episode of *The Simpsons*, as well as the movies *The Social Network* and *Inside Job*). At the World Bank, to his credit, he crusaded for investments in girls education in low- and middle-income countries. However, he also spearheaded the imposition of harsh neoliberal economic policies in the early 1990s. These policies, lacking protections for the vulnerable, contributed to many deaths globally - a phenomenon described in this reader as "social murder".

While at the US Treasury, Summers and like-minded colleagues such as Robert Rubin, and Alan Greenspan were at the center of the Great Recession (2008-09) that still reverberates in 2025. For example, despite warnings of wide-spread chaos, Summers led the fight against regulation of financial derivatives and campaigned for bank deregulation. The ensuing financial crisis triggered a host of social, economic and political crises costing trillions of dollars and affecting the lives and livelihoods of millions of people. The failure of neoliberalism contributed to the rise of populism,[6] post-neoliberalism and today, the emergence of the far-right.

---

[5] https://www.bankingsupervision.europa.eu/press/speeches/date/2024/html/ssm. sp241104~e6126e18d5.en.html

[6] The recession fueled right-wing populism. Across developed economies, ordinary people watched in disbelief as governments bailed out financial institutions—handing out $32 billion in executive bonuses—while they endured severe hardship. Their anger grew amid a cultural backlash against shifting traditional values, driven by self-expression movements (such as those advocating for LGBTQ rights, racial justice, and religious tolerance) and large-scale immigration.

Neoconservative Hawks In the late 1990s, geopolitical events fell under the sway of another type of extremist - neoconservative hawks who favored a foreign interventionist policy and the idea of achieving peace through military strength. Most notable was the Project for the New American Century (PNAC), a Washington-based right-wing think-tank that came to dominate the Bush administration. Their top priority was regime change in Iraq and 9/11 provided the "opportunity". Despite world-wide protest and warnings from national security, military and international law experts, Iraq was invaded in 2003. This decision spawned a network of long-lasting crises - the rise of Iran, new forms of Islamic radicalism, years of conflict and terrorism, democratic backsliding and the emergence of extremists.

Neo-reactionary movement (NRx) The crises described in this collection exemplify the kind of leadership that brought them about – one that privileges the present over the future, the rich over the poor, and the powerful over the powerless.

Yet none of this is enough for those who believe 'might is right' and "more" is possible. Although Trump's disruptions of Washington and the global order are reflective of the MAGA agenda, Project 2025 and the expectations of his base, they are perhaps more comprehensible when considered through the lens of the neo-reactionary movement (NRx) that now permeates his administration. NRx stems from the work of political philosopher Nick Land, and Curtis Yarvin, a neo-reactionary blogger (and Silicon Valley Prophet), funded by tech elites, such as Peter Thiel.

Described by the *Financial Times* as a strange and disturbing political philosophy,[7] NRx is a pro-tech movement that envisions states run with business-like efficiency, led by a dictator or king - monikers Trump ascribes to himself. Once on the fringes, it is linked to Elon Musk (who

[7] https://www.ft.com/content/02217acf-ac64-49c2-acd5-ef4f107f014c

co-founded PayPal with Thiel), JD Vance, Michael Anton (Director of Policy Planning), Steven Miller Deputy Chief of Staff, and a "revolutionary vanguard" of conservatives in the White House that grew up reading Yarvin's blogs.[8] A DOGE advisor told the Washington Post that it was "an open secret that everyone in policymaking roles has read Yarvin.[9]"

NRx regards democracy as an outmoded conceit incompatible with liberty. It is anti-egalitarian, antihumanitarian, and committed to deconstructing the administrative state. The neo-reactionary movement aims to dismantle what it calls "the cathedral", defined as a collusion of academia, mainstream media and democratic institutions that, in its view, drives a misguided progressive agenda of equality, justice and redistribution based on the premise that people are equal. The neo-reactionaries are anti-woke and assert that there are societal hierarchies based on race, ethnicity, and gender — and vow a return to this "natural order". Yarvin, for instance, links race to IQ and describes slavery "a natural human relationship".[10][11]

The presence of neo-reactionary ideals in Trump's administration is evident in his efforts to concentrate power in the executive branch, his contentious cabinet selections, and his policies: cuts to the federal civil service (DOGE), elimination of EDI programs, reductions in social security, attacks on press freedom and academia, deportation without due process, and a disregard for the judiciary. These actions are often carried out with striking nonchalance. For instance, the once-influential Musk tweeted (February 3, 2025) that he could have attended a party but instead "spent the weekend putting USAID in the woodchipper.[12]" Russell Vought, co-lead author of Project 2025 and head of the Office of Management and Budget said, "We want the bureaucrats to be

---

[8]   https://www.politico.com/news/magazine/2025/01/30/curtis-yarvins-ideas-00201552

[9]   https://www.washingtonpost.com/politics/2025/05/08/curtis-yarvin-doge-musk-thiel/

[10]   https://www.thenation.com/article/politics/curtis-yarvin/

[11]   https://www.platformspace.net/home/nrx-a-brief-guide-for-the-perplexed

[12]   https://x.com/elonmusk/status/1886307316804263979

traumatically affected…We want to put them in trauma".[13] He succeeded. In the Spring of 2024 Yarvin proposed expelling all Palestinians from the Gaza Strip and turning it into a beachfront luxury resort with Jared Kushner as developer – a set of ideas nearly identical to Trump's "Riviera of the Middle East".[14]

Vance's behavior—berating President Zelensky in the White House, lecturing European allies on democracy, and embracing Germany's far-right, Nazi-curious AfD—exemplifies this trend. The rise of JD Vance underscores public concerns about NRx. He adopted what critics describe as his "weird and terrifying techno-authoritarian ideas" from his friend Yarvin, while his political ascent was bankrolled by a network of tech billionaires, including Thiel.[15] These financiers supported his Senate campaign and lobbied Trump to select him as his running mate. Commentators warn that Vance's rise marks "a significant, unsettling turn in American politics, reflecting the mainstreaming of neo-reactionary ideologies."[16] In the eyes of some, Vance is the likely successor to Trump.[17]

At Trump's January 20, 2025, inauguration, the front row of the crowded Rotunda was reserved for tech billionaires like Bezos, Cook, Zuckerberg, and Musk, while cabinet members were relegated to the second and third tiers.[18] Yet, during the inaugural weekend's glitzy gala at Coronation Hall—a celebration of the neo-conservative elite's ascent—Yarvin was the unofficial guest of honor.[19]

---

[13] https://www.youtube.com/watch?v=oBH9TmeJN_M On May 20, 2025, the Washington Post reports that fired are indeed traumatized. See https://www.washingtonpost.com/investigations/2025/05/20/federal-workers-trump-mental-health/

[14] https://www.newyorker.com/magazine/2025/06/09/curtis-yarvin-profile

[15] https://newrepublic.com/article/183971/jd-vance-weird-terrifying-techno-authoritarian-ideas

[16] https://www.platformspace.net/home/nrx-a-brief-guide-for-the-perplexed

[17] https://www.youtube.com/watch?v=KtNiiCMW5vc&t=8s

[18] https://vp.nyt.com/video/2025/01/20/132802_1_20vid-photo-id-inauguration-71852_wg_1080p.mp4

[19] https://www.politico.com/news/magazine/2025/01/30/curtis-yarvins-ideas-00201552

***

The Over-reach of a Maximalist Government As 2025 draws to a close, Donald Trump is—for now—taking a victory lap following what he perceives as wins over universities, the corporate media, the judiciary, the administrative state, the scientific community, and on tariffs. His incursions into California, his takeover of Washington, and his ventures into state capitalism are all part of his quest to become the CEO of everything before him—a strategy that evokes Yarvin's NRx playbook: "It wouldn't be unlawful; you would simply declare a state of emergency" or just claim national security.[20] Yet, the "dark enlightenment" looms over a landscape where democracy is no longer strong enough to stop autocracy.

---

[20]   https://www.vox.com/policy-and-politics/23373795/curtis-yarvin-neoreaction-red-pill-moldbug

Introduction

This reader presents *prima facie* evidence that acts of "social murder" and "crimes against humanity" have contributed to - or resulted from - the polycrisis which in turn, has demonstrably worsen the prospects for human and planetary health.

To begin with, social murder refers to the foreseeable and avoidable premature deaths caused by the deliberate and structural exposure of people to high-risk conditions—whether through acts of omission or commission. This concept gained traction in the early 2000s amid rising inequality and the emergence of multiple crises. Examples include implementation of indiscriminate austerity measures, deregulation, privatization, failure to mitigate or adapt to the climate crisis, and weak responses to COVID-19 and other pandemics.

The Grenfell Tower fire in London, England, is often cited as an instance of social murder, but the term also encompasses other public policy failures related to the social determinants of health. Experts warn that Trump administration's shutdown of USAID could cost 14 million lives by 2030.[21] Similarly, reductions in U.S. health infrastructure, life science research and innovation will lead to foreseeable and avoidable deaths of many Americans. Likewise, the July 4th passage of the "big, beautiful budget" means 11.8

---

[21] https://www.thelancet.com/journals/lancet/article/PIIS0140-6736(25)01186-9/fulltext

million adults and children risk losing access to healthcare—outcomes that ought to be labeled as "social murder."

In addition to social murder, this reader examines "crimes against humanity", acts that are "committed as part of a widespread or systematic attack directed against any civilian population" such as forcible transfer of population, extermination and persecution. It also cites examples of war crimes, acts of genocide and genocide.[22]

Articles in this collection are drawn from publications that I produced over two decades. About half of these have appeared in *The Lancet* or the *BMJ* in various forms but mainly as opinion pieces. Others come from publications supported by NGOs such as Christian Aid, Action Aid, and Save the Children. Others have been published in *The Guardian* (UK) newspaper, the Institute of Development Studies' (UK), *Working Papers* and journals such as the *International Journal of Clinical Practice*, the *Canadian Medical Association Journal* (CMAJ), *Canadian Journal of Public Health, New England Journal of Medicine*, and the *American Psychologist*.

The reader is divided into five parts. Part One provides *prima facie* evidence of social murder and crimes against humanity across a range of topics - from immigration policies, deportation, and forcible transfer of population to torture, war, pandemics, austerity, deregulation, and ecocide. Part Two examines epidemics and pandemics in the context of social murder. Part Three explores the relationship between inequalities, and leadership and acts of social murder while Part Four focuses on lessons learned and identifies potential paths forward. Part Five consists primarily of perception data—the «voices» of members of the international donor community (expats) whom I interviewed and consulted while working in countries such as Tanzania, Zambia, Kenya, Madagascar, and Senegal. This section aims to provide insight into the thoughts, words, and actions of often conflicted individuals tasked with implementing unjust policies they may or may not have agreed with—a dilemma relevant in 2025 as neo-reactionaries target people forced to either resist or submit.

---

[22] https://www.usip.org/sites/default/files/MC1/MC1-Part2Section1.pdf

PART ONE:
Acts of Omission and Commission

PART ONE:
ACTS OF OMISSION AND COMMISSION

Most at risk of social murder and crimes against humanity are vulnerable populations: people typically without the power to control the things that matter most in their lives. President Trump's second term sometimes called "Trump Unrestrained", has made the world's vulnerable more vulnerable and increased their numbers.

Part One comprises 22 articles, beginning with a short *Lancet* (2025) piece which examines Trump's dismissal of scientific evidence during COVID-19 which killed 1.2 Americans. It asks whether, with his appointment of RFK Jr, he is again rejecting science and creating a pathway for disease spread – a worthy question as measles cases hit record highs in the summer of 2025. In a similar vein, a *Times of Israel* (2025) piece briefly reviews five global crises where again, evidence of impending danger was ignored.

Many readings in Part One explore a world where some voices are valued less than others and, more broadly, where some people belong and others do not. The worldwide proliferation of national border walls and fences since 2000 serves as a metaphor for defining who belongs and for rising levels white nationalism, ethnic nationalism, populism or anti-migration sentiments. Far-right rhetoric inflames these divisions such Trump's description of migrants as "animals" or his claim that "there are a lot of bad genes" in the U.S., or Michael Anton's (U.S. Director of Policy Planning at the State Department) assertion that "'Diversity' is not 'our strength'; it's a source of weakness, tension, and disunion."

With the walls and rhetoric come policies and programs that appear designed to threaten, deter, and inflict suffering. Sometimes, cruelty is the point. Stephen Miller reportedly the most powerful actor in the White House, has taken a maximalist position on immigration (including ICE raids, using the Alien Enemies Act and threatening to suspend *habeas corpus*). Trump's immigration and deportation policies are, in the eyes of some, a "crime against humanity"[23] and a violation of US and international law.[24] Trump's response to accusations of extraconstitutional leanings is "He who saves his country does not violate any law."[25]

Britain too, has a long history of xenophobia and cruel anti-immigration initiatives. Prime Minister Starmer warned in May 2025, the country risked becoming "an island of strangers" (an unworthy comment he soon retracted). A decade earlier, Britain's *hostile environment* ("Go Home") policy, its treatment of the "Windrush generation, Brexit, and Rwanda policy, have been variously described as "state crimes", breaches of international law [26] and, "worse than a crime, a mistake". Several readings address instances of "forced removals" and "population transfers" in other countries as crimes against humanity.[27]

---

[23] https://opiniojuris.org/2025/05/23/trumps-deportations-as-an-emerging-crime-against-humanity/

[24] https://www.genocidewatch.com/single-post/mass-deportations-violate-u-s-and-international-law

[25] https://www.nytimes.com/2025/04/08/us/supreme-court-trump-confrontation.html The justices' new approach appears to have multiple goals: to stay out of the political fray, to maintain their legitimacy and, perhaps most important, to avoid a showdown with a president who has relentlessly challenged the legitimacy of the courts.

[26] https://www.opendemocracy.net/en/beyond-trafficking-and-slavery/is-johnsons-rwanda-plan-a-crime-against-humanity/

[27] https://sencanada.ca/en/newsroom/ridr-cruel-and-unusual-as-draconian-solitary-confinement-continues-corrections-minister-and-government-fail-to-heed-sen-

In contrast to the US and UK, Canada is seen as a global leader in welcoming newcomers. Yet at the micro level, walls serve as a metaphor for Canada's mistreatment of Indigenous peoples—embodied by prison walls, cells, and walls of solitary confinement. Canadian prisons too often violate the United Nations Mandela Rules, which prohibit prolonged solitary confinement—a practice considered torture and a crime against humanity.

Two-thirds of Indigenous prisoners have endured solitary confinement and, at any given point in time, they represent 50% of the solitary confined population.[28] Levels of self-harm and suicide correlate with these figures.

Several articles examine how austerity measures lead to foreseeable and avoidable premature deaths In the UK for instance, deep cuts were associated with an additional 335,000 deaths and have been repeatedly described as social murder.[29] Elsewhere, the British Medical Journal (BMJ) refers to austerity as "COVID's little helper". Several readings point to the link climate crisis and austerity – which may be pertinent to the July 2025 floods in Texas. These readings show the consequences of deregulation, regulatory failure and downsizing the administrative state. In March 2025, EPA Director Lee Zeldin for example, enacted sweeping deregulation, declaring, "We are driving a dagger straight through the heart of the climate change religion." By the end of July, Zeldin said he would revoke the scientific determination that "planet-warming greenhouse gases are a threat to public health".[30]

This section concludes with an examination of the 2003 Iraq War and the Israel-US/Gaza conflict. The two share commonalities: both were

---

ate-committee-recommendations/

[28] https://policyoptions.irpp.org/magazines/january-2022/the-use-of-solitary-confinement-continues-in-canada/

[29] https://policyoptions.irpp.org/magazines/january-2022/the-use-of-solitary-confinement-continues-in-canada/

[30] https://www.nytimes.com/2025/07/29/climate/epa-endangerment-finding-repeal-proposal.html

driven by extreme right-wing conservatives who seized the opportunity to act on long-standing agendas. Both are associated with war crimes, high number of civilian deaths—particularly among children—and the deliberate undercounting of those deaths, and the failure of media to provide unbiased reporting.

Is Trump again preparing a pathway for disease spread?

Chris Simms[31] Lancet February 2025

The World Health Organization (WHO) recently issued a statement imploring the global community to end its "collective amnesia" over COVID-19. According to psychiatrists and cognitive psychologists, "collective amnesia" may signal unprocessed trauma and can be a useful coping mechanism for "forgetting" bad memories.

However, there is another type of "collective amnesia" which occurs when collective memories are shaped by people and processes that promote memory ignorance and denial of historic or scientific facts, and these can lead to epistemic injustice. During the 2024 presidential election campaign, Mr. Trump repeatedly claimed "we did a phenomenal job with the pandemic" a claim that persists in his personal website. Despite 1.2 million American deaths, the most of any country, Trump gets little pushback on his false claims—this from a population burdened by "Covid amnesia", "lockdown fatigue" and "move-on" politics.

Rather than doing a "phenomenal job", evidence shows that prior to January 2020, the Trump administration made a series of decisions that may have meant the US lost the opportunity to tackle the outbreak early on and instead, helped clear a pathway for its spread—the implication being that it may have contributed 100s of thousands avoidable US deaths and a portion of the 7.2 million deaths worldwide–or worse still, the outbreak could have been confined to a crisis not a tragedy.

Among the most consequential decisions were those informed by Trump's scepticism of all facets of US relations with China including

---

[31] https://www.thelancet.com/journals/lanam/article/PIIS2667-193X(25)00003-1/fulltext

CDC's very presence in China. During the period 2018–19, 70% of CDC's staff in its China office were cut, despite more than 30 years of successful collaboration. One US official who worked in the China office at the time of the cuts said, "the CDC office in Beijing is a shell of its former self". A former US embassy official in China said the cuts "left only a skeleton staff in place, and the US government without the eyes and ears on the ground". In July 2019, Dr. Linda Quick, a renowned expert in identifying emergent diseases was removed from her job.A former CDC official who held a similar role from 2007 to 2011 commented, "If someone had been there, public health officials and governments worldwide could have acted much more swiftly."A critical error was the Trump administration ending cabinet-level dialogue with China (that existed during the Bush and Obama years) which allowed heads of health security to connect. When the crisis hit, the US had few points of contact to fathom what was happening.

In 2017, the US was the best placed country (other than China) to avert a global pandemic first, because CDC correctly identified China as presenting a unique disease threat and second, it focused its health investments on "high-leverage intervention points" to prevent, detect, report, and respond to an outbreak.

Not today. Over the last four years, Trump has exerted his influence on an obsequious Republican party to politize public health to levels detrimental to the next four years. This is reflected in the (Republican-dominated) Select Subcommittee Report on the pandemic (December 4th, 2024) which concludes that "masks and mask mandates were ineffective at controlling the spread of COVID-19," that "unscientific lockdowns caused more harm than good" and "Covid-19 vaccine mandates caused massive collateral damage and were very likely counterproductive." It is seen in the nomination of John F. Kennedy Jr as head of Health and Human Services (HHS) together with a team of vaccine contrarians. It is reflected in recent efforts to revoke FDA approval of the polio vaccine (December 13th, 2024) and in a Gallup poll showing only 26% of Republicans and Republican-leaners (half as many as in 2019) believe it is extremely important for parents to get their children vaccinated.

Coincidentally, on the same day Trump announced Kennedy's nomination (November 14, 2024), the CDC published an article in its *Morbidity and Mortality Weekly Report* on a 2023 measles outbreak in Samoa. It began with a description of the infamous 2019 measles outbreak that resulted in 6000 cases and more than 80 deaths, a tragedy associated with Mr. Kennedy›s visit to the island and his sharing of antivaccination misinformation locally. Writes one chronicler, "I'll never forget what Kennedy did during Samoa›s measles outbreak".

In a country where 40% of COVID-19 deaths were reportedly vaccine-preventable, adopting an anti-science, conspiracy-style approach to public health risks enabling another fatal pandemic. For a traumatised population, "collective amnesia" may be a healthy coping mechanism but it is unhealthy for making public policy. For political leadership to engage in "collective amnesia" by both creating a false narrative and prescribing a ludicrous way forward, does an injustice to millions of Americans who suffered the coronavirus and to those who may succumb to the next outbreak.

Warnings Gone Unheeded

The Times of Israel, January 2025[32]

Chris Simms

———◆———

In the months leading up to the October 7 massacre, repeated warnings from female border soldiers about suspicious Hamas activity were ignored by their superiors. According to Anat Peled, reporting in the *Wall Street Journal,* the soldiers' observations were dismissed since the Israeli security services considered Hamas to be tamed and, the soldiers, who were at the bottom of the IDF hierarchy, were not taken seriously because they were women.

Review of important global crises reveals similar patterns, where women raise alarms about impending dangers based on information that contradicts conventional wisdom. They are often met with condescension, labeled as overly emotional, panicky, or alarmist and their concerns therefore dismissed, ignored, or even met with anger and aggression.

One example of this occurred on August 6, 2001, when a President's Daily Brief (PDB) titled "Bin Laden Determined to Strike in US" was presented to George W. Bush. The PDB was prepared by members of a small group of women CIA analysts known as the "Sisterhood," "the girls," or disparagingly as, "a bunch of chicks". It warned of "suspicious activity," referenced the World Trade Center, plane hijackings, and the presence of al-Qaeda operatives in the U.S. These women, the first to identify and track the rise of Osama bin Laden and al-Qaeda, struggled to have their voices heard and when they did, it was often a sexist response. After meeting with one analyst, CIA Director George Tenet

---

[32] https://blogs.timesofisrael.com/warnings-gone-unheeded/

described her as "a woman quivering with emotion." The White House considered the PDB "historical reporting of old data" and left it like a letter unopened and unanswered.

Another example concerns the efforts of Brookley E. Born to secure regulation of over-the-counter derivatives, particularly "swaps" that contributed to the Great Recession. In 1998, as head of the Commodity Futures Trading Commission (CFTC), she appeared before Congress to warn that the ballooning derivatives market "threatens our economy without any federal agency knowing about it." She faced strong opposition from Larry Summers and Alan Greenspan, who told Congress there was "no clear evidence" to support the proposed regulation. According to many commentators, Summers, known as the enforcer, "ran over" Born and "shouted her down". Born said Summers' stridency "made me very suspicious and troubled." One CFTC colleague remarked that Born was seen as "someone they could flick off their hand like a fly." In 1999, Congress stripped the CFTC of any authority to regulate derivatives, and Born resigned.

Two compelling examples, particularly when considered together, are the stories of Dr. Nancy Messonnier and Dr. Rachel Carson. On February 25, 2020, Dr. Messonnier became the first high-ranking U.S. official to warn that coronavirus would upend American life. In contradiction to Trump's claim two days earlier that "This is very much under control," she stated at a media briefing on COVID-19 that, "It's not so much a question of if (community spread) will happen anymore, but rather more a question of exactly when." The next day Trump said, "Within a couple of days, it's going to be down to close to zero." However, he was enraged by Dr. Messonnier's warning, and demanded her firing, evoking for many his catchphrase, "You're fired! Get out!" She was promptly removed from public briefings on COVID-19, reassigned to another role in April, and was persuaded to resign in May.

Decades earlier, Dr. Rachel Carson published her landmark book *Silent Spring* (1962), which warned of the indiscriminate use of pesticides, particularly DDT. She faced intense personal and professional criticism from the chemical manufacturing industry, public officials, and parts of the media, including *Time* and *U.S. News & World Report*. *Time* described her as "hysterically over-emphatic," and dismissed the book as an "emotional and inaccurate outburst." In contrast to today, the 1960s were considered a golden era for science, and Carson received broad support from the scientific community, President Kennedy and the American public. Her book led to a decade of environmental legislative initiatives and the establishment of the EPA in 1970.

In the aftermath, Born (who won the JFK Profile in Courage award) was described as "the hero of the Great Recession", the CIA analysts as "the women who saw 9/11 coming", Messonnier, the "truth teller" and Rachel Carson, "the mother of the environmental movement". How many lives and livelihoods could have been saved had sense and science prevailed, had gender not been an added issue? As to the parents of the *tatzpitaniyot, the* killed and captured, they also are asking.

Trump 1.0 and 2.0 "Get out, stay out"
The Rise of Walls and the Decline of Values: From Trump to Calais

Lancet, November 2016[33]

Walls as metaphor This article was published in November 2016, coinciding with Donald Trump's election. It was written with him and his campaign refrain, "Build that wall, build that wall" in mind. In 2025, with the immigrant detentions, disappearances and deportations, it seems especially relevant. I introduce 'walls' as a metaphor for the way they separate, for those they keep out or keep in, in the way they are built (perhaps representing the gradual accumulation of resentment) or suddenly rise up (flare up) over-night and for the way they frighten and cause despair or obstruct our view of deeper problems. They symbolize the fear and resentment that permeate a fractured global community in crisis. Walls suggest failure, a reaction to the consequences of not planning ahead, of failing to mitigate and adjust to risks that gave rise to the walls in the first place.

◆

Breaking down walls, removing barriers, and opening pathways for cooperation and collaboration have long been at the core of international and global health – at least conceptually. Resistance to these goals and their underlying values has typically been ideologically or economically driven, reflecting the self-interest of powerful actors. However, the obstructions these actors create have never been as conspicuous, widespread, symbolic, or impactful as they are today.

The figure shows the number of walls and fences erected on national borders during the period 1945-2015. It depicts a modest increase from 1945 until 1989 when the Berlin Wall came down and then shows a sharp rise, especially over the last 15 years. Many of the nearly 70 walls have been built recently in Europe where countries are attempting to cope with a profound

---

[33] For access to the original article and footnotes, see tiny.cc/RiseOfWall

immigration crisis in which millions of people are on the move. Interestingly, the graphic representation of these trends actually conjures up the image of a bolstered wall.

The refugee crisis in Europe, the building of the wall in Calais, the dismantlement of the so-called "jungle" refugee camp and the plight of its children, have drawn global attention. Walls have become a metaphor for fear and resentment and for the overarching paradox that, while the global community is more interconnected than ever, it is becoming increasingly fragmented A particularly disturbing aspect of these trends is the anti-migrant, anti-Muslim, anti-ethnic rhetoric that accompanies them. This is perhaps epitomized in the speeches of Donald Trump (Republican nominee in the US presidential elections to be held November 8). A video shows Trump exhorting thousands of supporters with a refrain – "build that wall, build that wall" – evocative of scenes from the darkest days of 20th century Europe.[34]

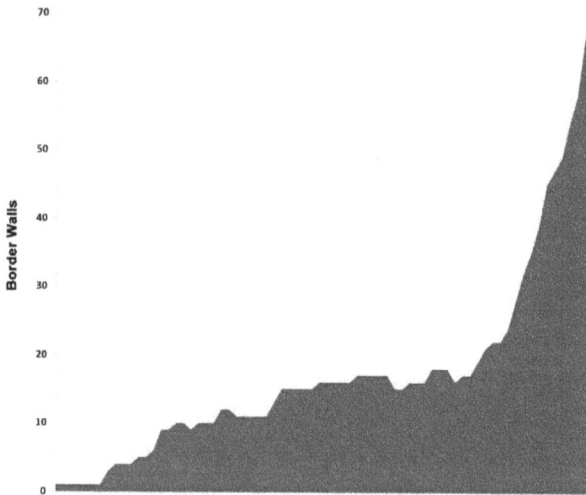

Fig. 1. Source: Update by Élisabeth Vallet, Zoé Barry, and Josselyn Guillarmou of statistics included in Élisabeth Vallet, ed., Borders, Fences and Walls: State of Insecurity? (Farnham, UK: Ashgate Publishing, 2014).

---

[34] https://www.youtube.com/watch?v=cBW8mTHDgvk

The plight of migrants and chaos along national borders appearing daily in the media is in sharp contrast to the vision and values of international and global health as originally conceived. For instance, Halfdan Mahler, Director-General of WHO during 1973-88 and who ushered in the Declaration of Alma Alta (1978) on primary health care (PHC), described the 1970s as a "warm decade of social justice". PHC envisioned removal of the barriers between health facility and the populations it served by focusing on simple and inexpensive interventions at the village level (essentially patient- or family-centred care).

For Igogwe Hospital, a 100-bed facility in the southern highlands of Tanzania, the adoption of PHC in the 1980s literally meant the removal barriers from the hospital compound and sending health workers out into the villages where they developed and strengthened a network of rural health centres, maternal and child health clinics, and mobile services. When HIV/AIDS hit hard, Igogwe had a range of initiatives a full 10 years before the international donor community.

Yet rural hospitals like Igogwe were the exception. Halfdan Mahler, recalls that when the International Monetary Fund and World Bank interposed their policies of structural adjustment and health reform, they created barriers to access as real as bricks and mortar. For the world's poorest, the 1990s became known as the lost decade.

The Consortium of Universities for Global Health distinguishes global health from international health, stating that the former refers to "the scope of problems, not their location", that it parallels a shift "in philosophy and attitude that stresses the mutuality of real partnership", and aims for "health equity among nations and for all peoples" – that is, a more level playing field without barriers. While most donor countries embrace these values (including the European Union), it is typically left to the non-governmental organization community which, together with its southern partners, works with ordinary people, their families, and communities to address the detrimental impact of walls along borders. For example, Christian Aid issued "Breaking down the barriers", Action

Aid, "Protect people, not borders", while Doctors without Borders' vision and mission are self-evident.

Walls are often used as metaphor for the way they separate, for those they keep out or keep in, for the way they are built (perhaps representing the gradual accumulation of resentment) or suddenly rise up (flareup) overnight, for the way they frighten, cause despair, or obstruct our view of deeper problems. Some of these metaphorical allusions ought to resonate with the global community. From a health systems point of view (or from a Donabedian analysis perspective) a wall – in that it exists at all – tends to imply inadequate inputs, poor process, poor outcomes, and generally mass failure – a scar on the global landscape. In his final address to the UN in September, US President Barack Obama stated that these walls paradoxically imprisoned those who build them.

Trump 1.0 and 2.0 - Resistance
Trump and the Role of Data Driven Resistance in Global Health
BMJ Opinion, 2017[35]

Trump's rhetoric and actions in 2025 align with the concept of "competitive authoritarianism," where elected leaders who aspire to autocracy reward corrupt allies, intimidate the establishment, and attempt to crush resistance. Steven Levitsky, an expert in authoritarian leadership, states, "We're pretty much screwed... The concentration of political, economic, and media power here is staggering. To my knowledge, this has never been seen in a democracy. This is uncharted territory." He notes that during Trump's first term, the establishment did resist—a dynamic I explore in this article. I also examine Canadian Prime Minister Stephen Harper's efforts to suppress dissent.

———————◆———————

"Resistance" is an evocative term common to the natural and social sciences where it denotes the act of resisting, opposing, or withstanding. In the so-called hard sciences it is easily identified and measured. A physicist, for example, will gauge resistance in ohms; in medicine, the intrarenal arterial resistance index (RI) is used to calculate resistance to blood flow; and in microbiology, drug resistance is measured by levels of minimum inhibitory concentration (MIC).

However, in the behavioural sciences, resistance is more subjective and often carries a moral dimension. Where acts of political oppression or social injustice are involved, questions may arise as to who is the aggressor and who is the resistor, although both may lay claim to the latter. (For example, while both the apartheid South Africa backed Mozambique National Resistance Movement and Nelson Mandela's armed resistance

---

[35] For access to the original article and footnotes, see tiny.cc/GlobalHealthTrump

appropriated the appellation résistance, physician or human rights groups that monitored war crimes in the region had no difficulty distinguishing between the two.)

Given President Donald Trump's actions over the past fortnight and the reactions they have elicited, a discussion of "resistance" seems relevant. His executive order to ban nationals of seven Muslim majority countries from entering the US – detrimental to the wellbeing of 100 000 immigrants and refugees and their families – caused spontaneous demonstrations at home and abroad.

The Wall Street Journal objected to the ban, saying it was based on weak analysis of incomplete data. Resistance came from multiple quarters, including US diplomats, the US attorney general, civil rights groups, and, eventually, by the federal courts, which have stayed the ban nationwide, at least temporarily. Trump's response to the stay was to tweet "the opinion of this so called judge" is "ridiculous."

Resistance to Trump's muzzling of government scientists who might object to his aggressive energy policy and dismantlement of environmental protections has drawn less attention yet is especially relevant to global health. His administration has for now banned federally employed scientists from disseminating material, including information on climate change, telling them to decline calls from reporters and cancel media meetings.

In addition, the Centers for Disease Control and Prevention (CDC) felt compelled to cancel a long-planned conference on climate change and health scheduled for this month. The executive director of the American Public Health Association said of the cancellation of the meeting: "We can take this as a strategic retreat." And public health scientists in the US Department of Health and Human Services, also muzzled, are concerned that they will be unable to comment on the impact on ordinary people if Obamacare is repealed.

The scientific community has responded by creating "a resistance movement" on Twitter, while well respected journals such as *Nature* and *Science* have been strongly advocating against the anti-science, anti-intellectualism movement sweeping in. Professional associations for science writers and public health officials have reacted with what they call "a great push" – to inform and influence public opinion.

However, Canada's experience with a coalition of government and powerful resource extraction industries suggests that the effectiveness of resistance may be limited. Prime Minister Stephen Harper (200615) gutted environmental regulations and muzzled federal government scientists. Not only did his government restrict their publications and media releases, they also sent political aids to monitor government scientists' presentations at conferences.

One indicator of the disquieting effect this had was revealed by a survey of 4000 Canadian federal scientists, which showed that 90% felt they were not allowed to speak freely about their work with the media, and that if they possessed knowledge of a departmental decision that could harm public health, safety, or the environment, 86% felt they would encounter censure or retaliation for speaking to the media about it.

A public health issue that re-emerged last week, and which seems to capture the irrationality of the anti-science sentiment of the new government – as well as the populism on which it is based – is Trump's long held belief in a possible link between the vaccination for measles, mumps, and rubella (MMR) and autism. His support for anti-vaccine activists (anti-vaxxers) recently drew attention when Robert Kennedy (a campaigner against MMR) said that he would head up a committee for the Trump administration to investigate the link (although Trump's team later said that nothing had been decided).

With the number of measles outbreaks increasing globally (due in part to the autism scare), *Nature* said that "scientists must fight back with the truth about the debunked link." However, like populism, this idea attracts because it panders to those that dwell in the domain of losses, on their fear and anxiety, who are vulnerable to post-truth, "alternate facts," and prefer anecdotes and personal stories rather than scientific data. Not surprisingly, research into the psychological profile of anti-vaxxers is consistent with populist desires: a need to feel empowered and to reject authority, especially when imposed by big government programmes or regulations.

The ultimate worry for some observers is that these trends may threaten democratic processes. In the Canadian experience, Harper's response to resistance from First Nations groups, demonstrations, and legal actions taken by environmental and human rights NGOs was ruthless: employing police and tax revenue agencies to harass and intimidate. In the process, he diminished the country's international reputation, from which Canada is only now recovering.

This month the Trump administration begins a concerted effort to dismantle the rules and regulations of the oil and gas and banking industries set in place by Obama to protect the environment and avoid a reoccurrence of the 2008 Great Recession. With Trump's party controlling Congress, an effective judiciary becomes particularly important. It is in this context that the president's anti-science posture, along with his mocking of (what he called) "the so-called judge" who stayed the ban on Muslims, worries many observers. Pursuit of autocratic rule and demagoguery that benefits the very rich is not what the founding fathers of the United States had in mind – and it needs to be resisted in all quarters.

Africville

What matters in the lives of many Black Nova Scotians often takes place in their absence, in rooms they have no way of entering or, sometimes, no way of leaving.

———————◆———————

Halifax is highly ranked for its livability and quality of life, yet for some, it has been about street stops and police violence, solitary confinement, the consequences of forced transfers of populations, exclusion from everyday public goods and services, and denial of the ability to voice dissent.

Only since 2020 did the story of slavery in Nova Scotia come fully to the fore. Reassuring fables portraying Nova Scotia as a haven for enslaved people and freemen escaping the US in the 18th and 19th centuries have been upended by what was deliberately erased - that it was also home to slave owners and traders. Records show that enslaved people made up more than 10% of the Halifax population in the mid-18th century, that they were dispersed through all provincial counties where racist perspectives thrived across generations. For the next two centuries, to be Black meant for many (though not all) a half-hidden ancestry of slavery, re-enslavement, bondage, servitude, endless segregation, poverty, and unactionable human rights.

The outright suppression of this history of slavery by institutions and political agents including grade schools, high schools, universities, and the media is now a source of deep anger.[36] [37] States Senator Dr. Thomas Barnard, the "erasure of our full history, the denial of that full history causes tremendous pain, trauma, and in essence, a sense of not belonging, not truly belonging to this country."[38]

And no story captures the essence of systemic and structural racism in Nova Scotia better than the story of Africville. This close-knit, segregated Black community on the margins of Halifax, thrived for 150 years with its own stores, post-office, and school. Its church, Seaview United Baptist was the social and spiritual center of the community. Sitting on the shore of Bedford Basin, in the northeastern end of the city, the tract was long coveted by both public and private sectors. Although residents paid taxes, the community was denied city services such as water, sanitation, garbage disposal, paved roads, and streetlights, despite decades of pleas and petitions.[39] Each time a resident or group of residents sought and were denied any one of these basic public goods or services by City Hall, it was an "act", and the accumulation of such "acts" over decades did as much to define Halifax as it did Africville.

Africville is widely cited in Canada as a case study in extreme environmental racism. On land adjacent to the community, the city issued

---

[36] https://www.thestar.com/news/gta/why-the-black-struggle-in-canada-has-all-but-beenerased-two-historians-explain-our/article_3478537b-4ab0-5c1c-85bd-210dd0fd-2da0.html

[37] For example, Nova Scotia's Fortress Louisbourg, a National Historic Site that has attracted millions of visitors since the 1960s, was home to 381 slaves—a long-suppressed fact that could not have escaped the notice of the multitude of research teams, including historians, archaeologists, anthropologists, sociologists, and psychologists. Only in 2021 did Parks Canada acknowledge slavery by promising to add an exhibit in 2023. Activist Theresa Brewster said, "Although it may be painful to tell the story of what really happened, and about the slaves, it has to be told." https://www.cbc.ca/news/canada/nova-scotia/parks-canada-fortress-slavery-louisbourg-1.6281735

[38] https://www.cbc.ca/news/canada/nova-scotia/nova-scotia-first-emancipation-day-slavery-reparations-history-1.6122800

[39] The Halifax Regional Water Commission (HRWC) reports that in 1952, through fundamental restructuring, it "transformed the water supply system into a modern, efficient and financially sound operation" – it just did not include Black residents of Africville.

permits for a fertilizer plant, abattoir, tar factory, open garbage dump and an incinerator. The media played a significant role in public perceptions of Africville. When it became clear in the 1950s and 1960s that the city intended to forcibly relocate residents of Africville from their homes, the community was increasingly described as a slum. Even well-intentioned social reformers were duped or cajoled into lending support for the demolition of Africville. Alongside those motivated by greed, they ignored the vibrancy of a settled social community, and rather than make amends for past "crimes against humanity" instead, committed themselves to still another – the uprooting of the entire population and razing Africville to the ground.[40]

Iconic images of belongings being loaded onto city garbage trucks persist like the racism that explains them. However, the Nova Scotia Archives and the Halifax Municipal Archives which have thousands of photographs and digitalized records related to Africville, do not have a single photo of the bulldozing of the homes or the Church which was ploughed under in the dead of the night, November 20, 1967. It is as if eyes were averted from the crime. Although it's unlikely the city will ever sit comfortably with the Africville saga, it remains comfortable enough to reject compensation claims knowing this rejection sits well enough with those who curate public opinion.

Today, decades later, as if it hadn't missed a beat, Nova Scotia continues to be home to the largest, most segregated, and racially persecuted Black community in Canada. Racism is most conspicuous in the justice system. A report showing Blacks in Halifax are six times more likely to be street-checked than whites was met with the police response that "there was nothing to apologize for" - a stance that was reversed at the insistence of the provincial Department of Justice. A Washington Post article by Halifax activist and columnist El Jones (recipient of the

[40] When in Cape Town, South Africa, in 1992, I noted that the timeline of events in Africville (District 8) coincided with the forced removal of the population of District 6 in Cape Town due to the apartheid Group Areas Act. Other aspects of the population transfer were also similar.

Order of Canada 2023) entitled "Black Canadians are suffocating under a racist policing system too" said of racist policing in Halifax and other Canadian cities, "we have long had the boot on our necks as well".[41] YouTube videos showing excessive use of force towards outgroups,[42] especially Blacks, young[43] and old, male, and female[44] are too common. A recent CBC investigative report[45] found that allegations of racism against Halifax police were dismissed by supervisors who found not a single case of wrongdoing.[46]

Once "inside" the Canadian justice system, Black inmates face harsher treatment than whites, serve longer sentences and are seven times less likely obtain parole than whites.[47]Following the murder of George Floyd, the Premier felt compelled to publicly apologize to Black Nova Scotians; he stated, "our system of justice, from policing to the courts to corrections, has failed many members of our Black community. A system that is supposed to keep you safe, but because of the color of your skin, you fear it".[48] Since then, a damning Report by a group of Dalhousie Law Scholars focused on solitary confinement, implicated the entire justice system.[49] Being Black in solitary for months on end seems like another

41   https://www.washingtonpost.com/opinions/2020/06/04/black-canadians-are-suffocating-under-racist-policing-system-too/

42   https://www.cbc.ca/news/canada/nova-scotia/laurence-gary-basso-guilty-of-assaultingpatrice-simard-1.5172280

43   https://www.cbc.ca/news/canada/nova-scotia/officer-charged-with-assault-bedford-place-mall-arrest-1.5753734

44   https://www.cbc.ca/news/canada/nova-scotia/halifax-mother-walmart-arrest-santina-rao-court-1.5468752

45   https://www.cbc.ca/newsinteractives/features/police-stops-bias

46   A senior official at my university annually leads a session on racism for my graduate students. She tells them that she and other Black Nova Scotian parents need to have "the conversation" with their children early on to help them navigate a system that is mostly white and that can pose risks. .

47   https://www.oag-bvg.gc.ca/internet/English/parl_oag_202205_04_e_44036.html

48   https://www.cbc.ca/news/canada/nova-scotia/apology-justice-racism-nova-scotia-1.5742914

49   https://digitalcommons.schulichlaw.dal.ca/cgi/viewcontent.cgi?article=1044&context=reports

instance of segregation, of not belonging,[50] and serves as a reminder that much of what matters in the lives of Black Nova Scotians does take place in their absence, in rooms they have no way of entering or sometimes, no way of leaving.

---

[50]   https://wellnesswithinns.org/press-release-blog/2020/8/12/downey-and-gray-v-attorney-general-nova-scotia-may-represent-a-new-chapter-in-prisoners-rights-in-nova-scotia

Character is Destiny

The phrase "character is destiny" originates from the Greek philosopher Heraclitus and is meant to suggest character determines our fate, not external forces. I begin this article, "Africville", with the view that "much of what matters in the lives of many Black Nova Scotians takes place in their absence". In 2021, a Nova Scotia five-judge panel seemed to concur; it sentenced a Black Nova Scotian man to house arrest and probation instead of the two to three years of imprisonment sought by the Crown. Speaking for the panel, Judge Anne Derrick stated now is the time to consider the impact of culture and race in sentencing. The Crown, not unexpectedly, objected since it was only doing what it had always done – seeking and securing harsher treatment and longer sentences for Blacks. To ensure compliance, the Public Prosecutions Office set out detailed policy guidelines for Crown Attorneys entitled, "*Fair Treatment of African Nova Scotian and People of African Descent*", a training program on cultural competence beginning with what it means to be Black in Nova Scotia facing a racist justice system. As for Heraclitus' Greece, the destiny of 10% of its population was enslavement - about the same as mid-18th century Halifax.

United Kingdom: Get Out, Stay Out!
Biocitizenship and Forced Removals
Lancet, July 2018 [51]

A state crime and breach of international law In May 2025, British Prime Minister Kiers Starmer said "we risk becoming an island of strangers", echoing Enoch Powell's "rivers of blood" speech. This article describes the "Windrush Scandal", a draconian response by the British government to illegal immigration and to growing anti-immigration sentiments. [52] For Prime Ministers Cameron and May, the political advantages of appealing to British nativism and anti-immigration sentiments through "go home" and "hostile environment" policies outweighed the risk of evoking the British colonial history of slavery in the Caribbean and increasing racial tensions. Indeed, being caught in the act of wrongfully detaining, deporting, or failing to provide due compensation to victims even had a certain political advantage for the government. The deliberate act of creating anxiety for hundreds of thousands of British citizens – a sense of not belonging or never having belonged – was an egregious transgression of British values. Like Britain's Rwanda policy, it is seen by many as a "state crime" [53] and a breach of international law. [54]

———————◆———————

There are researchers, including in the global health sphere, who have an interest in how lack or loss of power gets into the body and causes physical illness and mental anguish.

---

51 For access to the original article and footnotes, see: tiny.cc/Biocitizenship

52 The Financial Times reports that more than 10,000 belonging to the so-called Windrush generation "suffered harassment by immigration authorities and other bodies, who denied them re-entry to the UK and refused them healthcare or barred them from jobs or accommodation".

53 https://thebscblog.wordpress.com/2021/07/07/windrush-as-state-crime-britains-hostility-towards-racially-minoritised-populations/

54 https://www.opendemocracy.net/en/beyond-trafficking-and-slavery/is-johnsons-rwanda-plan-a-crime-against-humanity/

Farmer (and others)[55]have looked at questions of citizenship, power, and rights in the context of colonialism, a telling and far-reaching example of such disempowerment. They embrace the notion of biocitizenship – a concept that considers the ways access to limited social goods mediates the relationship between citizens and state and helps defi ne who "belongs" (as citizen) and who does not. This notion of biocitizenship provides a useful lens to interrogate how forced removals of established families and communities affect well-being.

A report from May 2018 by the think-tank Oakland Institute describes the burning of homes and uprooting of tens of thousands of Masai in Tanzania to make way for foreign-owned tourism development. Studies by the International Consortium of Investigative Journalists (ICIJ) show that the World Bank, sometimes failing to adhere to its own guidelines, funds projects that uproot communities – more than 3 million people over a 10-year period. Some forced removals harken back to colonial and post-colonial periods – for example, the resettlement of millions of Tanzanians in the 1960s and 1970s into 2500 villages, the uprooting of 1.2 million Kenyans, 2.5 million Algerians (1952-63) or millions of people from District 6 in apartheid South Africa (1960-83). These tragedies typically present as humanitarian crises and victims consistently speak of extreme anxiety, sadness, and anger.

A striking example of a forced removal policy which has drawn international attention is the still evolving British political crisis known as the Windrush scandal. In 2010, in response to rising levels of nativism, the British Home Office launched its draconian immigration campaign which became known in 2012 as its "hostile environment" policy. Designed to reduce the number of illegal immigrants, it forced landlords, employers, banks and NHS services to run immigration status checks on those, in effect, "who looked like or sounded like immigrants". The 2016 Immigration Act gave landlords the right to evict tenants who could not prove their citizenship. Caught up in this initiative were citizens known

---

[55] https://hcghr.wordpress.com/2009/09/19/colonial-roots-of-global-health/

as the Windrush generation, immigrants from the Caribbean (and else-where) who had arrived between 1948 and 1971 and given leave to re-main in 1971. Because they often lacked official documentation and the Home Office had destroyed their stored landing cards in 2010, they had difficulty proving their legal status. Thousands were deported or threat-ened with deportation, many lost access to social goods and employ-ment and most suffered anxiety. Unconscionably, the government knew of these injustices as early as 2013 and ignored them.

The destruction of Windrush landing cards (despite clear warnings they were vital to establishing legal status) seems to symbolize loss of biocitizenship. Indeed, a multitude of recorded interviews of Windrush victims show the impact of lost access to healthcare and other social goods as well as a sense of alienation, "unbelonging", betrayal and an-guish associated with separation from family. For some, these losses would evoke a life as a colonial subject, living without status or agency, without biocitizenship, in a region where race-based access to health and social services was a key incentive for independence.

With its "hostile environment", the British Home Office has linked current policy with its colonial past, parts of which officialdom had made every effort to suppress. Like most European colonial history, it is top-down, incomplete and therefore inaccurate. Archived material consists almost exclusively of military and administrative documentation, absent the voices of ordinary persons. It is selective: the destruction, disappear-ance, or ferreting away of embarrassing or unwanted colonial records is not unusual. What the Home Office has managed to resurrect and bring to the fore is a Caribbean history, one based on slavery (the importation of 1.6 million slaves) – egregious, profound exploitation across centuries. Only an extraordinary lack of mindfulness of the past and preoccupation with satisfying nativist sentiments could allow this to happen.

The Windrush scandal is now part of colonial history that historians report they want to write from the inside out as a "history of emotion". They have begun to focus on the "hostile environment" policy as one explicitly aimed at creating anxiety among immigrant populations. They will focus on those of the Windrush generation that were presented with NHS bills, refused social assistance, evicted from their homes, refused re-entry into the country; on families surprised by their loss of power, right, and citizenship. Inevitably, historians will link the promotion of nativist sentiments beginning in 2010 to the anti-immigration rhetoric and rise of nationalism and will conclude both were ill-judged and shameful.

Asian Development Bank Failing in Its Mission to Protect the Poor

The Guardian UK, March 3, 2014[56]

Forced Removals and Abandoned Values This reading examines an Asian Development Bank (ADB) rail project in Cambodia that involved the forced resettlement of hundreds of families, leaving them impoverished and contributing to child deaths. The ADB's independent watchdog found that the bank failed to consult affected families during the project's design and did not provide adequate compensation, suitable replacement housing, or basic services at resettlement sites. The uprooting of vulnerable populations is a recurring theme in this reader, as is the tendency of International Financial Institutions (IFIs) to overlook human rights and inequalities—issues they claim to prioritize.[57]

———————◆———————

In its efforts to reduce poverty in Asia and the Pacific, the Asian Development Bank (ADB) has placed good governance, civil society, accountability and information disclosure among its key themes. In a recent speech, the bank's president stated that improving "governance in our developing member countries is one of the central aspects of our work in promoting inclusive development".

According to a 180-page report released late February on a project to repair Cambodia's rail system, ADB is not, however, adhering to its own polices and procedure in these areas. The bank's internal watchdog, the Compliance Review Panel (CRP), said management needed to undergo a "mind-shift" in the way it deals with vulnerable populations. Its findings are similar to those identified more than a decade ago in relation to ADB's performance in Indonesia.

---

[56] For access to the original article and footnotes, see: tiny.cc/AsianDevBank

[57] https://www.adb.org/sites/default/files/publication/845451/common-threads-lessons-compliance-reviews.pdf

The panel was convened to investigate complaints from NGOs that the rail project, which entailed compulsory resettlement, impoverished hundreds of families and contributed to three child deaths. The report found that the bank had failed to consult the families affected in the design of the project, and did not provide adequate compensation, suitable replacement housing or basic services at resettlement sites. Neither did it establish an effective mechanism to redress grievances. The panel recommended ADB pay up to $4m in compensation for loss of income and land.

CRP's finding that the case was not an anomaly but represented systemic failure is particularly striking. It said ADB's operational, sectoral and regional staff needed to undergo a fundamental change in their approach to vulnerable populations and the handling of "resettlement, environment, and public disclosure and consultation". It was not acceptable that the bank's management tended to treat these priority issues as afterthoughts, it added.

CRP also found that when ADB was provided with evidence as early as 2010 that vulnerable households were being impoverished by the project, it chose to ignore it. It did seek the expert opinion of Michael Cernea from the LSE-Brookings Institute project on internal displacement in 2012, but when he submitted his findings, the bank refused to release the full report. Instead, it published only Cernea's recommendations and launched a video that touted the project's benefits while dismissing the notion that households were being harmed. It has so far refused to pay compensation.

CRP's findings are similar to those of a 2003 review of ADB's leadership in Indonesia's health sector during east Asia's financial crisis in that it failed in its mission to protect the poor and, having done so, sought to obfuscate the results.

During the crisis, the IMF persuaded Indonesia's government to cut spending in order to help repay western banks. Given concerns that poor households should not be seen to be bearing the burden of such austerity measures, an ADB plan was implemented to protect their access to healthcare. In 2000 the bank reported that it had succeeded in its main objectives, maintaining spending on primary healthcare and access and on the uptake of services targeting the poor. Its report led the donor community to conclude that the worst fears of catastrophic health impacts had been overstated.

In reality, primary healthcare spending fell by 25%, as did the number of children vaccinated. The use of services such as clinics and health centres generally frequented by the poor fell between 26% and 47%. After decades of steady improvement in life expectancy, infant mortality increased in 22 of 26 provinces by an average of 14% between 1996 and 1999.

The quality of ADB's response to the CRP report is notable given the bank's emphasis on information disclosure in its new public communication policy which promises to strengthen its response and its appeals mechanisms. It is also remarkable given the uncomfortable finding that while ordinary people were impoverished, the Australian private sector benefited from the Cambodia rail project.

In Indonesia, while primary healthcare spending was slashed, private companies in rich donor nations benefited from a dramatic increase in hospital spending, mostly on expensive equipment – a deplorable and unjust allocation of scarce resource, according to the World Bank.

For obvious moral and practical reasons, ADB ought to reverse its stance and pay the compensation CRP recommended for families affected by the Cambodian rail project. Not to do so would imply that it does not accept the panel's findings and that it has failed to acquire the insight it is accused of lacking. This in turn implies a continued risk of it making egregious errors without redress for ordinary people.

Missing and Murdered Women.
Photo: Renegade98 / Flickr.com (CC BY-SA 2.0)

Canada's Murdered and Missing Aboriginals

BMJ, May 2015[58]

Crimes Against Humanity This reading presents prima facie evidence that the Government of Canada knowingly caused the foreseeable and avoidable premature deaths of vulnerable Indigenous peoples through acts of commission and commission. It examines the crisis of Canada's 1189 murdered and missing Indigenous women and girls (MMIWG) and the dismissive response to the crisis by the Harper government (2006-15), law enforcement, the media and civil society. After his election in 2015, Prime Minister Justin Trudeau established the National Inquiry into MMIWG which published a 1200 page Report four years later. The Report estimated 4,000 lives were lost and made 231 recommendations. Only two of these have been fully implemented.[59]

———◆———

How would you know and what would it matter if the invisible disappeared? The self-described "invisible" are Canada's aboriginal women, and the "disappeared" are the 1189 aboriginal women and girls who have been murdered or gone missing since 1980 – young aboriginal women being five times more likely to die as a result of violence than non-aboriginal women of the same age.

As to who knows and who cares, grieving families claim few take notice and most don't care. They cite Prime Minister Steven Harper as a case in point; although he made "safe streets and safe communities" and

---

[58] For access to the original article and footnotes, see: tiny.cc/MurderedMissing.
[59] https://www.cbc.ca/newsinteractives/features/cfj-report-cards

"putting victims first" top priorities, they do not seem to apply to aboriginals. When asked about the murdered and missing, many of them children, he told national television: "Um, to be honest it's not high on our radar" – as if to confirm they were literally "invisible."

These families hold similar views about the justice system. Police responsiveness across the country was awarded an average 2.8 out of 10, according to just released results of in-depth interviews with 110 of these families. Concurring with this is a recent report by the UN Office of the High Commissioner for Human Rights, which states that the "Canadian police and justice system have failed to effectively protect Aboriginal women, hold offenders to account, and ensure that victims get redress." It therefore accused Canada of "grave violation of human rights."

As to media coverage, aboriginal leadership cites quantitative and qualitative analyses showing that aboriginals receive three and a half times less coverage than white women, and reporting is "detached in tone and scant in detail" compared to intimate portraits of murdered or missing white women. CBC's recent launch of a database of photos of the murdered and missing women startled many Canadians – showing that a disturbing 25% of the victims are obviously younger than 20 years of age.

A slow withering: Helping to explain how aboriginal women have been marginalized to the point of "invisibility" is a series of federal policies that have withered away many of the threads that connect individuals – to a sense of self, to family, and to community. One means of gaining insight into this process is to consider the relatively uncommon term "deracination" – an evocative word that casts more than one shadow. It is variously described as to uproot, extirpate, to remove, or separate from a native environment or culture.

An early example of deracination is the federal government's Indian Residential School system (1880s-1996), an assimilation program with the explicit purpose (according to the prime minister's apology in parliament in 2008) to "remove and isolate children from the influence of their homes, families, traditions, and cultures" – that is, "to kill the Indian in the child." The rational for the schools was set out by John A Macdonald, Canada's first prime minister, who stated:

"When the school is on the reserve, the child lives with his parents who are savages; he is surrounded by savages, and, though he may read and write, his habits and training and mode of thought are Indian ... he is simply a savage that can read and write."

With this racialized view in place, pervasive and systemic physical, sexual, and psychological abuse of children soon followed on – including medical and nutritional experiments, even the use of a makeshift electric chair. Trauma experienced by many of the 150 000 children rippled through families and communities, accumulating over generations, and manifest today as epidemic levels of suicide, substance abuse, fetal alcohol syndrome, violence, and incarceration.

Two other forms of deracination affected aboriginal women. The first is the well-known forcible confinement of aboriginals to reservations, often a gruesome spectacle; it was achieved on the western plains for example, by deliberate acts of genocide and starvation.

The second (which exacerbates the first) was the usurping of women's traditional leadership and social roles within tribes (especially in matrilineal societies) by colonial legislation (such as the Indian Act of 1876). For instance, if women married non-status men, they and their children lost their status, often resulting in loss of band membership and the right to remain in the community. This forced many to move to urban areas where they typically live at the margins: poor, transient, socially excluded, and sexually exploited. Between 1950 and 2015, aboriginal urbanization grew from 13% to 60%. One indicator of these grim events is that aboriginals now represent an astonishing 44% of the girls in youth custody.

Aboriginal women want an inquiry: Several obstacles stand in the way of Canada's First Nations effectively tackling the murdered and missing crisis and its root causes. The more than 600 aboriginal groups scattered across the country are located mainly in remote northern communities or in impoverished urban enclaves. First Nations do not have a strong political voice.

Another important obstacle is that for Mr. Harper the murdered and missing do not represent a systemic, sociological problem. This contradicts the findings of more than 40 studies done since 1996. Indeed, research released last week by the University of British Colombia shows that a parent attending a residential school was a strong predictor of women and girls being assaulted later in life; it also showed that sexual abuse in childhood increased the probability of assault 10-fold.

Another obstacle is that Mr. Harper seems prepared to go to unusual lengths to limit criticism of his position. For example, in 2012 Mr. Harper defunded dozens of native women's health organizations that were critical of his government on disparities, violence against women, and underlying causes. He defunded the National Aboriginal Health Organization (NAHO), which was Canada's only organization dedicated to developing common health policies for all aboriginals. He cut all funding to the National Aboriginal Women's Association's national database, which tracks cases of missing and slain aboriginal women.

Reversing 50 years of non-partisan support for civil society, Mr. Harper said, "If it's the case that we're spending on organizations that are doing things contrary to government policy, I think that is an inappropriate use of taxpayer's money and we'll look to eliminate it."

Nevertheless, aboriginal women are right to say that the way forward is to have a public national inquiry into the murdered and missing. It will help identify root causes, reveal gaps in basic services, create better coordination among police services and departments of justice, provide an opportunity for the grieving to have their stories told, and contribute to a greater public awareness of past injustices – especially those related to colonialism and racism. In other words, the way ahead is to make the invisible more visible and increase public awareness so more people would know and more would care.[60]

---

[60] Terminology relating to Indigenous people has changed over time. In Canada, the term "Indigenous" is preferred over "Aboriginal" and includes First Nations, Métis, and Inuit. Phrases such as "Canada's Aboriginals" are not acceptable since they imply ownership by newcomers.

Global Health and Altruism: The Case of Canada and Its Treatment of Refugees

BMJ Opinion, September 2015 [61]

Cruel and Unusual This article describes the maltreatment of refugees by the Harper government, which the Supreme Court described as "cruel and unusual." The article then describes Justin Trudeau's reversal of these policies when he assumed the premiership in October 2015. According to a 2019 United Nations report, Canada took in more refugees than any other country in the world in 2018, surpassing the US which has 10 times the population. When President Trump issued a ban on non-Americans, from seven Muslim-majority countries, Trudeau responded with the promise, "To those fleeing persecution, terror & war, Canadians will welcome you, regardless of your faith." [62]

———————◆———————

Last year, government cuts to basic health services for refugees – especially those meant for women and children – outraged Canadian physicians to the point of petitioning the courts to intervene. The Federal Court agreed with the physicians, and in ordering the restoration of these services, it described the conservative government's policy as "cruel and unusual."

Indeed, the past 10 years have not been easy for refugees hoping for sanctuary in Canada. And when Canadians, already disturbed by photos of the Syrian child Aylan Kurdi washed up on the beach of Turkey, learned that members of his family in British Colombia had applied to sponsor him and were turned down, many might have concluded "right country, wrong time."

The reality is that over the past decade Prime Minister Stephen Harper has dramatically altered Canada's international posture. Eschewing

---

[61] For access to the original article and footnotes, see tiny.cc/HealthAltruism
[62] For access to the original article and footnotes, see tiny.cc/HealthAltruism

multilateralism as a "weak nation strategy", he has embraced what he called at Davos the principle of enlightened sovereignty, the natural extension of enlightened self-interest." He confirmed that "do-good" policies that benefit others globally would need to benefit Canada as well. This, of course, contrasts with the notion of "doing good" without anticipation of material reward – altruism. It also means that in Canada today, immigrants and refugees are treated very differently.

Immigrants have been traditionally welcomed in Canada as they are by Mr. Harper's government – especially if they are well educated and with personal resources. According to enlightened sovereignty, this works because it benefits both parties.

Refugees, in contrast, are discouraged from seeking entry and are treated badly if they succeed. In 2014, Canada accepted 23 000 refugees, down from 35 000 in 2005. As to the Syrian refugees, a paltry 188 Syrians have obtained government assistance to enter Canada (another 857 have been privately sponsored).

This diverges from Canada's strong record of accepting refugees on humanitarian (altruistic) grounds – for example, tens of thousands from Vietnam and Kosovo. In both cases, mass sponsorships were arranged by a proactive government that sent immigration teams overseas to facilitate processes. The former chair of the Immigration and Refugee Board of Canada says we have the expertise to do this again, but "this government has decided not to." Under this government, any immigration teams sent overseas have had the explicit purpose of dissuading refugees from coming. Mr. Harper's first public response to the photos of Aylan Kurdi – stating that a military response is needed to address the root causes of this refugee crisis – is perhaps revealing.

The larger context

The Canadian government's treatment of refugees is part of a large whole that, to some extent, is predictable. Research shows that rich countries that are generous to vulnerable populations at home (as measured by government support to individual households, including family allowances, disability and sickness benefits, and unemployment insurance) are also altruistic towards poor countries – as measured by overseas development assistance (ODA). Countries less generous internationally than their peers typically have weaker social safety nets, greater inequalities, and less social trust at home.

For example, between 2006 and 2014, Canada's ODA budget fell from 0.33 to 0.24, (as a % of gross national income), which is "far below [the] average DAC [Development Assistance Committee] country effort of 0.39%", according to a 2015 report by the Organization for Economic and Development. Under the "sovereignty" and "self-interest" labels, Mr. Harper adopted a foreign policy known as "economic diplomacy," which saw ODA become skewed toward trade and commerce and away from development and human rights, away from Africa and towards Latin America – i.e., where there would be demonstrable benefit to Canadian business.

On the domestic front, over the same 10 years, Canada's social safety net has been significantly weakened by conservative leadership that embraced small government, individualism, and free markets. Familiar programs such as unemployment benefits and social housing budgets have been cut by 50%; virtually all pro-poor programs have been cuts, cancelled, or redirected. Indeed, outcome data collected by UNICEF show that in 29 rich countries, Canada now ranks 28 of 29 for childhood immunization, 22 of 29 for its infant mortality rate, and 29 of 29 for early child education. Vulnerable populations explain a large part of these outcomes.

Levels of altruism (or selfishness, its opposite) may change with shifting political leadership or ideology. Unhappily, a decline in generosity seems to spread faster through sectors than a rise, since those vulnerable to change have little or no voice. Nevertheless, Canada needs to begin to rebuild its former self. Until then, for most would-be refugees Canada must remain a foreign country – and perhaps too for many Canadians as well.

World Bank Reforms Must Embrace Racial Equality and Accountability

The Guardian (UK), November 27 2012 [63]

Racism in the World Bank This article looks at deep racial inequalities in World Bank (WB) staffing in Washington, D.C. that have beleaguered the institution for decades. The article's publication in the Guardian drew many letters from readers including from the WB itself. As a UN agency headquartered in the US, the WB is not required to follow US laws to collect race-based data or provide independent arms-length assessment of claims of discrimination. The Bank's refusal to address the subject angered critics who were concerned how these inequalities might influence policy decisions which are intended to address disparities. For many critics, the racial inequalities within the WB help explain the Bank's failure to tackle Sub-Sahara's HIV/AIDS crisis until the early 2000s. Following the rise of the Black Lives Matter campaign, David Malpass, President of the World Bank announced the launch of a task force [64] and a series of initiatives to address racism within the institution, including promises to change behavior and culture within the Bank. However, almost identical promises were made 10, 20 and 30 years ago. [65]

———————◆———————

At the World Bank IMF annual meeting in Tokyo this month, Jim Yong Kim promised to bring in an era of reform saying: "While I'm excited by how much the bank has changed around openness and results

---

[63]   For access to the original article and footnotes, see tiny.cc/WorldBank

[64]   https://www.worldbank.org/en/news/factsheet/2021/11/11/the-world-bank-group-addressing-racism-and-racial-discrimination#:~:text=The%20Task%20Force%20is%20also,conversations%20are%20respectful%20and%20constructive.

[65]   I spoke with many people interested in the main findings of this article, including Maxine Waters, Chair of the US Black Women's Caucus, and lawyers with the US Department of Justice in Washington. The messages, brimming with frustration, carried the same sentiment: "We know the World Bank lacks diversity, but as a UN agency, they are exempt from US laws." I also spoke with staff at the World Bank; they were largely dismissive of the findings. Their views are reflected in World Bank's Monica Oldham's response to the Guardian, Nov 28, 2012 (available online).

and accountability, I believe the bank can go further". One step in this direction would be for the bank to address racial inequalities in its staffing at the senior level and to become open and accountable about its progress towards this end.

At issue is the conspicuous under-representation of African Americans at senior levels of the bank. In 1978 William Raspberry reported in the *Washington Post* that there were only three black Americans, out of 619 Americans working at the World Bank. Thirty years later (in a report titled "Racial discrimination at the World Bank: a review of the treatment of black employees in recruitment, retention and justice decisions" the Washington-based Government Accountability Project (Gap) reported that of more than 1,000 American World Bank staff of professional grade, four were African-Americans.

The many studies the bank has undertaken over the years have generally acknowledged that race-based discrimination "is evidenced in management's hiring and promotion decisions, attitudes and behaviours" and that a culture of bias, stereotyping of in-groups and outgroups exist within the work environment. In response, the bank took several positive steps including launching a racial equality programme in 1998, the office of diversity programmes in 2001, the diversity and inclusion leadership awards in 2003, and in 2009, a code of conduct that addressed diversity, inclusion and discrimination.

Yet to most observers, these anti-discrimination policies have been largely cosmetic. Racial discrimination persists and even the bank's own diversity newsletter reports that "despite considerable talk about the diversity and inclusion agenda – and new policies designed to advance it – the impression lingers among many World Bank Group staff that culture change lags far behind".

A fundamental first step towards redressing discrimination, according to the bank's team for racial equality (TRE), is to develop "accurate and complete databases" and use them "as indispensable management tools for monitoring the status and progress of black staff". This is consistent with Kim's call for openness and accountability. Yet the bank categorically refuses to track the number of African-American employees and, instead, collects information on national diversity based on passports – an exercise that it recognises is inadequate and misleading (pdf).

From the point of view of bank employees with a discrimination complaint, the situation is substantially worsened because they do not have recourse to national laws and must rely on the World Bank administrative tribunal (Wat); the tribunal almost never finds for the complainant. According to the Gap (pdf), review of the records since 1996 shows that Wat found no instances of discrimination in any of the cases that came before it.

A recent article in Forbes Magazine said the bank "is so obsessed with reputational risk that it reflexively covers up anything that could appear negative, rather than address it". This is an extraordinary conclusion to reach yet, for an institution that claims that "diversity and inclusion are at the heart of how we define organizational and professional excellence" (pdf) then fails to provide an effective internal grievance system for those harmed suggests an organisation more concerned about reputation than it is about justice.

The bank is vulnerable to still more far-reaching critiques. Chronic inequalities may draw attention to past failures to deal with development challenges such as Africa's HIV/Aids crisis, malaria and tuberculosis in the 1990s where severe under-representation of Africans on its board of governors and in regional offices, and the general lack of an African voice, show that inequalities affect output and outcomes. The bank, as the lead donor in SSA's health sector in the 1990s, allocated $552m to HIV (1986-96): $160m went to Brazil, a middle-income country with an HIV prevalence rate of less than 1%, while $274m was received by Africa. In any organisation, raced-based discrimination will inevitably have a detrimental effect on its legitimacy, credibility, effectiveness and staff morale.

Kim told the global community this month in Tokyo that he wants to "bend the arc of history". Dealing with its long-standing inequalities in Washington DC and its own institutional weaknesses is a good place to start.

The World Bank in Kagame's Rwanda

Lancet, August 2017[66]

World Bank "a human rights-free zone" This piece describes the World Bank's uncritical support of the Rwandan government under the leadership of Paul Kagame, which Kim Yong Jim praised as "a model for the entire world," despite numerous reports of government repression, violence, and torture. Since its publication, new evidence has emerged that shows continued intimidation of the population, unjust imprisonment of opposition leaders and extrajudicial assassinations overseas. In 2024, The Economist describes Rwanda as a land ruled by fear.[67] Members of the US Congress are increasingly distancing themselves from the regime. Furthermore, claims by Kagame (and the World Bank) that Rwanda has undergone an "economic miracle" are inconsistent with existing evidence according to the Financial Times. This situation adds to the perception that Bank ignores human rights in client countries and treats them "more like a disease than universal values and obligations", and that its operational approach to human rights is "incoherent, counterproductive and unsustainable". The US State Department Human Rights Report on Rwanda paints a dire picture of a despotic regime.[68] An internet search of "Kagame" and "crimes against humanity" yields numerous reports of war crimes and human rights abuses as well as his support for the M23 Movement in Congo.

———————◆———————

On August 4, 2017, Paul Kagame was re-elected President of Rwanda for a third term, winning 98% of the popular vote and extending

---

[66] For access to the original article and footnotes, see tiny.cc/KagameRwanda

[67] https://www.economist.com/middle-east-and-africa/2024/03/25/three-decades-af-terrwandas-genocide-the-past-is-ever-present

[68] https://www.state.gov/reports/2023-country-reports-on-human-rights-practices/rwanda/

his 17-year rule to at least 2024. Many observers are wary of these results and cite extraordinary levels of fear and intimidation to help explain the margins. Given Rwanda's continued status as a beacon of development success, how should the international community respond?

Commentary last month by the *Economist* (entitled "Intimidation nation") and *The Wall Street Journal* (entitled "Rwanda's success story adds a dark new chapter") raised questions similar to those raised a year earlier in a Lancet Comment which acknowledged Rwanda's economic progress, yet described reports of a country of repression, violence, and torture. It noted in particular the claim that 60 journalists had been "threatened, arrested, kidnapped, beaten, assaulted, abused, imprisoned, expelled, or killed for questioning or criticising Paul Kagame and his government". The *Financial Times* provides the grisly details of events cited by *The Lancet*, stating that "political opponents are regularly imprisoned. Some have been killed, including those who have fled into exile".

In counterpoint, the World Bank president Kim Yong Jim in a 2-day visit to Rwanda in March 2017 (during the pre-election campaign) said "I am here to say to President Paul Kagame and the Rwandan people that the World Bank Group is ready to help in any way that they can and that we believe in the future of Rwanda and we believe that it will continue to be a model for the entire world". Jim's declaration came at a time when Diane Rwigara, an accountant and human rights activist, had undertaken a campaign to bring the Kagame government to task for abuses of civil rights and intimidation of the Rwandan people.

These differing perspectives are partly explained by the Bank's disinclination to concern itself with human rights abuses in borrowing countries. It cites its "political prohibition" from involving itself in a local politics. A report by a United Nations rapporteur assessing this policy and its consequences found that "political prohibition" is "misplaced legalism". It stated that "the World Bank is currently a human rights-free zone. In its operational policies, in particular, it treats human rights more like an infectious disease than universal values and obligations."

The Bank's recently published policy framework ignores this criticism and (according to observers) it further weakens its stance on human rights by relegating them to a non-binding "vision" statement. The framework further bolsters a value system that places primacy on results, not on the means by which they are achieved; it may open new pathways that undermine good governance or democratic institutions.

The framework also provides part of the context that enabled Jim to declare his enthusiasm that Rwanda was "a model for the entire world". This is not a shared view and the *Economist* states just the opposite – "many Africans see Paul Kagame's Rwanda as a model. They are wrong". Kagame's "model", it says, sends the message that "authoritarianism is more likely than democracy to bring stability and growth". The overemphasis on results rather than how they are achieved may lead to mis-steps or unwise decisions: the fact that Jim made a 2-day visit to Rwanda in the run-up to a national election and then offered effusive support for Kagame seems inappropriate and surely ironic, given the Bank's "political prohibition". Needless to say, it was exploited by the state-controlled media.

Although Kagame once said that if he was unable to groom a successor by 2017, "it means that I have not created capacity for a postme Rwanda. I see this as a personal failure", he in fact has methodically warded off (or eliminated) nascent threats to his power. The most recent example being Diane Rwigara, who decided at the last minute to run for President in May 2017; within days of her announcement, she was demeaned on the internet and prevented from registering despite meeting the requirement set out by the electoral commission.

The international community ought to take Kagame at his word – that his presence in this month's election is an indicator of a basic failure on his part and, since it was considered a success by many donors, that it is a sign of their failure as well. It represents confusion about their stated institutional values and how far they have drifted from their mission and vision.

The naiveté of the global community to accept the astonishing margin of victory of 98% and 90% turnout is probably inversely proportional to its continuing guilt over its failure to respond to the 1994 genocide. However, the World Bank with its "political prohibition" in particular ought to take stock of what it is and where it's going – even addressing ancient questions of whether it's more interested in growth than poverty, and in disbursement than health outcomes.

UK: "get out, stay out"
Brexit and the Vengeance of Unintended Consequences
BMJ Opinion, July 2017 [69]

Brexit is another type of border wall. Brexit is broadly seen as a "disaster" and in 2025, Prime Minister Kiers Starmer is attempting to reset EU-UK relations. This reading explores the decision-making processes that led to Britain's withdrawal from the European Union. Early on, politicians doubled down on ill-conceived policies that risked the economic and social health of the nation. Their decisions were heavily influenced by confirmation bias, a refusal to acknowledge mistakes, encapsulated by the signature claim by British Prime Minister David Cameron, "I've no regrets in calling the EU referendum". Ongoing commentary and analyses by the left and right acknowledge the negative social and economic impact of Brexit especially during the "cost of living crisis". The COVID-19 Inquiry also heard testimony that Brexit severely undermined the NHS's capacity to respond to the pandemic. Brexit led to an increase in attacks against "foreigners" and other hate crimes. Research reveals Brexit votes are correlated with increases in mortality.[70]

———————◆———————

Decades before the advent of complexity science, H L Mencken wrote that "For every complex problem there is a solution which is clear, simple, and wrong." These solutions typically complicate existing problems while creating new ones.

Local and global health communities likely have lessons to offer political leaders at risk of opting for these kinds of solutions, which have been influenced by inadequate information, weak analysis, perverse incentives, cognitive or emotional biases, or a focus on the short rather than long term.

---

[69] For access to the original article and footnotes, see tiny.cc/BrexitConsequences

[70] https://www.ncbi.nlm.nih.gov/pmc/articles/PMC7002930/

Such decisions usually have negative unintended consequences and, when they represent a doubling down on past "do nothing" policies or non-decisions, accidental decisions, or what might be termed "slouching towards a decision," they may signal a serious threat to overall population wellbeing. They also may be relevant to the calamity confronting Britain as it now attempts to deal with Brexit.

Two examples of unintended consequences are global warming and antibiotic resistance: the first the result of unrestrained economic growth, and the second the result of unchecked use of antibiotics. They are so called "long wave events" that evolve over a protracted period, foment a culture of their own, create self-supporting structures and processes, and desensitise decision makers and blunt their sense of urgency – thus pushing further out the probability of an effective response.

Scientists advocating for change will sometimes seek to address their long wave aspect by presenting decades of change in data visualisations, time lapse videos, or event animation to spark a sense of urgency and underscore the need for action.

For instance, a two-minute time lapse video[71] by Harvard researchers shows the beautiful and terrifying manoeuvres of bacteria (over a twoweek period) as the cells adapt to graduated levels of antibiotics. The video captures "evolution at work" and explains how, enabled by poor antibiotics stewardship, antibiotics have transitioned from a 20th century medical miracle to a 21st century public health crisis. In a similar fashion, scientists have sought to capture the progress of CO_2 build-up and the effects of global warming on the environment. NASA's animated time lapse video of Arctic ice loss (1984-2016) shows the 90% depletion of "old ice"; other amination effectively depicts global temperature change between 1850 and 2016.[72]

Although a time lapse video to capture the sequelae of Brexit is years

---

[71] https://www.youtube.com/watch?v=plVk4NVIUh8

[72] https://www.theguardian.com/environment/2016/may/10/see-earths-temperaturespiral-toward-2c-rise-graphic

or decades out (if it happens at all), it's nevertheless interesting that many observers evoke the time element in the opposite direction, repeatedly citing Brexit as "a slow-motion car crash" – the point of which is to stress the inevitable. Early signs of this "calamity" include doubling down on a largely accidental decision, little or no expressed remorse for the results, and no acknowledgement of a swiftly moving chain reaction (the causes of causes and results of results). For example, Prime Minister David Cameron's escalating commitment to a referendum he never wanted followed by his claim in its aftermath that he had no regrets are consistent with his successor's (Prime Minister Theresa May) ambivalence about Brexit followed by her subsequent claim that she had "no regrets" about calling an election meant to strengthen her position to negotiate Brexit, which in fact did the opposite.

As this unfolds, dozens of experts are warning of the detrimental effects Brexit will have throughout all sectors of the British economy over the short and long term. Predictions made by the British Medical Association say that it will have huge negative implications for the medical professions, and not just by compromising the workforce – patient safety, public health, and medical training standards all stand to lose out too. According to the Royal Society, 29% of the UK academic workforce (and more than 50% of PhD students) are from overseas. In addition, the number of nurses from the EU registering to work in the UK fell from 1116 in May 2016 to 85 in May 2017.

Many also expect that it will negatively impact research funding, medical innovation, and the pharmaceutical sectors. Furthermore, few would deny that Britain will lose influence as an actor in global health – an area that it has led over the past two decades.

H L Mencken warned of the perils of ill-conceived problem solving, and now complexity science provides the details of how this is a trap that governments and those creating public policy must be particularly wary of. Yet clinicians confront complexity and the risks of unintended consequences daily – whether it relates to new (or old) drugs or procedures, electronic records, trying to balance efficiency with equity, or, indeed, the risk that clinical practice guidelines might inadvertently stifle innovation or obfuscate local context. They therefore might reasonably expect some semblance of the same from their political leaders. For surely politicians must also abide by a modicum of good stewardship and some form of "do no harm."

Economic Crisis and Mortality

International Journal of Clinical Practice, 2010 [73]

Budget Cuts and Social Murder In the health sector, walls serve as a metaphor for the barriers vulnerable populations face. These barriers are shaped by income, residence, education, race, ethnicity, and religion, and their negative effects intensify during economic crises. This article examines three crises to demonstrate how free-market policies and economic upheaval disproportionately reduce access to healthcare, worsen health outcomes, and increase mortality risks for certain groups. It presents prima facie evidence that the World Bank, IMF, and US Treasury were complicit in social murder by knowingly exposing vulnerable populations to foreseeable and avoidable risks, leading to premature deaths through acts of omission or commission.

◆

The economic crisis that began on Wall Street and the European banking sector and spread across the globe has become a social crisis that is hitting hard the well-being of ordinary people in both rich and poor countries.

The principal pathway through which economic crisis diminishes health status and increases mortality risk is through its poverty effects including rising rates of unemployment, prices, currency instability, household debt and reduced personal assets, lost health insurance and cuts in health spending. Many of these commonly reduce access to effective healthcare in any given population. They may also lead to malnutrition, hunger, increased levels of stress and depression, changes in personal habits such as alcohol and tobacco use and contribute to cardiovascular disease, respiratory infections, chronic liver disease and violence.

Beyond the particular severity, intensity and longevity of any given crisis, two variables affecting outcomes are pre-existing levels of

---

[73] For access to the original article and footnotes, see tiny.cc/EconomicCrisis

vulnerability and the quality of responses to the crisis – at the individual and house-hold level, as well as community and national levels.

In low-income countries it is estimated that between 53 and 200 million people will become impoverished by today's crisis and, according to the World Bank, an average of 200,000–400,000 more children a year, or a total of 1.4–2.8 million, may die. About 40 countries are 'highly exposed to poverty effects and another 80 are 'moderately exposed'. The UN estimates that incomes in Africa will decline by 20% and, that there will be up to 100 million new cases of malnutrition globally leading to more illness and mortality. These estimates are on top of last year's food and fuel crisis, which impoverished 100 million and resulted in 44 million cases of malnutrition.

Conditions that lead to greater mortality risk in developing countries are pre-existing high levels of poverty and fragile economies. High burden of disease, weak infrastructure and very limited resources means poor countries are especially vulnerable to economic crisis. They are structurally vulnerable to external forces over which they have little control including declining exports, foreign investment, access to capital, remittances and most critically, declining levels of development aid. With respect to the latter, poor countries are chronically exposed to rich countries' failure to deliver on aid pledges even during times of prosperity; during economic recession disbursement rates tend to shrink still further. At the G20 London summit, the world's economic powers which had committed US$5 trillion to their own economies, had nothing to say about poverty, hunger and stress and cuts to public health spending in less affluent nations.

In contrast, rich countries are relatively protected from the most egregious aspects of economic shock thanks to high standards of living, good public infrastructure, and access to effective healthcare and education – the very factors that gave rise to high rates of life expectancy. Yet healthcare systems and social safety nets (SSNs) (as measured in social transfers such as family allowances, disability and sickness benefits, formal day care provision and unemployment insurance) vary widely in rich countries. In Europe evidence suggests that SSNs are softening the effects of the crisis while in the United States, the only rich country without universal healthcare and a limited SSN, ordinary citizens are especially vulnerable to the crisis.

Not surprisingly, access to affordable healthcare has become a critical aspect of the crisis for many Americans either because job loss often means loss of health benefits or because household budgets are increasingly strained. According to one survey, more than half of chronically ill adults did not obtain 'recommended care, fill prescriptions, or see a doctor when sick because of costs. A new Kaiser Foundation poll shows that 6 in 10 Americans have taken steps to delay or skip healthcare over the past year. This poll together with a spate of other studies show that ordinary Americans are turning to home remedies, over-the-counter drugs, pill-splitting, not filling a prescription, skipping screening, cancelling appointments, or avoiding medical advice entirely. American family physicians report that this shift in health-seeking behaviour is resulting in substantive health problems that could have been prevented and increased emergency hospitalizations including diabetes, chronic lung disease and cardiovascular disease.

These trends will not lead to increases in national mortality rates; they will however increase health inequalities, especially those defined by race, ethnicity and place of residence. In a cluster of southern states, for example, where infant mortality rates are two to three times higher than the national average and on par with many poor countries, and prevalence rates of diabetes, obesity and hypertension are highest, mortality could increase; female-headed households are especially vulnerable.

The quality of response to the crisis also determines health outcome. In poor countries the most vulnerable, women and children, depend on effective response by their government and the donor community to protect them from economic crisis – both of which have a poor track record. When Zambia was hit by economic crisis in the 1970s and 1980s, the International Monetary Fund (IMF) and the World Bank persuaded government to cut spending, advice that did not include taking steps to protect the poor. Public health sector spending was cut by 50%; the way these cuts were applied had a deleterious effect on the poor: rural expenditure was cut by 50% while urban care remained relatively protected; primary healthcare was cut in favour of curative care; and drug and supplies were cut in favour of salaries. Case fatality rates (CFRs) for acute respiratory infection increased by 65% and doubled for diarrhoeal disease, malaria, and malnutrition during the 1980s. The rise in CFRs was explained by reduced quality of healthcare and delay in seeking treatment due to rising direct and indirect costs. The proportion of children dying before reaching the age of 5 increased from 150 to 191 deaths per 1000 live births.

In Indonesia during the East Asian Financial Crisis (1997–1999) the government was persuaded by the IMF and the donor community to cut spending in order to repay western banks; this led to a 25% cut in primary healthcare spending upon which the poor depended while donors increased their support of hospitals by selling them western goods and equipment (used by the non-poor). The percentage of children vaccinated against tuberculosis (with BCG), diphtheria, pertussis, tetanus (DPT), poliomyelitis and measles fell by 25% and the use of services such as clinics and health centres used by the poor fell between 26% and 47%. Spending on drugs fell 25% as prices increased due to currency devaluation. After decades of steady improvement in life expectancy, infant mortality increased in 22 of 26 provinces by an average of 14% between 1996 and 1999.

In the United States, response to the financial crisis has evolved. Initially, state, and local governments confronted with massive deficits and no more room to aggressively raise taxes responded by cancelling bold proposals to expand health insurance coverage, cutting existing services and implementing cost containment actions were taken such as pharmacy control, benefit reduction, eligibility cuts. Medicaid, the state-federal health programme intended to deal directly with the nation's large health disparities, was cut in 19 states this past fiscal year and more and larger cuts are scheduled for this year. The Obama administration has sought to reverse these some of these trends by expanding the child health insurance programme (CHIP), protecting access to healthcare by the newly unemployed (COBRA), targeting stimulus funds at state healthcare systems and promoting a universal healthcare agenda.

In this issue, Falaga and others review the literature which describes the influence of economic crisis on mortality. Their findings and today's current crisis ought to be of concern to public health officials and decision-makers in terms of what the outcomes might have been had more effective and equitable social policy been in place before the crisis, had immediate and effectives steps been taken during the crisis and the lessons that can be learned to inform future policy.

As to the way forward, governments and the international community first need to avoid past mistakes that have typically led to cuts in public health spending aimed at groups with little or no voice or political power and instead focus on financing essential healthcare services that target vulnerable populations. Second, more reliable data, better monitoring, research and analysis are needed to track countries' situations and guide responses. Third, issues of good governance that challenge some developing countries and all international financial institutions need to be addressed; their democracy deficit and lack of accountability, transparency and dialogue undermine the credibility upon which they depend. Fourth, in this, the most serious downturn since the Great Depression, social protection measures that protect income and the well-being of those at greatest risk are essential and ought to be a priority. Fifth, donors need to meet their commitments and resist pressure to cut aid in favour of at-home priorities. This is more likely if there is political leadership and co-operation between Ministries of Health, Finance, and regional and global health institutions as well as academia and civil society.

It would be indefensible if, in the end, the world's most vulnerable who are the least to blame for this crisis are left to bear its brunt through the death of two million children while rich countries, whose greed and imprudence led to this crisis (by their own account), walk away relatively unscathed and only vaguely aware of the misery left in their wake.

Trump 1.0 and 2.0:
Russian Dolls: Revealing Trump's Diminution of the Common Good
BMJ Opinion, June 2017 [74]

Budget Cuts and Social Murder Elon Musk described Trump's "Big Beautiful Bill" as "a disgusting abomination," but he missed the key point: it transferred wealth from the poor to the rich, stripping millions of their Medicare coverage. During his first term, Trump enacted major tax cuts, disproportionately benefiting the wealthy, while slashing government spending. This article explores the effects of Trump's deregulation and downsizing policies across multiple scales—global, national, state, community, household, and individual. The title references a recursive process, where outcomes reinforce themselves, illustrating a spiral of self-interested, irrational, and biased policies with lasting consequences.

◆

A few weeks ago, two of Donald Trump's top advisers, H R McMaster and Gary Cohn, astonished many in the world community when they wrote in *The Wall Street Journal* that "The president embarked on his first foreign trip with a clear-eyed outlook that the world is not a 'global community' but an arena where nations, nongovernmental actors, and businesses engage and compete for advantage."

This worldview is the antithesis of the values and priorities of the global health community and its search for collaboration and equity across borders. A review of Trump's policies on a descending scale from global, regional, national, state, community, household, to individual reveals – like the recursion in a set of nesting Russian dolls – a theme of presumed selfishness and competitive struggle. By examining in sequence Trump's policies, the threat that they pose to people's health and

---

[74] For access to this original article and footnotes, see tiny.cc/RussianDolls

wellbeing and the communities in which they live becomes clearer.

Firstly, at the global level, Trump has taken several measures to "put America first" at the expense of other nations' health. His exit from the Paris Climate Accord (on 2 June), described by the *Economist* as "unconscionable and fatuous," could, according to physicians and research scientists, lead to a public health disaster – comprised of increased levels of respiratory, heart, and infectious disease and mental health disorders.

Similarly, his cuts to US global health spending by 25% (US$2.2 billion) will have a worldwide impact – notably for women, according to MSF. They include budget cuts of 17% for HIV/AIDS programs in the poorest countries and of 11% for efforts to fight malaria. Funding for family planning and maternal healthcare programs may be eliminated entirely (with proposed budgetary cuts of US$524 million); experts claim that this will lead to 3.3 million more abortions, 15 000 more maternal deaths, eight million more unintended pregnancies, and 26 million fewer women receiving maternal and child healthcare.

Secondly, at the regional level, Trump has been dismissive of collaborative arrangements between nations (including the United Nations, NATO, the North American Free Trade Agreement, and the Transpacific Partnership), which seek to promote peace, prosperity, and human development. He has claimed, for example, that the European Union would break up in 10 years and that Europe will be "unrecognizable"; in this context, he is a strong supporter of Brexit – itself a threat to "key aspects of health and healthcare." A spokesperson for the United Nations secretary general has stated that Trump's decisions will "make it impossible for the UN to continue all of its essential work."

Thirdly, at the national level, Trump is cutting spending on social welfare while pursuing his deregulation agenda – both of which will be detrimental to health and healthcare. Massive cuts to the Environmental Protection Agency (EPA) will diminish programs that address occupational health and safety; air, water, and soil quality; and even basic regulations meant to protect children from lead in paint.

Critics of H.R. 1628, the American Health Care Act (Trumpcare), which replaces Obamacare, have focused on how the act jeopardizes coverage for pre-existing conditions such as asthma, diabetes, and heart disease, with its proposal to allow states to waive rules that currently stop insurers from charging new customers more because of their medical history. Trump's plan, which is predicted to leave 23 million fewer people with healthcare insurance by 2026, has flummoxed even the most hardened observers.

Fourthly, in devolving responsibility for social safety nets to states, Trump sidesteps equity as a core public health principle. According to the Brookings Institute, "historically, equity has been a key justification for federal involvement" – and in the US there is strong reason for adherence to this. Research shows that states with the largest African American populations tend to have the weakest social safety nets. The Office of Minority Health reports that black children are four times more likely to be admitted to hospital for asthma than white children and are 10 times more likely to die from asthma than white children. Coincidentally, the Office of Minority Health is also one of the many targets of Trump's budgetary cuts.

Fifthly, at the local level, Trump's policies have a direct impact on community services, such as neighborhood clinics, family planning and maternal healthcare, and chronic disease programs and health promotion. Popular grants that help to revitalize economically distressed communities, including the community services block grant (which normally addresses poverty and its health implications), will be eliminated, as well as billions of dollars for public housing and rental assistance.

Finally, at the individual level, Trump's policies look to some like "a war against anti-poverty programs" – an injustice perpetuated by the view that individuals are responsible for their own welfare and cannot depend on the state. The secretary of housing and urban development, Dr. Ben

Carson, underscored this perspective when he recently described poverty as a "state of mind." Trump is also calling for cuts to meals on wheels and a 25% cut in the food stamp program; when asked about these proposed cuts, an important Republican committee member could not bring himself to state that "people are entitled to eat."

The assertion by Trump's advisers that there is no "global community" is similar to Margaret Thatcher's observation "there is no such thing as society." Thatcher's statement – "there are only individual men and women and there are families … and people must look after ourselves first" – reads much like Trump's advisers' declaration: "An are na where nations, nongovernmental actors, and businesses engage and compete for advantage." In these circumstances, without a moral code, a sense of the greater good, or a commonwealth, the last of the Russian dolls (which in folklore is meant to be a pleasant surprise) is neither surprising nor pleasing.

The British and Canadian Health Systems at 70 and 60

BMJ Opinion, March 15 2018[75]

Budget Cuts and Social Murder This reading examines the British National Health Service (NHS) and the Canadian hospital system as they celebrated their 70th and 60th anniversaries, respectively. It explores the challenges faced by leaders making decisions within Complex Adaptive Systems (CASs), where control is decentralized, and outcomes can be unpredictable, random, or even chaotic. In such contexts, decisions often prioritize short-term gains, which can lead to long-term negative impacts on health and well-being. For example, the reading analyzes the 2012 decision by a small group of British politicians to implement significant cuts to social spending. Research suggests that these austerity measures (2012–2019) are associated with an estimated 335,000 excess deaths—a phenomenon repeatedly described as social murder. In 2025, experts warn that due to austerity and failure to invest, the NHS is now on the brink of collapse.

———————◆———————

This July the British NHS and Canadian hospital insurance systems will celebrate their 70th and 60th anniversaries, respectively. Both healthcare systems – like many in high income countries – are in crisis, although neither is about to collapse.

Health systems are known as complex adaptive systems (CASs) and this leaves them vulnerable to a whole host of weaknesses that can prey upon them. There is typically no single point of control within them, and the behaviour of groups and individuals belonging to these structures (including politicians, bureaucrats, providers, patients, and their communities) can be unpredictable, random, and chaotic. They tend to have their own values, rules, and objectives, and are often in conflict with one another – sometimes without knowing precisely why or with whom. Normally CASs adapt and self-adjust to internal changes or outside pressures

---

[75] For access to the original article and footnotes, see tiny.cc/UKCanadaHealthSystems

– what the NHS select committee calls "its daily struggles" – through so called "single loop learning." But when ongoing pressures accumulate or new ones threaten, simple corrective measures are no longer adequate.

These pressures take the form of the very factors that drive health systems: a bulging demographic cohort (increasingly burdened by chronic disease, comorbidities, and fragility) attempting to pass through a structure rife with bottlenecks. The existence of these bottlenecks (at the input, throughput, and output stages) indicates an underfunded, understaffed, and under-performing healthcare system, which is weakened by a highly polarised and divisive political environment.

A common (and not unexpected) thread to both crises is the links between austerity, access to effective healthcare, and outcomes. In Canada for example, total health expenditure as a percentage of GDP has fallen since 2010, while waiting times have hit all time highs and performance indicators all time lows. The UK has witnessed similar trends.

Another commonality is the failure to plan ahead and to rely instead on short term, reactive, ad hoc decisions. A recent NHS select committee report concluded that a "culture of short termism seems to prevail in the NHS and adult social care. The short-sightedness of successive governments is reflected in a Department of Health that is unable or unwilling to think beyond the next few years." For example, rather than embrace the recommendations of the Barker Commission (the antithesis of short termism in the long span of its review, which looked back to 1948 and forward through the rest of the 21st century), the UK government has let social care decline to the point that it is little more than a "threadbare safety net". Elsewhere, seemingly random promises of £350 or £100 million injections into the NHS are revealing indicators of this short termism.

In Canada where there is no national health plan and services are delivered by the provinces and territories, short termism is often the hallmark of cash strapped governments – a reality exemplified in workforce planning or rather the lack of it. Increased demand, staff shortages, and overwork manifest in physicians leaving the profession or retiring early, low morale, and very high levels of burnout. GPs' feelings of being undervalued and not respected are worsened by deep inequalities, which see some specialists (such as radiologists and ophthalmologists) earn salaries five times greater than GPs. The NHS is similarly plagued by the linked phenomena of low morale and burnout and is struggling to hold onto its workforce.

Too often the complexity of these health systems is met with ill-conceived efforts to improve them, which take the form of centralisation of structures or concentration of power. In the UK this was seen in the unfolding of the 2012 Health and Social Care Act, which was put together by a handful of politicians in 12 days, and which ultimately breached the trust between the medical profession and politicians. Over the past four years the government has played a blame game with the NHS crisis, alternately pointing the finger at NHS management, patients, and GPs and hospital doctors.

In Canada, an almost identical situation exists. Governments have sought to deal with complexity and the reality that there's "no single point of control" by alternately centralizing and decentralising services, assembling or dismantling local health authorities, all the while bemoaning the bureaucracy, professional associations, and irresponsible patients.

The paradox is that this July both the NHS and Canadian Medicare have a number of reasons to celebrate their successes. Medicare is still seen to embody Canadian values and the NHS remains a "national religion." Cross country data also show that for most indicators the UK performs well against its peers.

However, neither the NHS nor Medicare is sustainable. Instead of being stuck on the endless loops of detecting and correcting errors, both healthcare services need a systems approach (double-loop learning), which occurs when the error is "detected and corrected in ways that involve the modification of an organisation's underlying norms, policies, and objectives."

The idea of taking a systems approach to these healthcare services is not new, yet its implementation has so far failed to materialise, perhaps falling at the hurdles of tackling difficult questions and confronting powerful stakeholders. It takes discipline to avoid knee jerk reactions to a crisis – the temptation is to concentrate power or eschew responsibility. Yet fiscal sustainability will only be achieved by taking into account the value of public health and prevention and what we know of the social determinants of health: you need to plan for the long term with patient centered care as the driving force.

A Rising Tide: the Case Against Canada as World Citizen

Lancet, May 2014[76]

Ecocide, a crime against humanity Canadian Prime Minister Stephen Harper (2006-15) was a precursor to President Donald Trump 1.0. This article reviews Harper's tenure, especially his pursuit of a $600 billion resource development strategy, a move that recalled 200 years of colonial history and maltreatment of Indigenous populations. Harper's policies foreshadowed the Trump era of deregulation, down-sizing government, muzzling of scientists, weakening of democratic institutions, human rights abuses, increasing inequalities and environmental degradation. For example,scant difference exists between Harper's labeling of the Kyoto Accord as a "socialist plot" and becoming the first leader to opt out of it and, Trump dismissal of climate change as "a hoax" and then his subsequent withdrawal from the Paris Accord.

———————◆———————

A generation ago, Canada was perceived to be an exemplary global citizen by the rest of the world: it took the lead on a host of international issues, including the Convention of Child Rights, freedom of information, acid rain, world peacekeeping, sanctions against South Africa's apartheid regime, and humanitarian and development assistance – much of this under conservative leadership.

During recent years, Canada's reputation as a global citizen has slipped,

---

[76]   For access to this original article and footnotes, see tiny.cc/RisingTide

in recent months more precipitously than ever before, and in new directions. The Climate Action Network recently ranked Canada 55th of 58 countries in tackling of greenhouse emissions. Results of other analyses show a government systematically removing obstacles to resource extraction initiatives by gutting existing legislation, cutting budgets of relevant departments, and eliminating independent policy and arms-length monitoring bodies.

Canada's reputation is further undercut by its silencing of government scientists on environmental and public health issues: scientists are required to receive approval before they speak with the media; they are prevented from publishing; and, remarkably, their activities are individually monitored at international conferences. These actions have outraged local and international scientific communities.

A survey done in December 2013, of 4000 Canadian federal government scientists showed that 90% felt they are not allowed to speak freely to the media about their work, and that, faced with a departmental decision that could harm public health, safety, or the environment, 86% felt they would encounter censure or retaliation for doing so. These trends are affected by the Canadian leadership's view that multilateralism is a "weak nation policy" and by its embrace of what it calls "sovereign self-interest", perceived as the conspicuous pursuit of economic goals and goals of resource-extraction industries. This world view is reflected in Prime Minister Stephen Harper's response to demands for him to end asbestos mining when he promised that "this government will not put Canadian [asbestos] industry in a position where it is discriminated against in a market where it is permitted" – a response that cast a pall over all Canadian environmental issues.

Domestically, claims by Canada's First Nations communities (whose traditional lands and territories encompass many of the country's natural resources), that environment and livelihoods are being destroyed by the oil sands, tailing ponds, and pipelines used in the oil industry, have been met by the Government tightening the flow of information. In addition to muzzling its scientists, the Government eliminated Statistics Canada's long-form census (a key source of data on vulnerable groups), defunded the First Nations Statistical Institute, shied from adequately measuring toxic air pollutants, and engaged the Canadian Security Intelligence Service and Royal Canadian Mounted Police to monitor indigenous activists and environmental groups, subsequently sharing this information with industry stakeholders. Revelations in January 2014, that the watchdog body mandated to oversee these agencies is led by lobbyists for the resource industries have startled even the most seasoned observers. Previously a leader in freedom of information, Canada is frequently cited for its decline in openness, most recently by the Center for Law and Democracy, in co-operation with the Madrid based Access Info Europe, which ranked it 55th of 93 countries, down from 40th in 2011.

Harper defends withdrawal of federal funding for non-governmental organisations (NGOs) that are critical of governmental policy, a reversal of a 50-year tradition of non-partisan support for civil society, saying: "if it's the case that we're spending on organisations that are doing things contrary to government policy, I think that is an inappropriate use of taxpayer's money and we'll look to eliminate it." Consistent with this logic, the Government was able to continue funding NGOs skeptical of global warming and supportive of the asbestos industries.

As for proscribing a way forward, it makes no sense to make recommendations that presume a level of political commitment that does not exist. However, if "self-interest" is the motivating force behind this Government's actions, it ought to develop and implement a global health strategy. Such a strategy would help set priorities, guide decision-making, and create efficiency and cooperation. A global health strategy would also prompt greater fairness and, with less to hide, greater transparency.

Trump 1.0 and 2.0: Ecocide
Deregulation Amid Fires and Hurricanes
BMJ Opinion, September 2017[77]

Ecocide, a crime against humanity Set against the two major climate disasters of
2025, the Texas floods and the California fires, EPA Director Lee Zeldin publically
committed to "the greatest act of deregulation in the history of the United States" - to
remove from the agency any authority to regulate green house emissions. This article
reviews hurricanes Harvey and Irma, which struck the Houston, Texas and the Florida
Keys in 2017. It raises questions about the impact of the simultaneous deregulation of
land development and "game-changing" deregulation of the EPA. It also raises questions about US's influence on global initiatives to tackle the climate crisis.

———————◆———————

Deregulation is at or near the top of the neoliberal agenda in most
liberal democracies, inspiring governments to cut back their regulations
and free up the private sector to flourish as it will. However, for many
observers, deregulation is undermining democratic processes to benefit
the few and producing results to the detriment of many. The colossal
disasters seen in Houston, Florida, and Grenfell are (or ought to be) reminders of this.

---

[77] https://blogs.bmj.com/bmj/2017/09/27/chris-simms-deregula-
tion-amid-fires-and-hurricanes/

As was noted recently in an editorial in the *BMJ*, "if public health is concerned with the prevention of illness, injury, and premature death" it must help to address the political and social determinants of health that underlie disasters like these. And those who would champion public health mustn't turn away from speaking truth to power – to those that set the narrative, control the media, silence the powerless, and make the rules and regulations.

Houston and Florida, recently hit by hurricanes Harvey and Irma, have been described as ticking time bombs due to intense population growth and the unwise, unregulated development of coastal areas set against a background of global warming. Scientists characterise the floods as a design problem: Houston is a city built on cement sprawling onto coastal prairie land, and Florida has absurdly erected high rises on barrier islands and marshes, swamps, and wetlands. Both are also marked by governance that has in recent years ignored the environmental vulnerability of these regions and encouraged development in its place.

As has been described elsewhere, Houston is a city organised "around one principle: unfettered development. Houston has no zoning regulations." Research reports by Texas A&M University that focused on the development of Greater Houston's wetlands describe a city disinclined to embrace an effective regulation process. One study showed a loss of 70% of Greater Houston's wetlands between 1992 and 2010, another revealed a half-hearted process for approving permits, and another showed widespread disregard for fulfilling permit conditions.

Despite environmental warnings by experts, the previous head of the Harris County Flood Control District (in Houston) criticised scientists and conservationists for being "anti-growth", complaining last year: "They have an agenda … their agenda to protect the environment overrides common sense in a lot of cases."

Meanwhile, analysts warning of the greatly increased risk of disaster in Tampa, Florida (along with other US coastal cities) are ignored by government and industry. As was a 2013 World Bank and OECD analysis of 136 cities at risk of floods and storm surge, which placed Tampa and Miami in the top 10.

In 2011 Florida's governor led a campaign of deregulation: eliminating the state watchdog agency presiding over development, cancelling a landmark growth management law, and devolving power to business dominated local government. An official with the International Code Council observed that local "jurisdictions don't want to take the time, effort, or political capital or money to invest in improving their [building] codes," even though this neglect shores up environmental problems for the future.

The Florida Center for Investigative Reporting also claimed that the governor allegedly enforced an unwritten gag on state employees, including Department of Environment (DEP) employees. For example, one DEP employee said, "We were told by the regional director that we were no longer supposed to say 'global warming,' 'climate change' or 'sea level rise" – an echo of President Donald Trump's recent silencing of employees at the Environmental Protection Agency.

Indeed, for those hoping for national leadership to halt this kind of careless development, Trump's election as president seems to put an end to that prospect. A month before the floods, he signed an executive order to reverse Barack Obama's tightened regulations for flood standards. He had argued that "This over-regulated permitting process is a massive, self-inflicted wound on our country – it's disgraceful – denying our people much needed investments in their community." I would query the phrases "our people," "over-regulated permitting process," and exactly what is "disgraceful."

Elsewhere, the wildfires that have raged around the world over the past year (from Canada to southern Europe) prompted the journal *Nature Plants* to last month publish an editorial focusing on how these "natural events" are being converted into "unnatural disasters." It stated that the interactions between urban planning, global warming, and forest management "are conspiring to make the relationship [between humanity and nature] ever more destructive."

London's Grenfell fire is the antithesis of a natural disaster, yet it and the charred skeleton of the tower are stark reminders of the risk of ignoring evidence-based rules and regulations and the complaints these oversights generate, while instead decrying red tape and clamoring for a "bonfire of regulations."

Although neoliberalism is couched in the concept of "freedom," we have to ask what kind of freedom it offers and who it benefits. For those concerned with "the prevention of illness, injury, and premature death," whether individually or as a group or association, they need to call out those who seek to put profits and growth over public health and safety.

There are few new lessons to learn from these natural events and unnatural disasters. What does begin to emerge though is that failing to heed those lessons that have long been available will yield more frequent and profound events than most of us have seen before.

Canada's new government: Climate change, "regulatory capture," and "cathedral thinking"[78]

BMJ October 6, 2016

Ecocide, a crime against humanity Ecocide is defined as "unlawful or wanton acts committed with knowledge that there is a substantial likelihood of severe and widespread or long-term damage to the environment being caused by those acts." This article examines how Canadian resource extraction industries dominated the government agencies tasked with regulating them, a phenomenon known as "regulatory capture." This dynamic was particularly evident during the tenure of Canadian Prime Minister Stephen Harper, when the oil, gas, and mining industries were given free rein, significantly harming the environment and planetary health.

◆

It's a year this month since Justin Trudeau was elected as Canada's 23rd Prime Minister, ending a decade of conservative rule under Stephen Harper. By most accounts he has set a progressive and inclusive agenda at home, while internationally he has eschewed populist sentiments (seen in many countries)—welcoming instead 25 000 Syrian refugees, re-engaging with UN agencies, and endorsing free trade.

Despite this promising start, evidence suggests that he has paid inadequate attention to the influence of resource industries on public policy making—the outcome of which is detrimental to environmental and public health and, inevitably, human rights. The type of influence exerted by Canada's oil, gas, mining, and pipeline industries is known as regulatory capture. Predominant during the Harper years (but widely reported as cleaned up by Trudeau), "capture" implies that "regulatory agencies eventually come to be dominated by the very industries they were

---

[78] Chris Simms (2016) "Canada's new government: climate change, regulatory capture and cathedral thing" BMJ Opinion, October 6, 2016 https://blogs.bmj.com/bmj/2016/10/06/climate-change-regulatory-capture-and-cathedral-thinking/

charged with regulating." Physicians, nurses, and their professional associations across the world have focused on the detrimental effects of climate change on health and the benefits of tackling climate change. Advocacy groups, such as the UK Health Alliance on Climate Change, have committed themselves to taking action: "in this unequal battle with big business" they have divested their fossil fuel holdings, lobbied policy makers and politicians, and sought to improve our understanding of the ultimate impact of anthropogenic carbon dioxide emissions (and other gases and aerosols) on health.

Resource extraction industries have typically sought to do just the opposite. Whether in the private or public sectors, they have pursued practices similar to those used by tobacco companies: to thwart regulators and to manage public perceptions of the risks associated with their industry.

For example, recent revelations suggest that the review of a proposed $16 billion Canadian oil pipeline (Energy East)—the longest in North America if completed—was marred by "regulatory capture." The pipeline is contentious because it could facilitate a 40% increase in oilsands production, has been estimated to potentially produce an extra 32 million tonnes of greenhouse gas emissions each year, and will obliterate promises on climate change Trudeau made in Paris.

Yet it's been reported that panel members of the National Energy Board (NEB) (the regulator charged with independent assessment of energy projects) met privately and improperly with businessmen representing the pipeline industry, including Energy East, in direct contravention of their mandate. Panel members including the chairman were obliged to recuse themselves—bringing to a juddering halt this gargantuan pipeline project.

Within the resource extraction industries (like the tobacco industry) some have been pulled up for going out of their way to obscure how they achieve "regulatory capture," the means by which their consultants influence government and how they suppress unwanted health information. For example, at its recent annual general meeting (AGM) in Calgary, the management of one of the world's largest oilsands producers successfully defeated a shareholder motion (that nevertheless had 40% support), which would have forced it to reveal the "payments it makes to lobbyists, trade associations, and grassroots campaigns to influence public policy."

Prompting the shareholder movement in the first place was information revealed by whistleblowers who claimed that "Suncor was one of the biggest impediments of the passage of two pieces of pivotal legislation on tailings management and water use in the oil sands." Furthermore, the parent company of another large oilsands producer is being investigated by 17 attorneys general in the US for trying to suppress information on the risks of climate change. Not surprisingly, the strategies adopted by state prosecutors are the same as those they successfully used to pursue tobacco companies.

Another instance of flawed process is seen in the approval by the Trudeau government of an $8.8 billion hydro dam in northern British Colombia, known as Site C. Its 83 km reservoir will flood traditional lands and sacred burial grounds of First Nations people. Scientists say that the environmental effects of Site C will be "greater than for any project ever assessed under the history of the Canadian Environmental Assessment Act."

More than 250 scientists, the Royal Society of Canada, and First Nations leadership describe the review process as expedited, nontransparent, and sidestepping normal environmental assessment. It abrogates the UN Declaration on the Rights of Indigenous Peoples and ignores Trudeau's explicit promise to obtain "prior and informed consent" from First Nations. Ironically, the Minister of Justice whose intervention is needed to halt construction actually campaigned against the dam before being elected to Parliament, calling it an assault on the "pristine" environment and a prime example of riding roughshod over indigenous peoples.

Her failure to even comment on the dam is a reminder of the power of power.

Physicians fighting climate change would not refute Trudeau's responsibility to protect Canada's future prosperity, yet they would strenuously object to "regulatory capture" and hope to see better balance between economic, environmental, and human rights goals. Trudeau promised as much in his online mandate letters to each of his ministers, including health, environment and climate change, indigenous and northern affairs, and energy. He directed the latter to modernize the NEB, "restore robust oversight," and "regain public trust" in environmental assessment.

The 2016 Global Risks Report says that climate change (and failure to take steps to mitigate it) is the greatest risk facing the world community - one that underlies other risks such as drought, political instability, migration, and terrorism.

An interesting approach to addressing these perils - one whose values are the antithesis of the selfishness and short-sightedness associated with regulatory capture is "cathedral thinking." Recently cited by Stephen Hawking, it is an architectural metaphor that envisions today's generation investing its time and resources to benefit future generations. The notion of cathedral thinking stems from medieval times when architects and artisans embarked on building a cathedral knowing they would never see the end product. It implies a shift not only from individualism to the greater good, but to the greater good of the future.

Justin Trudeau, with high favourability ratings at home and growing international stature, is well placed not only to end "regulatory capture," but to provide fresh leadership on climate change and good global governance.

Canada's Fort McMurray Fire: mitigating global risks

Chris Simms Lancet August 2016

Ecocide In the spring and summer of 2023 and again in 2025, media outlets likened the eerie orange haze from Canadian wildfires—which engulfed U.S. East Coast cities like New York, Boston, and Washington, D.C., as well as parts of the Midwest—to "the surface of Mars." This article examines the 2016 Fort McMurray fire in Western Canada. The disaster was fueled by climate change, El Niño, and forest fragmentation, deregulation, budget cuts to prevention programs, and a disregard for scientific advice. At its core, however, was the outsized influence of industry lobbyists and unchecked resource extraction. By the summer of 2025, wildfires reached their second-worst levels on record, leaving Toronto with the world's second-worst air quality.

———————◆———————

On May 1, 2016, a colossal forest fire began to sweep into Fort McMurray, a boomtown centred in the middle of the Alberta oil sands in Canada. Over the ensuing 3 weeks it grew to more than 3000 km², forced the evacuation of 88 000 residents, destroyed thousands of homes and buildings, and is expected to negatively affect the gross domestic product. The fire is seen by many as another natural disaster linked to climate change, El Niño, and forest fragmentation. Furthermore, the National Aeronautics and Space Administration's Goddard Institute for Space Studies reported that last month was the hottest April on record globally—and the seventh consecutive month to have broken global temperature records.[79]

Events in Fort McMurray are relevant to many in the field of global risk and climate change. For example, the UN Office for Disaster Risk Reduction seeks to tackle hazards before they become disasters through

---

[79] Scientific American reports 99 percent chance 2016 will be the hottest year on record. http://www.scientificamerican.com/article/99-percent-chance-2016-will-be-the-hottestyear-on-record

a culture of prevention, a thorough understanding of risk, by ongoing review of policies and priorities, and by good governance in support of collaboration and partnership.

Although Prime Minister Justin Trudeau sought to avoid casting blame in the midst of so much suffering (and fortitude), several aspects of the fire are striking. First, the public and private sectors failed to take notice of repeated and explicit warnings by forestry experts of the risks of rapid expansion of resource extraction industries northward into boreal forests without taking measures to mediate those risks.[80] Fort McMurray is seen by scientists as a "huge oil complex [built] in the middle of a forest ecosystem that is designed to burn—forests regenerate themselves through fire". [81]

Second, even as the forests became increasingly dry and dangerous, the Alberta provincial government made large cuts in its 2016 spring budget to forest fire preparation, including prevention and mitigation; it halved its base wildfire management budget. Cuts to basic programmes such as FireSmart that included initiatives such as tree thinning, suggests a poor understanding of the immanent risk by the decision makers.[82]

Finally, risk reduction and prevention depend on good governance. The relationship between the public and private sectors lacks transparency, and Canadian resource industries fight hard to keep it that way. For example, one week before the fire (April 28, 2016), at its annual general meeting in Calgary, Canada, the management of the largest oil sands producers successfully defeated a shareholder motion (that nevertheless had 40% support), which would have forced it to reveal its funding of

[80] Canadian Council of Forest Ministers Canadian Wildland Fire Strategy: A vision for an innovative and integrated approach to managing the risks. http://cfs.nrcan.gc.ca/bookstore_pdfs/26218.pdf

[81] Pittis D Sometimes it takes a disaster like Fort McMurray to make us prepare for the next one: Don Pittis. CBC News (Toronto). http://www.cbc.ca/news/business/fort-mcmurray-disaster-risk-prevention-1.3567955

[82] Henton D Did cuts to fire program budget have a role to play in Fort McMurray Fire? Calgary Herald (Calgary). http://calgaryherald.com/news/politics/did-cuts-to-fireprogram-budget-have-a-role-to-play-in-fort-mcmurray-fire

lobbyists, trade associations, and grassroots communications—which are widely seen by the public, and whistleblowers, as pivotal in preventing environmental legislation.[83] The parent company of another large oil sands producer is among several oil companies being investigated by 17 attorney generals in the USA for trying to suppress the risks of climate change.[84]

The Fort McMurray fire is one more example of failure to mitigate. As the fire spread to oil sands work camps near Fort McMurray and then crossed the border into the province of Saskatchewan—at least one voice of reason was heard. Christy Clark, Premier of British Columbia (where 80 fires are now ravaging the province), said that because of climate change things are getting progressively worse, "and we are girding for what is going to come next". She called for implementing a national forest fire plan.[78] This requires national leadership, open and honest collaboration with industry, and dedicated resources.

[83] Prystup M Suncor on expansion spree in down oilpatch. The Tyee (Vancouver). http:// thetyee.ca/News/2016/04/29/Suncor-Expansion-Spree/
[84] Gibson K says team up to take on the fossil fuel industry. CBS News (New York). http://www.cbsnews.com/news/states-team-up-to-take-on-the-fossil-fuel-industry/ [78] Cheadle B Climate change sparking need for national forest fire plan: Christy Clark. *The Globe and Mail* (Toronto). http://www.theglobeandmail.com/news/british-columbia/climate-change-sparking-need-for-national-forest-fire-plan-christy-clark/article30083692/

WAR

This section examines the 2003 Iraq War and the Israel-US/Gaza conflict. The two share commonalities: both were driven by extreme right-wing conservatives who seized the opportunity to act on long-standing agendas. In each case, there were high numbers of civilian deaths, deliberately undercounted. Most corporate media failed to meet their own journalistic standards in their reporting on these conflicts which were marked by numerous war crimes. Political cowardice in wealthy nations, especially the UK and US, facilitated and prolonged the violence.

Iraq
Mr. Blair "Was the enterprise worthwhile?"

———————◆———————

On 29 January 2010, in the final minutes of the afternoon session of the Chilcot Inquiry, its Chair, Sir John Chilcot, pointedly asked Mr. Blair, "Was the enterprise worthwhile?"

Blair's response to the Chair was to single out one item to substantiate his claim that the invasion was justified. He stated that, as a result of removing Hussein, Iraq's child mortality rate had fallen from 13% in 2000–2002 to 4% in 2010. However, Mr. Blair's claim was inaccurate. The child mortality rate during 2000–2002 was not 13%; it was between 4% and 6%, meaning his figures were overstated by two to three times.

On February 17, 2003 Blair first cited these erroneous data to help rationalize the invasion of Iraq. The Foreign and Commonwealth Office (FCO) and the Department for International Development (DfID) had warned the Prime Minister's office that these figures were unreliable and came from an untrustworthy source. A FCO memo (endorsed by DfID) stated:

"There are no truly reliable figures on child mortality; the source of the only available data was a study conducted with the Iraqi regime's 'help,' which relied on some Iraqi figures. The latter have proved questionable."

The Prime Minister's office ignored these warnings, and Blair proceeded to cite a 13% mortality rate as fact—with a certainty that mirrored his claims about weapons of mass destruction (WMD) – claims, in the words of the Chilcot Report, were made "with a certainty that was not justified."

In fact, Blair was subject to a string of allegations that he deceived the public. [85] [86] In response, he said "I did not mislead this country. There were no lies, there was no deceit, there as no deception". [87] It was notable however that after the release of the Chilcot Report, in a televised BBC interview, Sir John Chilcot stated simply that Tony Blair was "not straight" with the British public. [88]

Blair continues to insist that by removing Saddam Hussein, the war "was worth it"[89] - here too, with a certainty that was groundless. The war in fact precipitated the rise of Iran and new forms of terrorism. According to the World Bank, its governance indicators show that "states in the region are no more politically stable, effectively governed, accountable, or participatory than they were two decades ago." [90] On July 7, 2025, the 20th anniversary of the 7/7 attack in London, which killed 52 people and injured 750, the former head of counter-terrorism said the UK's participation in the Iraq war increased domestic radicalization and extremism.[91] It is estimated that 4.6 million people have died indirectly in post 9/11 war zones.[92]

[85] https://www.theguardian.com/commentisfree/2010/jan/29/tony-blair-chilcot-iraq-inquiry
[86] https://www.independent.co.uk/news/uk/politics/the-case-against-blair-15-charges-that-have-yet-to-be-answered-2190375.html
[87] https://www.c-span.org/video/?412303-1/british-prime-minister-tony-blair-chilcot-iraq-report
[88] https://www.google.com/search?sca_esv=ca6797ecbd91f455&q=john+chilcot+interview&tbm=vid&source=lnms&prmd=nvimbstz&sa=X&ved=2ahUKEwi6hZCPpbWEAxVUMlkFHTVoAXQQ0pQJegQIDxAB&biw=1366&bih=599&dpr=1#fpstate=ive&vld=cid:9ddf6263,vid:2tPygSfzEBg,st:0
[89] https://www.c-span.org/video/?291738-8/tony-blair-british-iraq-inquiry-part-4
[90] https://www.atlanticcouncil.org/blogs/menasource/how-the-war-in-iraq-changed-the-world-and-what-change-could-come-next/
[91] https://www.theguardian.com/uk-news/2025/jul/06/iraq-war-made-extremists-of-people-ex-police-terrorism-chief-looks-back-at-77
[92] https://watson.brown.edu/costsofwar/papers/summary

Box 1.3 Iraq War was Predetermined

A plethora of evidence suggests that the invasion of Iraq was pre-determined. One striking example comes from an anecdote recounted by Richard A. Clarke, the U.S. Counterterrorism Czar (see attached video). Late in the day of September 11, 2001, just before a meeting of national security advisors, Clarke recalls:

"We were standing around talking, waiting for the President to join us. Don Rumsfeld, the Secretary of Defense, was talking about bombing Iraq. I didn't understand. I said, 'I'm not getting this. It was al-Qaeda that attacked us. We have to go into Afghanistan now.' It had been a long, stressful day for him, for me. I thought perhaps somebody wasn't firing on all cylinders."[93]

The following day, President Bush somewhat irritably instructed Clarke and his aides to find evidence linking Saddam Hussein to the September 11 attacks.

---

[93] https://www.youtube.com/watch?v=KQAHMB_XnpA (cited at 1hr:26 minute mark)

I and the public know
What all school children learn
Those to whom evil is done
Do evil in return
—**W.H. Auden Collected Poems**

GAZA

———◆———

I sraelis, diaspora Jewry and friends of Israel everywhere ought to be aware that Israel is at risk of becoming a pariah state, a source of shame. So wrote Thomas Friedman in the *New York Times*, June 2025. He warned that Israel "instead of being seen by Jews as a safe haven from antisemitism, will be seen as a new engine generating it" and that people need to resist Netanyahu's "utter indifference to the number of civilians being killed in Gaza today" and his "ugly and nihilistic war".[94]

Israel's former Prime Minister Ehud Olmert claimed that his country is waging a "war of extermination: the indiscriminate, unrestrained, cruel, and criminal killing of civilians"[95] He told CNN, May 28th, 2025, "What else is it, if its not a war crime"?[96]

On June 27th, Haim Tomer, former head of Israeli Mossad Intelligence, said in response to the carnage, "stop it, stop it right now. On the spot. We have achieved enough."[97]

By late July and early August there was global outcry among world leaders over the deliberate starvation of Gazans. Two leading Israeli human rights groups, B'Tselem and Physicians for Human Rights Israel, for the first time, accused Israel of committing genocide in Gaza and taking coordinated action to intentionally destroy Palestinian society.[98]

---

[94] https://www.nytimes.com/2025/06/10/opinion/israel-gaza-anti-semitism.html
[95] https://www.haaretz.com/opinion/2025-05-27/ty-article-opinion/.premium/enough-is-enough-israel-is-committing-war-crimes/00000197-0dd6-df85-a197-0ff64a5c0000
[96] https://www.cnn.com/2025/05/28/middleeast/ehud-olmert-criticizes-gaza-war-oped-intl
[97] https://www.youtube.com/watch?v=-9RTR9bIh6o
[98] https://www.btselem.org/sites/default/files/publications/202507_our_genocide_

***

This collection is about "social murder" and "crimes against humanity"; its also about dehumanization, - the mental loophole that enables us to ignore or harm others.

The following pages examine Netanyahu's response to the October 7th massacre and the strategies that he implemented that gave rise sharp criticism even from "Israelis, diaspora Jewry and friends of Israel". However, I first begin by examining the tallying of civilian deaths in Gaza.

Reporting the Deaths At the time of the January 19th, 2025, ceasefire, the "official" Gaza death toll exceeded 46,000.[99] However, damage to Gaza's healthcare infrastructure diminished the Ministry of Health's ability to collect reliable mortality data. As early as November 2023, the ministry began relying on media reports.[100] This method is known as passive surveillance methodology (PSM). Experts warn that using PSM for estimating war zone mortality may capture as little as 10-20% of actual casualties. For example, during the Iraq war, PSM estimates allowed George W. Bush to claim 30,000 Iraqi deaths in December 2005, when there were, according to the Lancet (2006), up to 10 times that number of deaths.

The MoH reported that, as of June 30, 2024, there were 37,877 deaths and multiple sources reported 10,000 bodies buried under the rubble in Gaza. A 2025 Lancet study on traumatic injury mortality in Gaza found that these figures may undercount deaths by 41%. Using multiple data sources and capture-recaptured analysis, the authors estimated 64,260 traumatic deaths between October 2023 and June 2024.[101] This would mean that one year later, the death toll would be 80,000.

---

eng.pdf
[99] Israel claimed half of these were Hamas fighters.
[100] https://www.washingtoninstitute.org/policy-analysis/gaza-fatality-data-has-become-completely-unreliable
[101] https://www.thelancet.com/journals/lancet/article/PIIS0140-6736(24)02678-3/fulltext

A July 2024 Lancet article estimate indirect Gazan deaths – those caused for example, by untreated pre-existing non-communicable disease or communicable disease associated with collapse of public health systems or environmental degradation.[102] The MoH, reported that as of June 19, 2024, there were 37,396 direct deaths and another 10,000 bodies buried under the rubble. Given that indirect deaths in recent conflicts range from 3 to 15 times the number of direct deaths, the authors used a conservative multiplier of four, yielding a death toll of 186,000. One year later, July 2025, when 90% water and sanitation is destroyed, 92% of housing stock was damaged or destroyed, 94% of hospitals are damage or destroyed, and 75% of Gaza's population is at "emergency" and "catastrophic" levels of food deprivation caused by the 2025 blockade, this estimate is likely understated.[103]

Using a direct death toll of 80,000 and remaining with a conservative multiple of four, the number of indirect Gazan deaths would be 320,000.[104]

The Bombing Obliteration bombing (also known as saturation bombing) constitutes a war crime under Article 51 of Protocol I of the Geneva Convention. On January 16th, President Biden made the following statement in a televised MSNBC interview:

"I said, 'but Bibi, you can't be carpet bombing these communities'. And he said to me, 'well, you did it, you carpet bombed', not his exact words, 'but carpet bombed Berlin. You dropped a nuclear bomb.'"[105]

[102] https://www.thelancet.com/journals/lancet/article/PIIS0140-6736(24)01169-3/fulltext
[103] https://www.who.int/news/item/12-05-2025-people-in-gaza-starving--sick-and-dying-as-aid-blockade-continues
[104] A recent preliminary study by Michael Spagat (et al) estimated there were 75,200 violent deaths between October 7, 2023 and Jan 5 2025 and another 8540 due to starvation, disease and collapse of the health system. This total of nearly 84,000 deaths exceeds previous estimates. The violence of 2025 will greatly increase these numbers. https://www.researchgate.net/publication/392872177_Violent_and_Nonviolent_Death_Tolls_for_the_Gaza_War_New_Primary_Evidence
[105] https://www.timesofisrael.com/biden-recalls-telling-netanyahu-in-october-2023-you-cant-be-carpet-bombing-gaza/

This conversation drew attention because Netanyahu never denied IDF was carpet bombing. It was reported elsewhere as the day "Biden just gave away Netanyahu's whole game".[106]

The *New York Times* published an article on the MSNBC interview the next day. It did not include any reference to carpet bombing.[107]

Loosening the Rules Netanyahu's 'game' included changing the rules of engagement to give the IDF a free hand to undertake saturation bombing. On December 27th, 2024, the *New York Times* (belatedly) published a significant 6,000-word article describing how Israel, on October 7th, removed civilian protections and loosened its rules of war. These changes allowed mid-ranking officers to bomb non-priority targets, target low-ranking fighters, permit up to 20 civilian casualties. In certain cases, senior officers could authorize up to 100 - described as "crossing an extraordinary threshold for a contemporary Western military".[108]

Loosening of the rules also meant that "the military could target rank-and-file militants as they were at home surrounded by relatives and neighbors, instead of only when they were alone outside". This policy helps explain the frequent reports of entire families being obliterated - sometimes four generations killed in a single strike, and in some cases, more than 100 casualties.[109] It also helps account for the high death toll among women and children.

In July 2024, Oren Ziv, an Israeli journalist, provided details of his interviews with IDF soldiers and commanders. He stated, "It seems soldiers were shooting not for tactical or military reasons, but simply out of boredom—to pass the time or just because they could." He added, "The

---

[106] https://newrepublic.com/post/190365/joe-biden-benjamin-netanyahu-gaza-bombs

[107] https://www.nytimes.com/2025/01/17/world/middleeast/biden-interview-gaza-netanyahu.html

[108] https://www.nytimes.com/2024/12/26/world/middleeast/israel-hamas-gaza-bombing.html

[109] https://www.haaretz.com/middle-east-news/palestinians/2024-12-05/ty-article-magazine/.premium/entire-families-crushed-in-gaza-by-israeli-airstrikes-not-even-memories-remain/00000193-92bf-dfe8-a5db-fbff98170000

soldiers felt they could do whatever they wanted, that they wouldn't be held accountable. And all of this was done with the awareness of their commanders." [110]

Haaretz substantiated Ziv's claims in December with a report headlined, "No civilians. Everyone's a terrorist". Its subtext stated, "'Of 200 bodies, only 10 were confirmed as Hamas members': IDF soldiers who served told Haaretz that every Palestinian casualty was counted as a terrorist – "even if they were just a child." [111] *The Times of Israel* reviewed the Haaretz report the following day, noting one soldier as saying Gaza is a place "where there are no laws, where human life is worth nothing," and that Israeli soldiers are "taking part in the atrocities happening in Gaza." Another soldier claimed, "there are no innocents in Gaza." [112]

Total Urban Destruction Another part of Netanyahu's gameplan was to fulfill the promise - to flatten Gaza. A joint investigation by Israeli journalists Meron Rapoport and Oren Ziv asserts that a systematic campaign has been underway since 2024 to render Gaza unlivable by destroying buildings across the strip using bulldozers and explosives. [113] The purposive destruction was unrelated to any military activity. The report which focuses on Rafah, includes testimony from 10 soldiers involved in this operation, as well as videos [114] recorded by the soldiers themselves. [115]

One soldier said, "I secured four or five bulldozers (from another unit) and they demolished 60 houses per day". He said "The horizon is flat. There is no city". [116]

[110] https://www.democracynow.org/2024/7/12/israel
[111] https://www.haaretz.com/israel-news/2024-12-18/ty-article-magazine/.premium/idf-soldiers-expose-arbitrary-killings-and-rampant-lawlessness-in-gazas-netzarim-corridor/00000193-da7f-de86-a9f3-fefff2e50000
[112] https://www.timesofisrael.com/report-soldiers-say-open-fire-policies-in-gaza-too-loose-leading-to-civilian-deaths/
[113] https://www.972mag.com/israel-gaza-total-urban-destruction/
[114] https://x.com/orfialkov/status/1912843644001722397
[115] https://x.com/BwMnhm/status/1922272688346697836
[116] https://www.democracynow.org/2025/5/20/gaza_destruction_972_mag

No Witnesses Netanyahu's game plan included denying foreign press access to Gaza and "targeting" Palestinian journalists and media personnel. As of September 2025, more than 250 journalists have been killed, making this the deadliest conflict for journalists in history. On August 10, 2025, a well-known correspondent, Anas al-Sharif was deliberately killed along with four other journalists. The IDF claimed he was a member of Hamas. According to +972 Magazine, there is an IDF "legitimization cell" tasked with identifying reporters who could be smeared as undercover Hamas fighters.[117]

Inside Israel, the press is tightly controlled and censored. Gideon Levi, appearing on British television in June 2025, stated that Israeli media largely ignores events in Gaza and that Jewish Israelis are comfortable not knowing about the suffering of Gazans.[118] Evidence suggests they have a positive view of IDF and its actions in Gaza. According to a poll conducted by the Israeli Democracy Institute in June and published August 5, 2025, 78% of Jewish Israelis think the military "is making substantial efforts to avoid causing unnecessary suffering to Palestinians in Gaza" and 70% broadly trusts IDF's reporting of Palestinian casualties.

***

US Complicity Netanyahu's strategy relied on continued backing from the US President and Congress. Biden, the most pro-Israel of all US presidents up to that point, told Netanyahu on October 18, 2023, "Whatever you need, you've got it". From Trump, Netanyahu secured nearly unconditional support including for the transfer of Palestinians out of Gaza.

Robust military, diplomatic and technical support for Israel has been well documented.[119] Israel reportedly financed 70% of the conflict through US assistance. To many, this makes the US complicit in highly

---

117 https://www.theguardian.com/world/2025/aug/15/israeli-military-unit-reportedly-tasked-with-linking-journalists-in-gaza-to-hamas

118 https://www.youtube.com/watch?v=QVZjNx1ThFw

119 https://www.972mag.com/lavender-ai-israeli-army-gaza/

efficient and widespread acts of genocide. Of concern to many observers is the eagerness of tech companies like Google, Microsoft and Palantir to sell Gazan-killing" technology to Israel.[120]

One indicator of US legislators' support for Israel was the 50 standing ovations Netanyahu received when he addressed a joint session of Congress (July 24, 2024) and said, "give me the tools and I'll finish the job".

There are many striking examples of US complicity. For instance, it enabled Israel to use starvation as a weapon of war by failing to cut military assistance to Israel when it was blocking aid from entering Gaza (as required under the US Foreign Aid Assistance Act).[121] Although USAID sent Secretary of State Blinken a detailed 17-page memo[122] on Israel's misconduct, he mislead Congress May 24, 2024 by saying that "We do not currently assess that the Israeli government is prohibiting or otherwise restricting the transport or delivery of U.S. humanitarian assistance" – this at a time when 1.5 million tons of flour, enough to feed 1.5 million people for 5 months, was stranded 30 miles across the border. This at a time when Israeli's B'Tselem, stated simply that, with its blockades "Israel is committing the war crimes of starvation in the Gaza strip".[123]

The following week, the *Wall Street Journal* unconscionably published an article titled "Plenty of Food is Getting into Gaza".[124]

NRx and Project Esther Following the October 7 massacre, the Heritage Foundation traveled to Israel to implement a plan to dismantle the pro-Palestinian movement in the U.S. Known as Project Esther, it aimed "to

---

[120] https://www.business-humanrights.org/pt/latest-news/palantir-allegedly-enables-israels-ai-targeting-amid-israels-war-in-gaza-raising-concerns-over-war-crimes/
[121] Population, Refugees and Migration agreed with USAID's findings and the recommendation that the Foreign Assistance Act should have been triggered cutting off arms shipment to Israel.
[122] The State Department's own Bureau of Population, Refugees and Migration agreed with USAID's findings and the recommendation that the Foreign Assistance Act should have been triggered cutting off arms shipment to Israel.
[123] https://www.btselem.org/publications/202404_manufacturing_famine
[124] https://www.wsj.com/opinion/plenty-of-food-aid-is-getting-to-gaza-7da988cd

rebrand all critics of Israel and pro-Palestinian protesters as providing material support for terrorism," according to a May 18, 2025 *New York Times* investigative report.[125] It targeted universities, students, faculty, sought to remove curricula supportive of Palestinian rights and deport foreign students or faculty who advocated for those rights.[126] Stefanie Fox of *Jewish Voice for Peace* stated that while Project Esther involved a few smaller Jewish groups, but was primarily driven by far-right and evangelical Christian organizations and had little to do with Jewish safety. She noted that, given the Trump administration›s recent actions against pro-Palestinian voices, the Heritage Foundation is now «taking a victory lap."

Fox warned that the same suppression tactics could be used by government to target other groups – implementing for instance, Stephen Miller's immigration agenda.

US media Coverage of atrocities in Gaza by US mainstream media is a fraction of reporting undertaken by PBS, Democracy Now or Britain's, ITN (Channel Four News). It gives often Israel a platform to disseminate falsehoods. For instance, amid the blockade on food and supplies, when one million children were facing acute risk of starvation"[127] *NBC* ran the headline on April 17, 2025, "Aid Groups Describe Dire Conditions in Gaza as Israel Says There Is No Shortage of Aid."[128]

Elsewhere, a leaked *New York Times* memo directed its reporters not to use the word "Palestine" except in rare cases and advised against describing areas of Gaza as "refugee camps." It also recommended restricting terms like "genocide" and "ethnic cleansing," and avoiding the phrase

[125] https://www.nytimes.com/2025/05/18/us/project-esther-heritage-foundation-palestine.html
[126] https://www.democracynow.org/2025/5/19/project_esther
[127] https://www.gov.uk/government/news/aid-to-gaza-e3-foreign-ministers-statement-23-april-2025
[128] https://www.nbcnews.com/news/world/gaza-aid-shortage-israel-blockade-hunger-rcna201379

"occupied territory" when referring to Palestinian land.[129]

However, investigative journalists at the *New York Times* have produced important reports and essays on the Israel/US-Gaza conflict (included in these pages) on topics such as "loosening the rules of war", Project Esther and, how Netanyahu prolonged the war for his own political gain.

US media typically uses the passive voice when writing about atrocities in Gaza ("the most relied-upon tool of the oppressor".)[130] According to *Fairness in Accuracy & Reporting* (FAIR), while Israel openly declares starvation as a weapon, US media "hesitate to blame it for famine".[131] Interestingly, the *New England Journal of Medicine*, and the journals of the American Medical Association and the American Public Health Association used the passive voice to describe events in Gaza – this in sharp contrast to their uncompromising assessment of war crimes by Russia in Ukraine.

NRx, Ethnic Cleansing and US Media In the first month of his presidency Trump described Gaza as "literally a demolition site right now. Almost everything is demolished". He proposed that "we just clean out" the territory —not of rubble, but of people—a statement widely interpreted as advocating ethnic cleansing. He followed this with his bizarre "Riviera" video featuring a sunbathing Netanyahu. [132]

NRx's Curtis Yarvin first brought forward the idea turning Gaza into "Riviera of the Middle East" in the spring of 2024. He proposed expelling all Palestinians from the Strip and turning it into a beachfront luxury resort with Jared Kushner as developer.[133]

---

[129]   https://theintercept.com/2024/04/15/nyt-israel-gaza-genocide-palestine-coverage/

[130]   https://time.com/6695499/palestine-power-of-language-essay/

[131]   https://fair.org/home/as-israel-openly-declares-starvation Gazans -as-a-weapon-media-still-hesitate-to-blame-it-for-famine/

[132]   https://www.politico.eu/article/donald-trump-posts-gaza-riviera-ai-video-sunbathing-benjamin-netanyahu/

[133]   https://www.newyorker.com/magazine/2025/06/09/curtis-yarvin-profile

The month following Trump's allusion to ethnic cleansing, several commentators in the mainstream corporate media appeared to consider the idea. As reported by FAIR, Elliot Kaufman writing in the *Wall Street Journal* (WSJ), February 5, 2025, called Trump's 'proposal a "plan to free Palestinians from Gaza." [134] The same day the *WSJ* editorial board asked, "Is his idea so much worse than the status quo that the rest of the world is offering?"[135] A week later, Sadanand Dhume in the Wall Street Journal "If Indians and Pakistanis Can Relocate, Why Can't Gazans?" And writing in the *New York Times*, Bret Stephens observed that "Trump also warned Jordan and Egypt that he would cut off American aid if they refused to accept Gazan refugees, adding that those refugees may not have the right to return to Gaza. The president's threats are long overdue."[136]

Mainstreaming Extremism Netanyahu has led Israel for 12 of the last 14 years. Under his leadership the country has been exposed to sustained right-wing rhetoric and extremist narratives. During this time, the country shifted from "liberal democracy" to an "electoral democracy." This is primarily due to declines in transparency, the predictability of the law, attacks on the judiciary, the loss of civil liberties, and the elimination of democratic gatekeepers. Freedom of expression is increasingly restricted; the media is government-controlled, and surveillance has intensified under the "Spyware Law". Underlying the erosion of democracy and rise of authoritarianism is the far-right neo-reactionary belief in a hierarchically structured society.

Acts of incitement or calls for genocide—which would have led to arrest a decade ago—are now ignored. On "May 26, 2025, the AP (and other media outlets) reported that thousands of violent Israeli nationalists

[134] https://www.wsj.com/opinion/trumps-plan-to-free-the-palestinians-gaza-strip-for-eign-policy-middle-east-87ae687d
[135] https://www.wsj.com/opinion/donald-trump-gaza-hamas-palestinians-relocate-isra-el-benjamin-netanyahu-82f40f95?mod=e2tw
[136] https://www.nytimes.com/2025/02/11/opinion/trump-hamas-gaza-israel.html

paraded through Muslim areas of Old Jerusalem commemorating the conquest of the eastern part of the city.[137] They chanted "Death to Arabs", "Mohammed is dead", "1967 Jerusalem in our hand, 2025, Gaza in our hand" and singing "May your village burn".[138] According to Lindsey Hilsum, International Editor for Channel 4 News' (UK), reported that thousands chanted "kill the Arabs".

Contributing to these acts of incitement are far-right influencers such as Israel's Channel 14. In September 2024 three Israeli human rights groups accused the channel of providing a platform for genocidal rhetoric against Palestinians. The allegations included over 50 instances of calls for genocide and 150 statements advocating indiscriminate violence, mass expulsion, and starvation. [139] In late June 2025, the Guardian claimed the Israeli airwaves were filled with pro-genocide propaganda by lawmakers and public figures and published a sample of some of the worst.[140]

A series of polls and surveys provide insight into Israeli society, in particular, the way it relates to Gaza and its people. For example, A poll by the Jerusalem-based Israel Democracy Institute found that 73% of Israeli Jews between the ages of 15 and 24 described themselves as right-wing (compared to 46% of Jewish Israelis aged 65 and older). An analysis of these poll results, that drew on extensive interviews with young Israelis, suggests that, for many years, they have been exposed primarily to right-wing rhetoric and extremist narratives.[141]

---

[137] https://apnews.com/article/israel-palestinians-jerusalem-nationalist-march-ben-gvir-0c6471592182aac205115150d1b3a552

[138] https://www.pbs.org/newshour/world/thousands-of-israeli-nationalists-chant-death-to-arabs-during-annual-procession-through-jerusalem

[139] https://ww.haaretz.com/israel-news/2024-09-24/ty-article-magazine/.premium/israels-channel-14-has-repeatedly-called-for-genocide-against-palestinians-in-gaza/00000192-1f2e-d515-a1fa-5f3e99550000

[140] https://www.theguardian.com/commentisfree/2025/jun/27/israel-gaza-propaganda

[141] https://www.cnn.com/2025/03/28/middleeast/israel-young-people-extremist-views-intl-cmd

In June 2025, Haaretz reported "a grim" poll which showed that 82% of Jewish Israelis wanted the expulsion of Palestinians from Gaza.[142] A survey by the Institute for National Security Study in May 2025, showed that "64.5% of the Israeli public is not at all concerned or not very concerned about the humanitarian situation in the Gaza strip"[143]

Another survey undertaken in June 2025 by the Israel Democracy Institute asked the question, "To what extent should Israel take into account the suffering of the Palestinian civilian population in Gaza when planning military operations there?". The survey reported that "A clear majority in the Jewish sample (76.5%) think that Israel should not take the civilian population's suffering into account at all, or should only do so to a fairly small extent".[144]

A June 2025 poll conducted by the Israeli Democracy Institute, published August 5, 2025, asked "To what extent are you personally troubled or not troubled by the reports of famine and suffering among the Palestinian population in Gaza?". The results revealed that 58.6% Jewish Israelis answered, "not at all troubled" or "not so troubled" (23.4%).

Throughout the spring and summer of 2025, the world watched video footage of infants and children starving, and of tens of thousands of Gazans risking gunfire to access food. In these attempts, thousands were killed or wounded. On August 22, 2025, the UN officially declared a famine in Gaza. The replacement of an effective aid distribution system with the US-Israeli organization—absurdly named the "Humanitarian Relief Foundation"—appears designed to achieve military objectives and to humiliate Gazans. This assessment was confirmed in a report by Forensic Architecture and WPF entitled "The Architecture of Genocidal

---

[142] https://www.haaretz.com/israel-news/2025-06-03/ty-article/.premium/a-grim-poll-shows-most-jewish-israelis-support-expelling-gazans-its-brutal-and-true/00000197-3640-d9f1-abb7-7e742b300000

[143] https://www.inss.org.il/publication/survey-may-2025/?utm_source=active-trail&utm_medium=email&utm_campaign=Swords%20of%20Iron%20Survey%20Results%20-%20May%202025

[144] https://en.idi.org.il/articles/59568

Starvation in Gaza — March-August 2025."

In the US, a Gallop Poll released July 29 shows a rapid decline in support for Isreal's actions in Gaza - only 32% of US adults and more striking, among those age 18-34, only 9% supported Israel's actions in Gaza.[145]

Underscoring the words of Haim Tomer, former head of Israeli Mossad Intelligence, "stop it, stop it right now. On the spot. We have achieved enough"[146], Elana Sztokman, an American writer living in Israel for the last 30 years recently shared her views. "I woke up and said, 'I can't just keep going on as if this is all OK, as if this is normal.'" "Right now, We, Israel, are starving and bombing a nation to death." "Genocide. This is genocide. This is purposeful, deliberate, unrestrained killing of a people."

Yuli Novak, the director of B'Tselem, said her organization's report "Our Genocide" "is one we never imagined we would have to write... But in recent months, we have been witnessing a reality that has left us no choice but to acknowledge the truth."

Throughout August, 2025, Israel was seeking ways to displace Palestinians to other countries (such as Sudan and Syria) while simultaneously preparing an onslaught of Gaza city - this without a word of objection from the United States.

At this point in time, September 2025, we may reasonably make two statements:

Israel's understanding of its actions in Gaza, is essential to its self-understanding and; the United States' understanding of Israel, is essential to its self-understanding.

---

[145] https://news.gallup.com/poll/692948/u.s.-back-israel-military-action-gaza-new-low.aspx
[146] https://www.youtube.com/watch?v=-9RTR9bIh6o

The Iraq War, Chilcot, and Cherry-Picking Data: How to Find a Way Forward
BMJ Opinion, July 2016[147]

◆

Crimes against Humanity The first week of July 2016 was a week to remember. A cluster of war related stories dominated the media, including the 100th anniversary of the Battle of the Somme (1 July), the death of Elie Wiesel on 2 July, on 3 July there was the deadliest bombing in Bagdad since 2003, three days later we had the release of the Chilcot report and the 45 minute response it drew from former Prime Minister Tony Blair, and on 8 July the deployment of NATO troops into Eastern Europe (for the first time since the end of the Cold War).[148]

These events tend to underscore the importance of careful assessment of past mistakes and taking measures to prevent their reoccurrence. A recent editorial in *The BMJ* noted that whether we are speaking of apologising for the Iraq war or when things go wrong for patients, "the need to be open and honest" is fundamental and is the best pathway to learning lessons and gaining closure.

Among the core issues examined by the Chilcot report were the rationale for going to war and acknowledgement of its consequences. The

---

[147] For access to the original article and footnotes, see tiny.cc/IraqWarChilcot

[148] Some observers had the impression that Obama was deliberately provoking or taunting Putin, with NATO's support. Sweden and Finland sat at the top table with Obama at the NATO meeting. https://www.theguardian.com/world/2016/jun/06/nato-launches-largest-war-game-in-eastern-europe-since-cold-war-anaconda-2016

following paragraphs briefly look at the Blair government's management of evidence related to Iraqi mortality and the much-debated contention that one thing the Chilcot report tells us is there were no attempts to mislead. It draws on declassified memos included in the Chilcot report, a review of Iraqi mortality studies, and related commentary.

On 17 February 2003 (a month before the invasion of Iraq) Prime Minister Tony Blair made the case for invasion, including among his reasons the description of Iraq as a "country where today, 135 out of every 1000 Iraqi children die before the age of 5."

The Chilcot report notes that these mortality data were based on UNICEF's Iraq Child and Maternal Mortality Survey (ICMMS), which, like most country studies of its kind, depended upon the goodwill of the country government. Detailed analysis of this survey shows that Saddam Hussein's regime was using fear and intimidation to manipulate outcome data in order to bolster their claim that economic sanctions imposed by the UN were killing children. Declassified memos show that the Department for International Development (DfID) and the Foreign and Commonwealth Office (FCO) knew the data they had were questionable, but still used them as material that would make the best case for war.

Several UN sponsored surveys between 2005 and 2008 found that childhood mortality rates had actually been between 40 and 60 per 1000 live births. Yet when Blair was asked by Mr. Chilcot on 29 January 2010 (in the last minutes of the afternoon session of the inquiry), "was the enterprise worthwhile?" in direct response, he again cited child mortality rates of 130 per 1000 live births (2000-02). He said, *"That figure today is not 130, it is 40. That equates to about 50 000 young people, children [alive today who would not be if Saddam Hussein had remained in power] ... that's the result that getting rid of Saddam makes."*

To me the inconsistencies between these assertions and other evidence available at the time dispel the notion that there was no misleading in the lead up to the war or during the post-conflict era. Indeed, the

Chilcot report raises similar concerns about manipulation of Iraqi civilian mortality data – again, by various ministries and political figures. For example, the foreign secretary argued, "We need to find ways of countering the damaging perception that civilians are being killed needlessly, and in large numbers, by Coalition forces." Elsewhere, the report cites the following communication between FCO and Blair's office in October 2004.

"You asked for an assessment of civilian casualties in Iraq, noting that we cannot let figures of 10-15000 go unchallenged as if we are responsible for all of them ... The FCO recommend(s) that we stick to publishing terrorist responsibility for civilian casualties in individual incidents. Underlying this is concern that any overall assessment of civilian casualties will show that MNF (Multi-National Force – Iraq) are responsible for significantly more than insurgents/terrorists."

The report points out that it was a mistake a "trial (mortality) monitoring exercise initiated by No 10 in November 2004 was not completed" and that "greater efforts were not made to determine the number of civilian casualties."

These signs of cherry-picking data, of setting aside unwanted results, and of giving in to vested interests are evocative of recent efforts to tackle corruption in the scientific process. Hiding trial data that cast doubt on the safety and efficacy of drugs or succumbing to commercial or academic pressure is not dissimilar to squelching data that would undermine government policy or yielding to political pressure. When it comes to corruption of process, "we have to have many more mechanisms, much more skepticism, and much more willingness to challenge."

According to the British NGO Iraq Body Count (IBC), the manipulation of mortality data as part of an overriding "concern to sustain support for operations Iraq" (the Chilcot report) is disgraceful. However, as IBC points out, the "report should be commended for very forensically and effectively laying it bare." When it comes to "the need to be open and honest," to lessons learnt and clearing the way for apologising, the report at least suggests a step in the right direction and the possibility of closure for some.

Given that the invasion of Iraq was based on inaccurate information and has led to enormous human sacrifice, there is a need for accountability and open public debate. Blair and Bush claim the war was "worth it". If their judgement of "worth" is based on a sanitized body count, their judgment is once again based on inaccurate information.

Iraqi War: Civilian Deaths, March 2003-June 2006

———————◆———————

Crimes against Humanity The 2003 Iraq war was a murderous war , but there are too few reporters, recorders, and reliable witnesses" to know just how murderous it was.[149] The Iraqi Body Count (IBC) project attempts to provide clarity by using cross-checked media reports to tally the number of deaths. Frequently cited by governments and media outlets, the IBC acknowledges that its counts represent only a fraction of the actual fatalities. Its website notes that "many, if not most, civilian casualties will go unreported by the media."[150] Critics of IBC's argue that passive surveillance methodologies in war zones typically capture no more than 20% of deaths; others claim this figure is as low as 10%[151] Additionally, the IBC uses mainly English-speaking sources and is seen to have pro-US bias. For the period March 2003 and June 2006, IBC reported there were between 38,725 and 43,140 deaths.[152]

For the same period, an influential *Lancet* study[153] by Burnham et al. (2006) estimated 601,027 violent deaths. It was criticised by many scientists for bias and a small sample size and politicians dismissed it as not credible. Two notable studies undermined the Lancet findings: the first, conducted by the Iraq Family Health Study Group (IFHSG) (2008) and published in the *New England Journal of Medicine*

---

[149] https://www.iraqbodycount.org/database/
[150] https://www.iraqbodycount.org/
[151] https://www.thelancet.com/journals/lancet/article/PIIS0140-6736(06)69491-9/fulltext
[152] https://www.iraqbodycount.org/database/
[153] https://www.thelancet.com/journals/lancet/article/PIIS0140-6736(06)69491-9/fulltext

(NEJM)[154], reported 151,000 deaths between January 2002 and June 2006. The second study, by Hagopian (2013), published in *PLoS*[155] used the same methodology as Burnham et al. and reported 465,000 deaths for the period 2003-2011.

Missing Witnesses: Both the *PLoS* and *NEJM* studies share a common limitation: uncertain findings due to the lack of eyewitnesses to confirm whether residents were killed or fled. For example, a *NEJM* Perspective article accompanying the IFHSG study highlights the instability of the Iraqi population during the post-invasion period, noting that an estimated 1-2 million Iraqis were displaced. It cautions that the dissolution of a household means "no one remains to tell the former inhabitants' story."[156] Similarly, the lead author of the *PLoS* study acknowledges that, after extensive reflection, "we were simply unable to account for the massive migration out of Iraq." Recent research estimates that following the 2003 invasion, 4-5 million Iraqis fled the country and more than 9 million were displaced.[157]

Bias: The discrepancy between the IBC and Burnham et al. mortality estimates (43,140 versus 601,027) is striking. Both studies have faced criticism for perceived political motivations. The publication of the Burnham study, released three weeks before the 2006 US midterm elections, was viewed by some as an attempt to sway voters; the *Wall Street Journal* referred to it as "the Lancet's political hit."[158] On the other hand, the IBC was depicted as pro-Western and overly aligned with the US government.

[154] https://www.nejm.org/doi/full/10.1056/NEJMsa0707782?query=recirc_curate-dRelated_article

[155] https://journals.plos.org/plosmedicine/article?id=10.1371/journal.pmed.1001533#:~:text=By%20multiplying%20those%20rates%20by,not%20counted%20due%20to%20migration.

[156] https://www.nejm.org/doi/full/10.1056/nejmp0709003

[157] https://www.csis.org/analysis/iraq-20-years-after-invasion-humanitarian-displacement-and-climate-change-challenges#:~:text=The%20U.S.%2Dled%20coalition%20invaded,moderate%20or%20severe%20food%20insecurity.

[158] https://www.wsj.com/articles/SB119991629103078813

Critics have noted that the IBC's co-founders also co-directed "Every Casualty," an NGO partially funded by the United States Institute of Peace (USIP), which has been labeled a "neo-con group." Despite these associations, there is no concrete evidence of undue influence, even though prominent figures such as the US Secretary of Defense (Donald Rumsfeld), the Secretary of State (Colin Powell), and the president of the National Defense University have served on USIP's board of directors.

Both studies have been accused of attempting to shape public debate by "anchoring" an erroneous number of civilian deaths. The IBC was the first to publish estimates of civilian deaths, which the US government quickly adopted. In December 2005, when questioned about the number of Iraqi civilian deaths since the invasion, George W. Bush referenced IBC data, stating, "I would say 30,000, more or less, have died as a result of the initial incursion and the ongoing violence against Iraqis."[159]

At a White House press conference in October 2006, Bush dismissed the *Lancet* study saying, "I don't consider it a credible report" and added, "Neither does General Casey and neither do the Iraqi officials".[160] Critics of the Lancet study argue that it was meant to produce shocking estimates that would resonate for decades. Some editorial staff at the *Lancet* believe that while the Burnham study may have overestimated civilian mortality, it helped shift the conversation towards a more accurate assessment of the death toll.[161]

In November 2006, I spoke with the long-serving Technical Director of ORC Macro's Demographic Health Survey Program, which has provided technical assistance for over 350 surveys across 90 countries.[162] He is likely the foremost expert on the type of household survey methodology

---

[159] https://www.washingtonpost.com/archive/politics/2005/12/13/bush-estimates-iraqi-death-toll-in-war-at-30000/4eb845a0-0310-4e28-b6e9-556a39c947cc/
[160] https://www.theguardian.com/world/2006/oct/11/iraq.usa
[161] See https://www.prwatch.org/node/7034
[162] https://dhsprogram.com/data/Guide-to-DHS-Statistics/Description_of_The_Demographic_and_Health_Surveys_Program.htm

employed by Burnham. He followed up with an email (see full email in Appendix 1) that outlined three key points."

"I do not find much fault with the analysis. Using the report's figures for deaths and exposure, I estimate just about the same number of deaths and confidence intervals. Indeed, the estimate that I produce using UN projections is slightly higher.

"A second point has to do with the sample size. Indeed only 47 clusters with 1849 households were interviewed. The confidence intervals are quite large due to the small sample size and give estimates that can vary by 100% between the top and bottom of the interval. Indeed, the confidence intervals overlap for the periods May 04 –May 05 and June 05-June 06, which means that one cannot conclude that there was a change in mortality between the two periods. Because of the small number of clusters, I think the analysis by province should not have been presented (only Baghdad has enough to present)."

Third, he wrote "the sampling procedure used could lead to some bias, in some areas to overestimate and others to underestimate mortality". He then listed these instances (full email Appendix I).

On March 19, 2023—exactly 20 years after the start of the Iraq bombing—I contacted Dr. Gilbert Burnham, the lead author of the 2006 Lancet study, to discuss his estimates of civilian mortality during the first 40 months of the war. He responded the following day, coinciding with the 20th anniversary of the land invasion of Iraq (see full email in Appendix I).

In his response, Dr. Burnham made several key points. He repeatedly emphasized the importance of local knowledge – knowledge of the community, its population, displacement patterns, and local perceptions of conflict levels across governates. He wrote, "In each area we engaged a local colleague familiar with the area to help in the sampling. Known to the community he or she also gave the teams a sense of security and help in negotiations for access where needed." This stood in sharp contrast to the approach of the Iraq Family Health Study Group (IFHSG) (2008) study where, as Dr. Burnham noted "Interviewers identified themselves as employees of the Ministry of Health, then under the control of Shiite cleric Moktada al Sadr. Those interviewed, therefore, would be wary of saying a brother or son or husband had been killed by violence, fearing retribution".

Dr. Burnham also acknowledged the small sample size. "My goal had been 100 clusters, but in extensive negotiations with the data collectors, 47 clusters was the maximum number they would accept for personal safety reasons—so that's where the number came from, and we recognized that this would give wide confidence intervals. The distribution of deaths among governates was widely confirmed by Iraqis conversant with the conflict. So, although statistical comparisons were not that strong, it was consistent with local opinion."

He highlighted the physical and moral courage of team members, writing, "The interview team did an amazing job, some spending nights in jail and being threatened for their life while doing the data collection. Afterwards, of course there were many threats and accusations against all of us. My Iraqi colleague had threats against his life and dropped out of sight for a while. His teenage son was involved in some mysterious setup event that resulted in him spending a year in prison. My colleague had to sell his mother's house and use the proceeds to buy off a longer sentence".

***

Whatever constituted the moral courage of the Burnham team—and others like it—was conspicuously absent in media reporting on civilian mortality. According to many accounts, it "surrendered its independence and skepticism, passing on propaganda as news."[163] Fairness & Accuracy in Reporting (FAIR), a well-respected national media watch group[164]

---

[163]   https://vimeo.com/33033186
[164]   https://www.loc.gov/item/lcwaN0000179/

noted that the press consistently downplayed civilian casualties, relegated such data to the back pages, and avoided publishing images of the dead. Corporate media showed little interest in the human cost of war or in amplifying dissenting voices. Their coverage overwhelmingly favored pro-war sources over anti-war sources by a ratio of 25:1. FAIR criticizes the media for "imposing ignorance" on the public which led to a significant underestimation of civilian deaths by the US and UK public, in 2006, the median estimate in the US was only 5,000 deaths.[165]

Conclusion I conclude this section by asking, What is the difference between President Biden telling Prime Minister Netanyahu, "whatever you need you will get" and Prime Minister Tony Blair writing his infamous memo to President George W. Bush in 2002, promising "I will be with you whatever" and then signing off, "Forever Yours"? In both cases, the word "whatever" emphasizes a lack of restriction—to any thing, any amount, no matter what. The "what" in "whatever" refers to the evidence, the ethics, and the inevitable outcomes.

On one hand, the word "whatever" conveys a lack restriction—implying "anything", "any amount", or "no matter what". On the other hand, it suggests disregard for evidence, ethics, or potential outcomes.

---

[165]   https://fair.org/home/how-many-iraqis-died-in-the-iraq-war/

Social Murder in the Time of Pandemic

Introduction: Social Murder in the Time of COVID-19

Photo: https://commons.wikimedia.org

Even before his inauguration on January 20th, 2017, Trump was repeatedly warned about the likelihood of a global pandemic and the urgent need for preparedness. For example, in 2016, Bill Gates cautioned him about the world's inadequate readiness for a "significant probability of a large and lethal modern-day pandemic." Gates emphasized that such a pandemic would pose the greatest threat to humanity, given global interconnectedness and the constant emergence of new pathogens[166] On January 11, 2017, Dr. Anthony Fauci stated there was "no doubt" the incoming president would face an unexpected infectious disease outbreak and stressed the need to strengthen global health surveillance.[167]

---

[166] Bill Gates delivered a lecture hosted by NEJM and Massachusetts Medical Society entitled "Epidemics Going Viral: Innovation versus Nature". https://www.washingtonpost.com/news/to-your-health/wp/2018/04/27/bill-gates-calls-on-u-s-to-lead-fight-against-a-pandemic-that-could-kill-millions/

[167] His warning came in a speech (click for video) at an event organized by the Center for Global Health Science and Harvard Global See Health Institute, https://www.healio.com/news/infectious-disease/20170111/fauci-no-doubt-trump-will-face-surprise-infectious-disease-outbreak

Trump ignored this advice and did the opposite. Not only did he fail to bolster pandemic preparedness, but he also began dismantling the U.S. structures and processes designed to prevent, detect, report, and respond rapidly to disease outbreaks. For instance, during 2017-2018, his administration sought to reduce the CDC's prevention activities in 39 of 49 countries;[168] in China, its staff was cut by 70%. These activities were crucial for training front-line workers to detect outbreaks and for strengthening laboratory and emergency response systems, with the goal of containing outbreaks at their source.[169]

Other examples include the dissolution of the White House's National Security Council Directorate for Global Health Security and Biodefense in May 2018. (See Box 2.1) His administration shelved the NSC's 2016 "Playbook for Early Response to High Consequence Emerging Infectious Disease Threats and Biological Incidents" [170] which, informed by lessons from the Ebola pandemic, provided clear guidelines for a coordinated government-wide response to future pandemics.[171] In June 2019, Trump issued Executive Order 13875, which mandated that the CDC disband its advisory committees – groups of professionals who advised the director on public health issues. In October 2019, the USAID program PREDICT, aimed at the "detection and discovery of zoonotic viruses with pandemic potential" was discontinued.[172]

The dismantling of these and other disease prevention measures removed critical barriers, facilitating the spread of disease and contributing to the foreseeable and avoidable COVID-19 deaths in the U.S. and globally. In this context, such actions are described as social murder.[173]

---

[168] https://www.wsj.com/articles/cdc-to-scale-back-work-in-dozens-of-foreign-countries-amid-funding-worries-1516398717

[169] https://www.washingtonpost.com/news/to-your-health/wp/2018/02/01/cdc-to-cut-by-80-percent-efforts-to-prevent-global-disease-outbreak/

[170] https://s3.documentcloud.org/documents/6819268/Pandemic-Playbook.pdf

[171] https://www.ncbi.nlm.nih.gov/pmc/articles/PMC9115435/

[172] https://www.vox.com/future-perfect/2019/10/29/20936921/usaid-predict-pandemic-preparedness

[173] There is also prima facie evidence that British Prime Minister Boris Johnson's government is guilty of social murder in the foreseeable and avoidable COVID-19 deaths of

Box 2.1 Early Warning System

Beth Cameron, the former senior director of the Directorate for Global Health Security and Biodefense (which was disbanded under the Trump administration), stated, "Our job was to be the smoke alarm — keeping watch to get ahead of emergencies, sounding a warning at the earliest sign of fire — all with the goal of avoiding a six-alarm blaze." The dissolution of the Directorate "left an unclear structure and strategy for coordinating pandemic preparedness and response". Operating within the White House, the Directorate would have facilitated coordination among multiple federal agencies and resources. Cameron added, "What's especially concerning about the absence of this office today is that it was originally set up because a previous epidemic clearly demonstrated the need for it."
174 175

Part Two comprises five readings which have a bearing on the COVID-19 pandemic and, in 2025, Trump's actions against the World Health Organization, USAID, the US healthcare infrastructure and science in general. The first is a BMJ piece describing the CDC's word ban and its general politicization during the first Trump presidency. For instance, staff were instructed to avoid terms like "evidence-based" and "science-based" during budget preparations.[176] Of particular concern was the insistence that CDC base "its recommendations on science in consideration with community standards and wishes".

The second article, published on the 100th anniversary of the 1918 flu pandemic, reviews of past pandemics (the Spanish Flu, Ebola, H1N1,

tens of thousands of British citizens.. See UK Covid Inquiry Report July 2024 https://covid19.public-inquiry.uk/wp-content/uploads/2024/07/18095012/UK-Covid-19-Inquiry-Module-1-Full-Report.pdf

174 https://dhsprogram.com/data/Guide-to-DHS-Statistics/Description_of_The_Demographic_and_Health_Surveys_Program.htm

175 https://www.nti.org/atomic-pulse/united-states-must-lead-fight-against-coronavirus/

176 The seven words were "evidence-based", "science-based", "vulnerable", "diversity", "entitlement", "fetus" and "transgender".

SARS, swine flu, and HIV). The lessons learned highlight the need for clear, transparent, and fact-based public health communication – findings that contrast with the Trump administration's pattern of denial, understatement, and false reassurances during the pandemic. For example, on January 24, 2020, CDC Director Redfield assured the Senate, "We are prepared for this." On February 25, Larry Kudlow, the White House economic advisor, asserted, "We have contained this. I won't say it's airtight, but it's pretty close to airtight." In May, Trump proclaimed, "With or without a vaccine… we're going back to normal."[177]

The third reading describes what Senegal can teach the West about dealing with Ebola and other pandemics. Senegal's response to Ebola stood out for two key reasons: first, it adopted a no-nonsense, science-based approach to public health leveraging existing structures and maintaining clear lines of communication, and ensuring full participation from civil society. Second, Senegal adhered to what Peter Piot (the co-discoverer of Ebola), called the "Three Ones" principle: a single national strategy coordinated by one agency and supported by one monitoring and evaluation framework. This approach, well-suited for responding to COVID-19, would have involved an all-of-government framework where states and local authorities took on essential front-line responsibilities, while the federal government deployed a national strategy to manage the pandemic's nationwide consequences.

The fourth reading details the World Bank's failed response to the HIV/AIDS crisis in Sub-Saharan Africa.[178] Despite being the lead donor in the fight against HIV/AIDS, it did not take substantive steps to tackle the crisis. Instead, it pursued neoliberal policies - such as user fees, privatization, austerity - that exacerbated the pandemic. These policies, driven largely by the influence of the US Treasury Department on the Bank, led to dwindling annual disbursements which fell to about $3 per infected person by the end of the 1990s, at a time when 30 million Africans were

[177] https://www.ncbi.nlm.nih.gov/pmc/articles/PMC9115435/
[178] See Guardian (UK) piece, "Racial Inequalities at the World Bank". Part One)

either dead or dying.

In 2003, to address this profound failure, US President George W. Bush stepped in with the largest aid package in history: the President's Emergency Plan for AIDS Relief (PEPFAR). With a budget of US$110 billion, PEPFAR tackled the crisis head-on and is credited with saving 26 million lives. On January 28th, 2025, Trump cut PEPFAR with immediate detrimental results. The actions of both the World Bank and Trump are described in this reader as social murder.

The fifth and final reading, "Pandemic: A Biography," draws on my experiences living in Tanzania and Zambia during the 1980s and 1990s HIV/AIDS crisis (refer to Box 2.2). This narrative employs a fanciful device, imagining a sentient pandemic that navigates Sub-Saharan Africa as if under its own volition, skillfully bypassing barriers and gatekeepers. In reality, the virus simply exploited paths of least resistance - deep inequalities, and inadequate leadership responses - factors that facilitated its spread, much like we observed during the COVID-19 crisis and which threaten the world community in 2025.

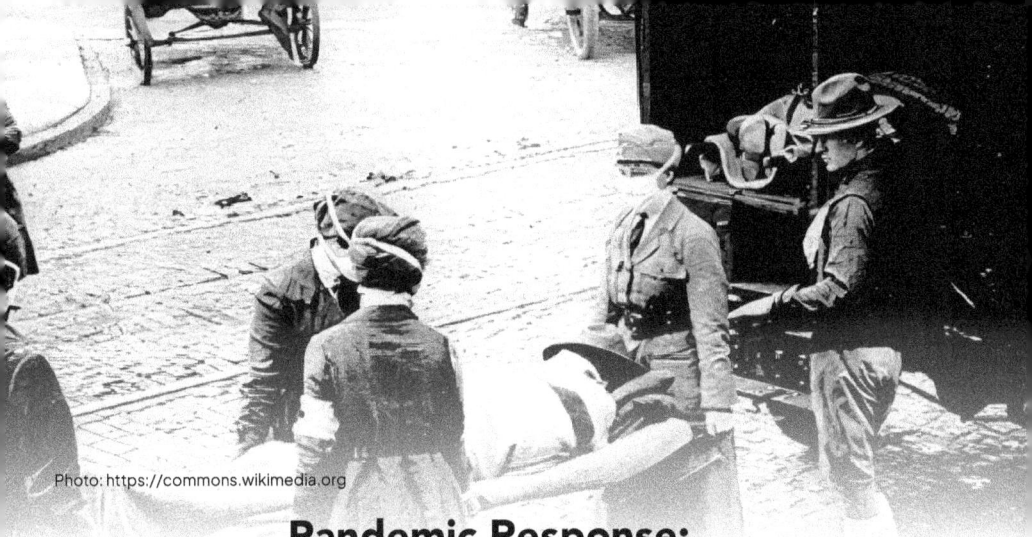

Pandemic Response:
Fear Is Inevitable, Panic Is Optional
Lancet, March 2018[179]

Pandemics Published on the 100th anniversary of the 1918 flu pandemic, this article reviews past pandemics including the Spanish Flu, Ebola, H1N1, SARS, swine flu, and HIV. It explores the opportunistic spread of the 1918 pandemic through networks established during WWI and the inadequate governmental responses it elicited. The article highlights lessons to be learned from these historical pandemics and serves as a warning about the increased frequency and lethality of viruses in our highly urbanized, globalized world. It emphasizes our lack of preparedness for such threats, presciently foreshadowing COVID-19.

◆

Research shows that when bad things happen, rational thought and communication typically give way to the irrational; we seem hardwired to blame others and sometimes assign intentionality. When the 1918 influenza pandemic spread to a world at war, belligerent nations quickly blamed one another, citing squalid trenches, overcrowded medical camps, unhygienic troop transport and staging posts – factors that often applied as much to the accusers as the accused. At the local level, the enemy within was often blamed – spies, immigrants, migrant workers, or simply

---

[179]   For access to the original article and footnotes, see: tiny.cc/PandemicResponse

those identified by their otherness. 100 years later, has anything changed?

In reality, the overlay of many factors fuelled the 1918 pandemic, including its timing (with the war), the particular susceptibility of young adults (of soldiering age) to the virus, prolonged comingling at close quarters, damp germ-infested environments, and indeed, the arcing transport networks between continents and countries. Data maps and visualizations of the pandemic18 help show its multiple and interconnected pathways and how it circumnavigated the globe five times in 18 months, killing an estimated 50 million people.

In 1918, many countries responded to the pandemic by censoring news, the aim of which was to avoid demoralising the population in a time of war. Instead of adequate, transparent, and targeted communication with the public and the institution of health measures, government officials in many (but not all) cases denied or understated the pandemic and provided the public with false reassurances – repeated refrains being "there is no cause for alarm" or "fear kills more than the disease". The disconnect between these messages and the sight, for example, of horse-drawn carts collecting corpses off city streets (the death in Philadelphia of 786 in one day and 12,000 in 6 weeks) was to transform an epidemic of fear into one of terror and panic. According to the Red Cross, it evoked images of the Black Death in the Middle Ages.

Three decades ago, Jonathan Mann described the HIV/AIDS crisis as consisting of two epidemics, the epidemic itself and reaction to it (the second of these being characterised by the displacement of evidence and science-based communication by fear and blame). The 1918 influenza pandemic has lessons to offer on both "epidemics", including (or especially) those where the epidemic is overstated or in some cases non-existent – i.e., where the contagion is principally fear or panic. For instance, after an outbreak of "swine flu" in 1976 at Fort Dix, USA, the National Immunization Program was launched, aiming to vaccinate "every man woman and child" (according to the US President then running for re-election). The National Immunization Program was seen as being motivated by politics rather than science and not directed by "effective communication from scientifically qualified persons" – the result of which was to engulf the nation in fear. After 40 million Americans had been immunised, no cases discovered outside of Fort Dix, and only one death and 13 hospitalisations, the National Immunization Program was abandoned and declared a debacle.

In similar fashion, the Ebola pandemic (2014) caused panic across the globe. In the USA, public health officials found themselves confronting not a disease epidemic (it had only seen four cases and one death compared to more than 11,000 deaths in west Africa), but rather a fear contagion that led to hysteria. Parts of the US media's reach outwards to cast blame (on African governments, health agencies, care providers, and even victims) simultaneously reached inwards to stoke fear. Again, risk and communication analyses show that what was needed yet lacking was robust and "comprehensive, transparent and easy to understand information on risks and the current degree of scientific uncertainty".

In between swine flu and Ebola was of course severe acute respiratory syndrome (SARS) in 2003, which caused a wave of irrational responses, fear spreading faster than the disease itself, devastating trade, travel, and tourism in a host of countries. It led to the development of the International Health Regulations (IHR), first tested by the H1N1 pandemic in 2009 that also led to panic and mass hysteria in many countries. Although WHO explicitly sought to avoid fear panic by taking measured responses, in some ways it fuelled anxiety. Evaluation of its response shows that it did not "acknowledge legitimate criticisms, such as inconsistent descriptions of the meaning of a pandemic"; after it declared a pandemic, a time when public awareness was particularly important, WHO "chose to diminish proactive communication with the media by discontinuing routine press conferences on the pandemic". Other communication failures included confusion over what could happen with what was most likely to happen.

Over the last 100 years, the global community has been relatively fortunate: SARS for example was an "easy problem to solve. Once clinical symptoms appear then there is ample time to isolate someone before they become infectious". Similarly, H1N1 was relatively a mild virus.

Today, however, a highly urbanised, globalised community is facing more frequent and more deadly viruses. For the Coalition for Epidemic Preparation Innovation (CEPI), backed by the US Centers for Disease Control and Prevention and the Bill and Melinda Gates Foundation, the worry is that viruses such as H7N9 will mutate to become transmissible from human to human. CEPI's repeated warning is that we react and don't plan. The most worrisome finding of the committee, in assessing the H1N1 response, was that the "world is ill prepared to respond to a severe influenza pandemic or to any similarly global, sustained and threatening public-health emergency". Indeed, data visualizations of the "next" epidemic are truly concerning. Larry Brilliant's observation that "outbreaks are inevitable, epidemics are optional" seems to apply both to pandemics and the social panic they spawn. There are rules and guidelines as to how to prepare for a pandemic and how to react and avoid panic: we ought to follow both as if our lives depended upon it.

What Can Senegal Teach the West about Dealing with Ebola?
BMJ, November 20 2014[180]

Social Murder: Safeguarding a Nation — This article explores Senegal's response to the 2014 Ebola pandemic, which mirrored its approach to the HIV/AIDS crisis from the previous generation. Senegal adopted a no-nonsense, evidence-based public health strategy that built upon existing structures, maintained clear lines of communication, and embraced full participation from civil society, deeply engaging local communities for cooperation and collaboration. In stark contrast, the responses of Canada, Australia, and the US to the Ebola threat were characterized as selfish and fear-based.. Lessons that might have learned from Senegal's successes, were largely by wealthier nations during the COVID-19 pandemic.

———◆———

Ten years ago, Peter Piot (the discoverer of Ebola) wrote the foreward to a collaborative effort on HIV strategies by nearly 200 scientists. He warned that an effective country response to the epidemic requires adherence to the so called "Three Ones" principle: a single national strategy, coordinated by one agency, and supported by one monitoring and evaluation framework. This advice applies as much to the Ebola crisis as it did to HIV – in rich and poor countries alike.

For those who focused on west Africa in this volume, it would come as no surprise to learn that Senegal has reportedly stopped Ebola "dead in its tracks." However premature or incautious this assertion may be, it is consistent with Senegal's no-nonsense, science based approach to public health – one that builds on existing structures and clear lines of communication, while embracing full participation by civil society and reaching deep into local communities.

In 1985, even before the first HIV case was officially reported as

<hr>

[180] For access to the original article and footnotes, see: tiny.cc/PandemicResponse

HIV, Senegal's national leadership, together with hundreds of community-based groups, had mobilized against the HIV crisis. As a consequence, prevalence rates were kept very low, and Senegal became recognized globally as a model of best practice – generously sharing its expertise across the globe.

Thus, when a young Guinean national infected with Ebola crossed into Senegal by road on 21 August 2014, he was quickly identified, isolated, and – while his 74 contacts were traced and tested – he was treated before being declared clear 42 days later. This was the result of resources, structures, processes, and protocols being put in place by a vigilant and proactive health system, which worked in concert with its global partners. Senegal again has lessons to teach the West, as well as its neighbors.

For in contrast, the West appears to have done just the opposite in some cases. Outwardly, the signs of its slow and ill prepared responses to Ebola are self-evident: no agreed upon strategy or coordination, contentious policies and protocol, and confused communication between various levels of government and would be partners.

Yet the West's failure reveals something more worrisome: a disregard for the global perspective, along with its implied benefits and responsibilities. In particular are the notions that more can be achieved by working together than going it alone, and that self-interest may be better served by contributing to the common good.

For example, as Dr. Anthony Fauci, from the National Institutes of Health, has warned that "the best way to protect Americans is to stop the epidemic in Africa," it makes no sense to disincentivize badly needed health workers who wish to help fight Ebola in west Africa by subjecting them to across the board quarantines. Yet in the United States, state governors resisted this advice – prompted perhaps by surveys showing that 80% of the population wanted some sort of quarantine.

In a similar vein, Canada and Australia issued visa bans for people from the three west African countries hit by Ebola, which is contrary to scientific evidence that shows these actions make the detection and tracking of individuals more difficult and dissuades countries from being forthcoming. These actions also run contrary to international law, the very laws that Canada helped draft in the wake of the SARS outbreak.

The World Health Organization asked Canada for an explanation, yet none was forthcoming except a tweet from a government minister that "we are a sovereign nation with a duty to protect our citizens" – a tone consistent with the government's view that multilateralism is a weak nation policy, and its embrace of the principle of "sovereign self-interest."

This rejection of the global health perspective also implies an under-estimation of global threats from existing or newly emerging infectious disease (EIDs) that may occur naturally, accidently, or deliberately. As Larry Brilliant, who worked on the smallpox campaign, warned, "outbreaks are inevitable; epidemics are optional."

We should remember that it took the international donor community until 2000 before it began to respond seriously to Africa's HIV/AIDS crisis, by which time 30 million were dead or dying – a full 15 years after Senegal tackled the crisis head on. Piot says that the response to pandemics is a "political concern," and it is strong leadership that the global community will need. So far, the west appears to be sleepwalking, as it quietly becomes increasingly vulnerable.

Trump 1.0 and 2.0
CDC's Word Ban: The Placement of Politics Over Science Is Part of a Larger Pattern

BMJ, January 3 2018[181]

Social Murder: Setting the Crime Scene — Early in 2025, Trump began gutting the US healthcare infrastructure including CDC and, as listed by the New York Times, identified 200 words that should be avoided or used sparingly.[182] This article, published two years before the COVID-19 pandemic, examines the conflict between science and politics under the Trump administration. It details the administration's efforts to slash CDC budgets, meddle in its operations, distort the truth, dominate the scientific community, and restrict media coverage. Similarly, the EPA saw the removal of terms like "global warming" and "climate change" from its official websites, labeled as "outdated language."

———————◆———————

Over the past few weeks, the Centers for Disease Control and Prevention (CDC) has been making headlines over reports that the agency had advised its officials not to use seven words in budget documents.

As with all language, the words scientists and doctors use can fall out of favour – sometimes even as the result of deliberate crackdowns and concerted efforts. This can even be a good thing when it is done with the intention of improving the communication of ideas and knowledge.

For example, medical journals and public health and safety officials had long sought to ban the word "accident" since it implies a random event, an act of God, or the inevitable. The CDC helped by developing a framework (based on intent and mechanism of injury) to standardise the grouping of injury data.

---

[181] For access to the original article and footnotes, see tiny.cc/CDCWordBan

[182] https://www.nytimes.com/interactive/2025/03/07/us/trump-federal-agencies-websites-words-dei.html

Yet this latest edict on language does not seem to have been done in that spirit. In contrast, the CDC has reportedly banned or advised against using the words "evidence based," "science based," "diversity," "entitlement," "fetus," "transgender," and "vulnerable" in its preparations of presidential budget proposals. All seven would be objectionable, yet the injunction against using either "science based" or "evidence based" is Global Health and Social Murder particularly worrisome since this is the basis for informed decision making and effective public policy – the glue that staves off chaos in liberal democracies. Instead of these essential terms, it has been reported that the CDC might use the watered-down phrase "CDC bases its recommendations on science in consideration with community standards and wishes."

The head of the CDC has responded to these reports by saying (in a way that leaves some wiggle room) that "there are no banned words at CDC" while other officials have said that this list is about offering guidance on the language that will be most effective with conservatives in Congress. Although the tone, wording, and source of the restriction on these words are unclear, the placement of politics over science is evident and part of a larger pattern.

Over the past 12 months, government employees in a multitude of US departments, including the Department of Health and Human Services (HHS), the Environmental Protection Agency (EPA), and the Department of Energy, have experienced similar pressures. Scientists at these organisations have had their research, conference, and media contact subjected to monitoring and surveillance; with the help of an external agency, even their emails are subject to scrutiny. The EPA has also witnessed the removal from official websites of so called "outdated language": the words "global warming" and "climate change." While a spate of emails between scientists (published by the *Guardian*) shows staff at the US Department of Agriculture have been told to replace references to climate change with weather extremes in their work (along with other terms).

Words and words as metaphors matter; they can influence what we think and how we act. Words mattered to a US judge who a decade ago banned cigarettes being described as "light" and "low tar", because this description could mislead the public about this product's potential to harm. They mattered to the Associated Press when it banned its writers from using the phrase "illegal immigrants" since it could create a biased picture, which compromises the wellbeing and safety of immigrants. Similarly, and yet in contrast, when Trump called global warming a "hoax" his words carried a meaning that later became manifest in his actions, such as turning away from the Paris Agreement and making wholesale cuts to environmental regulations.

The British government has intermittently attempted to muzzle health scientists and their research findings. For example, in 1988 it sought to have scientists sign a contract agreeing not to publish their findings if they went against government policy – the aim of which, said some commentators, was to control information and centralise power. Again, last year a British Cabinet initiative tried to ban researchers (who received government grants) from using their results to lobby for changes to laws or regulations. However, the actual banning of words themselves is more likely to be associated with authoritarian regimes. Former President Barack Obama, normally out of public view, recently evoked totalitarian Europe of the 1930s and warned of complacency in the midst of threats to democratic institutions.

Indeed, the words listed in the CDC's "word ban" are similar to those cited by Putin's authoritarian regime, which bans the promotion of LGBT culture, while giving Putin final say over the leadership of the Russian Academies of Science and Medical Sciences.

The year 2017 began with the banning of people from seven Muslim majority countries and ended with reports of the banning of seven words; both will affect the free flow of ideas and knowledge and, ultimately, the overall wellbeing of the nation.

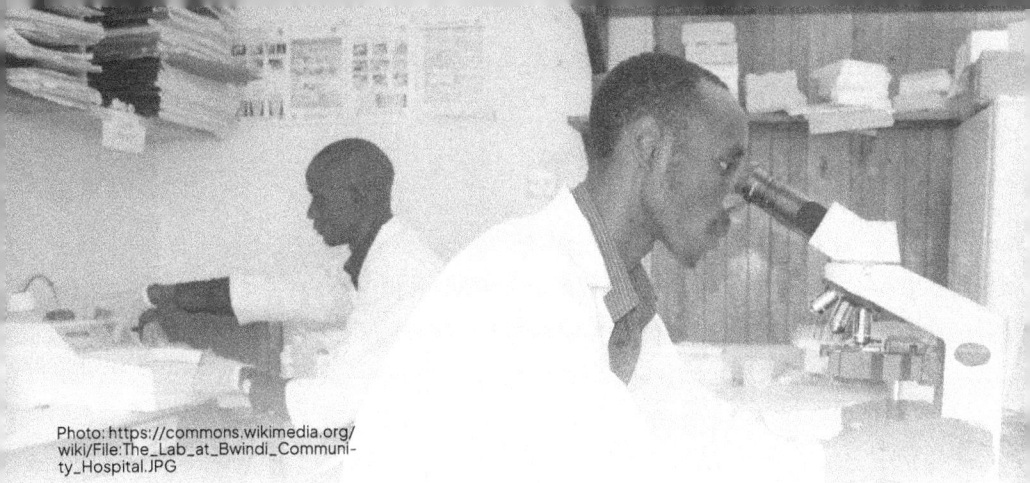

The World Bank and Sub-Saharan Africa's HIV/AIDS Crisis

CMAJ[183]

Between the early 1980s and 2000 the prevalence rate of HIV infection in sub-Saharan Africa increased from less than 1% to 12%, as illustrated in the prevalence maps in Fig. 1. This represents an increase in the number of people living with HIV infection from less than 1 million to 22 million. During this period, neither African governments nor the international donor community sufficiently prioritized HIV/AIDS or allocated adequate resources to help prevent and control its spread. In sub-Saharan Africa, the total amount of official development assistance actually declined in the 1990s, to about $3 per HIV-infected person by 1999. By this time, the international donor community had begun to focus on the HIV/AIDS pandemic and in 2000 began to send billions of dollars to sub-Saharan Africa to tackle the crisis. These investments appear to have had a positive effect: between 2000 and December 2005, HIV prevalence rates among adults were reported to have decreased in more than two-thirds of the countries in sub-Saharan Africa, falling from a mean rate of 10% to 7.5%.

◆

Although ultimate responsibility for responding to the HIV/AIDS crisis in a timely and effective manner rests with African governments, in reality it was the international donor community that determined Africa's health priorities, agendas and strategies over the last 40 years. It typically contributed about 20% of the funds needed to cover public health expenditures, and sometimes up to 30%–80% in the poorest countries. The

---

[183] For access to the original article and footnotes, see tiny.cc/WorldBankSSA

World Bank was the pivotal player in the international donor community in the 1990s. With a general mandate to reduce poverty and improve living standards, and a remit to promote access to essential services in the health sector, the World Bank exercised enormous fiscal and policy leverage over governments and the other members of the donor community. This influence was due to the fact that (a) the World Bank was sub-Saharan Africa's main development partner; (b) it was the lead donor in terms of finance and policy in Africa's health sector; (c) it often acted as the "umbrella funder," designing and implementing integrated health strategies to which other donors would contribute; (d) it attached "conditionalities" to loans that needed to be met by borrowing governments for the release of funds; and (e) it acted in concert with the International Monetary Fund, which also had great monetary and fiscal influence. Indeed, the World Bank frequently draws attention to its influence, citing its comparative advantage in dealing with governments through dialogue, analysis and lending. In its seminal document, Intensifying Action Against HIV/AIDS in Africa, it acknowledged its de facto leadership role and implied responsibilities, stating that "those who look back on this era will judge our institution in large measure by whether we recognized this wildfire that is raging across Africa for the development threat that it is, and did our utmost to put it out. They will be right to do so."

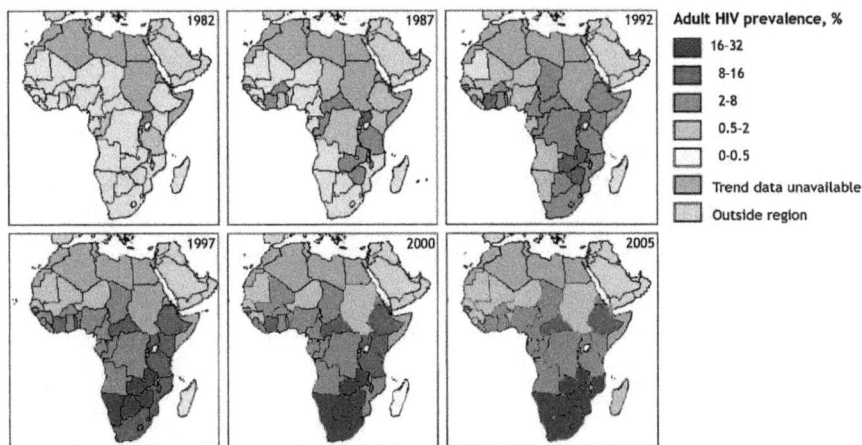

Fig. 1. Prevalence of HIV infection among adults in sub-Saharan Africa from 1982 to 2005. The first 5 maps show the dramatic rise in the prevalence of HIV infections among adults between 1982 and 1997; the remaining map and the map in Fig. 2 depict some of the improvements realized since 2000. [The first 4 maps were reproduced, with permission, from the 1998 UNAIDS report on the global AIDS epidemic; the last 2 maps were redrawn using UNAIDS data.]

As the largest contributor to HIV/AIDS intervention activities, the World Bank lent US$552 million globally between 1986 and 1996. However, these resources were inequitably distributed across regions. For example, Brazil, a relatively well-off country with a low HIV prevalence rate (less than 1%), received US$160 million, compared with US$274 million given to all of Africa, where many countries were virtually ignored until 2000. By 1999, the World Bank's Health, Nutrition and Population Unit had only 3 substantial AIDS projects in Africa, all of which were winding down, with no new projects in the offing.

Its own Operations Evaluation Department, whose mandate is to provide independent evaluations, analyzed what HIV/AIDS investments the World Bank did make. It found that, from public health and public economics perspectives, the World Bank failed to meet its own criteria. The 10 standalone HIV projects and the 51 projects with an HIV

151

component initiated between 1986 and 1996 lacked economic analyses of expected and actual results. In general, they also failed to focus on population groups at highest risk. In an internal analysis of the World Bank's investment in "best buys in public health and clinical services" for the period 1993–1999, Claeson and colleagues assessed the extent of investment in essential public health and clinical services. (These services were identified as essential in the 1993 World Development Report on the basis of disability-adjusted life-years averted and on available efficacy, effectiveness and cost data.) (10) The authors found that 44 (29%) of the 152 projects undertaken by the Health, Nutrition and Population Unit during 1993–1999 addressed HIV/ AIDS. Of those 44 projects, only 10 (23%) met the strict criteria used to define quality interventions in this domain (i.e., education on safe behaviour, condom promotion, treatment of sexually transmitted infections, and safe blood supply). In short, less than one quarter of the interventions met the World Bank's own quality indicators.

In reality, the World Bank in the 1990s was actually focused on health sector reform, not on HIV/AIDS. A review of key World Bank documents showed that it sought repeatedly and explicitly to deprioritize the HIV/AIDS crisis in favour of health sector reform. The review revealed that, in 1992, the World Bank had warned that, "an expanded role of the Bank in AIDS should not be allowed to overtake the critical agenda for strengthening health systems." The remarkable conclusion reached was that, as the decade progressed, increasingly "AIDS was even less strategically prominent in the Bank health sector strategy." To make matters worse, extensive data show that these very reforms, however badly needed, were poorly planned and underfunded and frequently had the effect of reducing access to effective health care, including services aimed at the prevention and control of HIV/AIDS. For example, with the promotion of cost recovery, it became commonplace to charge users for key HIVrelated services, including the diagnosis and treatment of sexually transmitted infections, blood transfusion schemes, voluntary counselling and testing, and antiretroviral therapy.

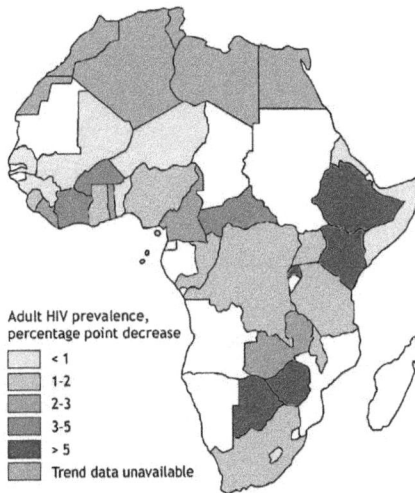

Fig. 2. Sub-Saharan countries in which the prevalence of HIV infection among adults decreased between 2000 and 2005. Source: UNAIDS data.

A series of institutional weaknesses identified in a review of the World Bank's investing activities in the health sector in the 1990s suggests that an effective response to the HIV/AIDS pandemic by the World Bank was an unlikely prospect from the outset. First, the World Bank operated as a bank and kept its core business processes and incentives "focused on lending money rather than achieving impact." Second, it had weak incentives and underdeveloped systems for monitoring and evaluation and therefore did not use its lending portfolio to systematically collect evidence on what works, what doesn't and why. Third, the World Bank failed to develop good dialogue and consultation with its partners and local stakeholders – often preferring to "go it alone." Fourth, it took a "one size fits all" approach to countries' situations that was insufficiently grounded in empirical evidence or institutional analysis of the local context. Fifth, it seldom placed sufficient emphasis on addressing determinants of health that lie outside the medical care system. Any one of these weaknesses would have severely undercut the effectiveness of the World Bank's response to the HIV/AIDS crisis. Collectively, they suggest the unchecked proliferation of ill-conceived, blueprint responses over a prolonged period from an institution out of touch with events on the ground. For example, upon reviewing levels of official development assistance targeting HIV/AIDS (about $10 per HIV-infected person globally and $3 in sub-Saharan Africa), the World Bank in 1997 concluded that "these allocations are remarkably large relative to national spending on the same problem and probably in comparison with international spending on any other disease. Perhaps only the international campaign to eradicate smallpox in the 1970s benefited from such a large preponderance of donor funds."

Box 2.1 Key institutional weaknesses of the World

- Bank's investing activities in the health sector in the 1990s
- Bank liked operations focused on lending money rather than on achieving impact
- Weak incentives and underdeveloped systems for monitoring and evaluation
- Lack of development of good dialogue and consultation with partners and local stakeholders
- "One size fits all" approach to countries' situations that was insufficiently grounded in empirical evidence or institutional analysis of the local context
- Insufficient emphasis placed on addressing determinants of health that lie outside the medical care system

Source: Johnston and Stout.12

In fairness, bilateral and multilateral agencies were generally no more effective than the World Bank in their response to the HIV/AIDS pandemic. However, none of these agencies was in comparable positions of leadership or influence. Furthermore, none of this critique removes the onus from African governments to do more: Uganda and Senegal have shown what can be achieved when there is strong political will, just as South Africa has shown the consequences of its absence.

Since 2000, the World Bank has made large investments in sub-Saharan Africa to tackle HIV/AIDS and has addressed some of its institutional weaknesses, the most obvious being that it offers grants rather than bank loans to finance interventions. A recent review of the World Bank's development effectiveness showed that 3 characteristics were good predictors of success: first, country assistance was focused and was in support of a country-owned program; second, the program was carefully aligned with government capacity; and third, strategies were based on analytical work that helped tailor them to a country's conditions. However, evaluation of the World Bank's HIV programs, while confirming substantial improvements in aid effectiveness, has identified areas that require immediate attention by the World Bank – the need to target HIV/AIDS intervention strategies at high-risk groups, to improve analysis of country-specific issues and to improve monitoring and evaluation of research activities – if it is to meet current challenges presented by the HIV/AIDS crisis in sub-Saharan Africa.

Box 2.2 Backstory

My work in Africa began in 1988 at a small mission hospital in the Mbeya region of Tanzania, where I coordinated community health activities. Located next to a truck stop on the Malawi-Zambia highway, this hospital became a rural epicenter for the HIV/AIDS crisis in Tanzania. Unlike most public health facilities in the country, this hospital boasted a well-funded HIV program. It featured Voluntary Testing and Counseling (VTC), health education, a condom distribution scheme, and robust social support networks, primarily supported by private entities and NGOs. In stark contrast, the Tanzanian government and the international donor community largely overlooked the crisis, failing to make significant investments until the early 2000s.In 1993, my work expanded to South Africa, Mozambique, Eswatini (formerly Swaziland), and Zambia, with the latter becoming a major focus of my research for the next decade. It was here that I witnessed firsthand the consequences of the donor and governmental prioritization of neoliberal policies at the expense of effective HIV/AIDS intervention.

Pandemic: A Biography

——————◆——————

Life of its own This piece is inspired by my experiences living in Tanzania and Zambia during the 1980s and 1990s. It employs a wholly imaginative approach to illustrate how epidemics and pandemics naturally migrate towards environments characterized by weak leadership and prevalent issues such as fear, anger, stigmatization, denial, victim-blaming, and self-interest. While this article highlights the World Bank's significant shortcomings in responding to the HIV/AIDS crisis a decade prior, it is important to differentiate between the organization's leadership and its field employees. The latter, based on my observations, were often among the most capable and insightful professionals in the sector.[184]

---

[184] My observations span Eastern and Southern Africa, East Asia, and the subcontinent. A poignant example involves Albertus Voetberg, a physician associated with the World Bank during the HIV/AIDS crisis. In late November 2002, around the time of the Mombasa bombing, we met in Nairobi. During our discussion, we touched on the beneficial impact of Kenyan President Moi's belated declaration of AIDS as a national emergency. Voetberg believed the "noise" generated by this announcement could significantly influence behavior change—a crucial lesson for leadership during any pandemic. Voetberg also shared insights into World Bank leadership, particularly concerning a confrontation with President James Wolfensohn (1995-2005) over his failure to acknowledge the HIV/AIDS threat. A group of scientists presented Wolfensohn with compelling data, urging him to recognize the crisis enveloping the developing world.
Further discussions with Sebastian Mallaby, author of The World's Banker and a journalist with the Washington Post at the time, revealed a critical view of Wolfensohn's leadership and his response to the pandemic. Intriguingly, Wolfensohn's lengthy (3,000-word) biography on the World Bank's website mentions HIV only once. Even more peculiar is that this solitary reference is the only mention of the pandemic across the extensive biographies of four Bank presidents from 1981 to 2005.

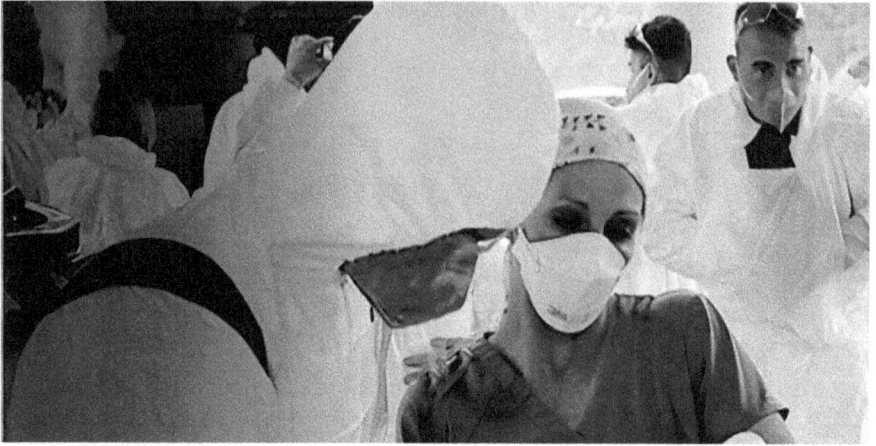

An employee at the West Oaks Nursing and Rehabilitation Center performs COVID-19 screening for National Guardsmen with Joint Task Force 176, May 12, 2020.

Photo: US Army National Guard Staff Sgt. Michael Giles, 36th Infantry Division Public Aff airs, The National Guard / Flickr (CC BY 2.0)

It's December 1999, Dar es Salaam, Tanzania. With just days to the Millennium, this Head of Aid, whom I have known both here and in Zambia, the quintessential 'constant gardener'[185] – diligent, self-effacing, modest – is overwhelmed. The source of his distress, like that of many in Africa's health sector, is the growing realization that as tens of millions of Africans are dead or dying from AIDS, few serious efforts have been made to tackle the crisis as most of the work being done is preoccupied with the World Bank's neoliberal reform agenda for Africa's health sector.

He says, "We saw the pandemic early on and then ignored it. We gave it free reign for at least 10 years and in the end, it dehumanized us". He looks at me. "It insinuated itself in me, in you, into the donor community

---

[185]   The Constant Gardener, a novel by John le Carré (2001), later made into a movie (2005) starring Ralph Fiennes and Rachel Weisz, portrays a self-effacing, dedicated, if naïve expatriate civil servant working in Sub-Saharan Africa who slowly discovers the various agendas at play in global health.

then swallowed us whole. We're in it and it's in us".

In his bewilderment he's taken to attaching inappropriate attributes to the epidemic; he describes it as self-directed, with a life of its own, taking orders from itself, with its own structure and function, anatomy and physiology, its own memory, a capacity for self-replication and self-annealing, and a collective 'intelligence' of sorts that helps guide it to where it will thrive and avoid where it will not.[186]

He imagines it meandering from Equatorial West Africa eastwards along the Trans-African Highway, along water and trade routes through Congo and Rwanda until reaching the Great Lakes region during Idi Amin's war. Here, it erupts, spreading swiftly into East Africa as if it found its true home – Uganda, Kenya, Tanzania and then Zambia and southwards as nascent epidemics become 'concentrated' and then 'generalized' and countries tumble like dominos.

And he imagines the epidemic mimicking the very virus that flows inside, that is, its ability to invade and destroy the systems that are meant to protect. He imagines its tentacles reaching into communities, moving undetected past public and global health systems intended to safeguard at-risk populations, confounding and disarming those very systems. First, use trial and error until you find prey that don't matter, whose hard death will go ignored – those who live at the periphery, the social margins, far from the centers of power, outgroups. Go to where there is a tumult, a fray, a dust-up; where there is war, forced migration, sexual violence, to where the advantaged and disadvantaged have just met. Go to where power clusters and rests undistributed, where another agenda predominates. Look up into the eyes of the gatekeepers as you slip past for any signs of reproach. Go safely now; you will know your success by their responses – fear, anger, abhorrence, denial, stigmatization, and ostracism. These are useful, they will resonate, they have the ring of truth. Now trade on your strength, your omnipotence; you are invincible, you easily

---

[186]   N. Christakis and J Fowler, Connected: The Surprising Power of Our Social Networks and How They Shape Our Lives, 2009 University of Chicago. USA

dissuade the dissuadable, the half-hearted, and even the final holdouts; you give them what they crave, an excuse for their docility.

Fourteen years earlier, when I arrived in Mbeya, in the southern highlands of Tanzania, this small community had already become an HIV epicenter in Eastern Africa. Staff at Igogwe hospital, a 100-bed mission facility near a truck-stop on the Zambia-Malawi highway, had been reporting "the slimming illness" (Ukimwi) at least since the 1970s. The hospital orphanage was home to many AIDS orphans. A place of arresting beauty, with undulating rolling hills and valleys over which is cast a net of tiny roads and footpaths connecting one family compound with another, one village with the next; along the nodes and threads of this network, the Wanyakusa and Wasafwa peoples stop to greet in repetitive fashion as if to affirm and secure the ties that connect. At a distance it looks like an enchanted mathematical 'fitness landscape'. Yet up close, I witness the virus sweeping through households and destroying communities while the donors, under the reins of the World Bank, looked on.

Four years later, in Zambia, where I had first met the 'constant gardener', he faces the conundrum *writ large*: on one hand, there is the World Bank's reform agenda for Zambia, and on the other hand, is one of the worst-hit countries in SSA's southern region. He is a player at the table, one that supports the Bank's idea of reform including cost recovery, privatization, and austerity. Yet early on the Bank makes clear where it stands, stating explicitly and repeatedly that "AIDS should not be allowed to overtake the critical agenda for strengthening health systems". And it did not.

Again, like the 'constant gardener', he initially does not get out into the field. However, the files have crossed his desk, he knows the material and has heard the stories: another economic crisis, the worst drought in 50 years, a 50% rise in childhood malnutrition, a doubling of childhood illness, a national poverty rate now at 90%, and a 20% rise in child mortality. And then he finds himself in the field, where the health sector has dissolved into chaos; he is in the Copperbelt, the North and Northwest, across to Malawi border areas and down to Mazabuka. And what he sees going from district to district is the spectre of human misery, empty shells that used to be rural health centers with nothing but the wind blowing through – without essential drugs or supplies, clinical staff no longer reporting for work because there are no patients – a parody of a once functioning health system. And now HIV rates have surpassed 20% and the pandemic exults.

Dr. Mahler, former Director General of the World Health Organization, is called in to investigate but in the end, he can only plead with the Bank. His team found chaos at the periphery, and he warned "it needs to be redressed". He said, "We exhort the reformers to listen carefully to the noise, the turbulence…within the system in order not to lose touch with reality on the ground". But World Bank Washington headquarters embargoes the "Mahler Report". Meanwhile, Bill Clinton and the US Treasury demur from entering the fray and the pandemic gathers and blooms like a murmuration, now rising phoenix-like above the great Zambia plateau – already turning southward to greet Thabo Mbeki.

The HIV/AIDS Crisis and the Right to Health[187]

———————◆———————

I t was in fact the HIV / AIDS crisis that clarified the connectedness between rights and health and revived the human rights approach to health care. This revival began in the 1980s in the United States, one of the first rich countries to become familiar with the 'hard death' associated with HIV / AIDS where the distribution of infection and access to healthcare were characterized by extreme inequalities, defined mainly by sexuality, race, gender and class. Here, influential Christian evangelicals lobbied against legislation that would have reduced discrimination while at the same time refusing to assist Africa – one 2001 poll showing that only 7% of evangelicals were prepared to donate to organizations that helped aid orphans in Africa. These realities gave rise to AIDS activist campaigning, an effective social movement that eventually spread to most industrialised nations. Its focus was to use intensive research and documentation to identify governmental human rights obligations and to expose failure to take timely and effective measures to fulfil these and then to set out the actions needed to close the gap. On a more global perspective, it was Jonathan Mann, a courageous American physician who headed up the World Health Organization's (WHO) Global Program on AIDS (GPA) between 1987 and 1996, that had insisted on a human rights-based approach to the pandemic. Other individual practitioners working in the South with non-governmental organizations (NGOs), first in mission facilities and then in later years with non-sectarian organisations, took a right-based approach to health with a focus on marginalised populations that eventually included those infected with HIV. Today most aid agencies and governments pay attention to human rights in health and integrate human rights obligations in their health activities both at home and globally.

---

[187]   For access to the original article and footnotes, see tiny.cc/HIVAIDS

Social Murder Inequalities and Human Rights

PART THREE
Social Murder:
Inequalities and Human Rights

U nregulated markets and austerity measures can exacerbate existing inequalities and foster new ones, particularly in environments with weak human rights protections. This section provide
prima facie evidence that states (or institutions) or their representatives
deliberately and structurally expose vulnerable populations to risks and
foreseeable, avoidable premature deaths. Part Three delves into not only
how the influential and powerful treat the vulnerable but also the extent
to which they will go to secure and maintain their advantages.

The first article focuses on the East Asian Financial Crisis in Indonesia
(1997-98), which was largely precipitated by the US Treasury and the
IMF encouraging smaller, successful nations to dramatically open their
capital markets to speculative, "hot money." I examine the IMF and the
US Treasury's response to Indonesia's financial crisis, which prioritized
bank preservation over the welfare of ordinary people, resulting in austerity measures that cut basic healthcare services relied upon mainly by
the poor, particularly in rural areas.

For Indonesians, the East Asian Financial Crisis was a humiliation.[188]
The widely distributed image in newspapers and the internet of President
Suharto hunched at a table signing an economic surrender agreement,

---

[188]   https://news-decoder.com/2015/07/09/greece-can-learn-from-asias-crisis/

while the IMF's Michael Camdessus glares down at him with arms folded reflected this national humiliation and is seen by some observers as a contributing factor in the rise of terrorism in Indonesia and the Bali bombing.[189]

I then turn to an analysis of 23 OECD countries that reveals a correlation between the generosity of nations in the Global North, as measured by their overseas development assistance (ODA), and their domestic social policies. Countries that are more generous internationally also tend to allocate more resources to social transfers domestically, leading to stronger social safety nets and lower inequalities. Conversely, those less generous abroad typically exhibit less domestic generosity and greater inequalities.

Against this backdrop, I explore the tenure of Canadian Prime Minister Stephen Harper (2006-15), focusing on his record concerning human rights and inequalities. The analyses suggest Harper exacerbated the marginalization of vulnerable groups such as drug users, refugees, immigrants, and the homeless. Furthermore, he utilized agencies like the RCMP, CSIS, and CRA to target perceived adversaries. His disregard for Canada's colonial history, his inadequate response to the crisis of missing and murdered Indigenous women and girls, and his reluctance to fulfill the Truth and Reconciliation Commission (TRC) recommendations have led to claims by the UN Committee on Human Rights (UNCOHR) that Harper rendered Canada's human rights stance "unrecognizable." In my view, Harper's governance foreshadowed the leadership style of Donald Trump.

Several reading focus on the United States. It is the world's wealthiest nation yet has high levels of poverty and inequalities. Several readings highlight how the American elite, representing entities like the AMA, pharmaceutical, and insurance sectors, have actively resisted universal

---

[189]   The number of terrorist attacks increased from 3 in 1998 to 61 in 1999, 101 in 2000, and 106 in 2001. In October 2002, the Bali bombings occurred in the tourist district of Kuta on the Indonesian island of Bali. The attack killed 202 people and injured 209 others.

healthcare. This resistance exploits two societal tendencies: first, a reluctance to support resource redistribution benefiting those with whom one does not identify; and second, a propensity to act against one's own interests when such actions affirm one's identity distinct from marginalized groups.

In the OECD study, the United Kingdom is an outlier among the 23 countries because it provided high levels of development assistance to low-income countries until June 2021, when Prime Minister Boris Johnson reduced donor aid. However, domestically, the UK reports high levels of poverty and significant regional and intergenerational inequalities. Prime Minister David Cameron's push for deregulation in 2012, which he famously termed a "bonfire of regulations," exacerbated these disparities. Many observers point to the Grenfell Tower fire as a stark illustration of how deregulation can amplify human rights disparities in the UK. This tragedy is often cited as a case of social murder. Furthermore, 14 years of Conservative-led austerity have deepened inequalities, correlating with 335,000 foreseeable and avoidable deaths from 2012 to 2019, a period also marked by accusations of social murder..

In short, these 14 articles show, on one hand, the risks associated with far-right policies ideologies – the 2008 providing the best example, and, on the other hand, the social and economic benefits of reducing inequalities.

Box 3.1 Price Fixing

Under collusive price-fixing schemes, consumers pay more than they would in an open market, with the poor disproportionately burdened, particularly when it comes to essential goods and services. In Canada, the United States, and most OECD countries, price-fixing is an indictable criminal offense.

In August 2024, the US Department of Justice (DOJ) sued RealPage for price-fixing rental rates, a practice that has harmed millions of American households.[190] In 2023, the DOJ fined seven major generic drug companies $250 million for their involvement in a price-fixing conspiracy.[191]Some observers might consider these acts a form of "social murder," as they deliberately and structurally expose vulnerable people to significant risk. On July 25, 2024, Canadian companies Loblaw and its parent company, George Weston Ltd., self-reported collusion and agreed to pay a $500 million fine to settle a "industrywide" bread price-fixing scheme. The other five major retailers, including Sobeys and Walmart, denied any involvement - raising the obvious question: Why would Loblaw and George Weston Ltd. self-report and agree to settle for a half a billion dollars if no other retailer colluded?[192]

[190] https://www.justice.gov/opa/pr/justice-department-sues-realpage-algorithmic-pricing-scheme-harms-millions-american-renters

[191] https://www.justice.gov/opa/pr/major-generic-drug-companies-pay-over-quarter-billion-dollars-resolve-price-fixing-charges#:~:text=In%20June%202020%2C%20Glenmark%20was,the%20same%20and%20similar%20conduc

[192] https://www.cbc.ca/news/business/loblaw-bread-price-settlement-1.7274820

Reassessment of Health Effects of the Indonesian Economic Crisis: Donors Versus the Data

Lancet, 2003[193][194]

Social Murder and austerity The deregulation of markets played a significant role in precipitating the East Asian Financial Crisis (1997-99). Influenced by the IMF and the US Treasury, the Indonesian government prioritized bank repayments over social spending during its crisis response. This article explores the consequences of these decisions, particularly the reduction in healthcare spending and its correlation with increased childhood mortality. Additionally, it highlights how the Asian Development Bank selectively presented data, obscuring the true impact of these policies. Over six months in Indonesia, I conducted dozens of interviews with representatives from donor agencies, international financial institutions, government bodies, and think tanks. A consistent theme emerged from these discussions: while safeguarding the banking sector was deemed crucial, it was widely acknowledged that it should not have come at the expense of the impoverished.

———◆———

Between the late 1960s and the late 1990s, gross domestic product in Indonesia grew by an average of 6–7% a year and poverty dropped from 50% to 10% – a feat accomplished without increasing inequality. Throughout this period, large investments were made in primary education, leading to almost complete enrolment at schools and sharp declines in illiteracy. In the health sector, a network of health centers and subcenters was established. Between 1980 and 1997, death rates in children younger than 1 year and 5 years fell by about 30% and 40%, respectively. Improved nutrition and access to basic healthcare services such as immunization and treatment of childhood illnesses including acute respiratory infection, diarrheal disease, and malaria were key factors in the upward trend in health status.

---

[193] Chris Simms and Mike Rowson
[194] See tiny.cc/HealthEffects

Health care during an economic crisis

In mid-1997, an economic crisis that began in Thailand spread quickly through the closely connected economies of East Asia and had a substantial and detrimental effect on welfare indicators in several countries. The crisis had an immediate bearing on the livelihoods and health of people in this region through three main mechanisms. First, income fell while unemployment rose, resulting in a striking increase in the rate of poverty. Second, rising prices for imported goods, such as pharmaceuticals, and in Indonesia's case, the basic staple of rice, led to severe shortages of essential goods. Third, economic collapse precipitated a decline in governments' social expenditures on health and education. However, debate exists about the extent to which health and other social indices were affected by the crisis, with some commentators arguing that the effects were much smaller than initially anticipated.

Indonesia was especially badly affected by the South Asian economic crisis, which posed an immediate threat to the wellbeing of low-income households. In response, the Indonesian government and its donor partners implemented a set of measures known as a plan for a social safety net for the health sector (JPS-BK), which aimed to mitigate the effects of economic decline on the health of poor citizens by protecting their access to effective health care. Opinion from within the international community holds that these measures have worked; the World Bank claimed that "catastrophic results were averted", and other agencies suggested that the dire predictions of the crisis' effects on welfare might have been overstated.

In its 2000 report to the Ninth Annual Meeting of the Consultative Group on Indonesia, the Asian Development Bank (ADB) stated that a key JPS-BK objective was to maintain spending on primary health care. They reported that during the crisis, the Government had maintained resources allocated to essential health services at the same level as those before the economic decline. A second key objective was to maintain the quality of services provided to the poorest sectors of the community

– quality being defined by indices such as attitudes and qualifications of health personnel, and the availability of basic medical equipment, supplies, and essential drugs. The ADB also uses rates of uptake of health services as a measure of quality of care. A third and related objective was to maintain access of vulnerable groups to essential health services. The ADB emphasised that to protect the health and nutrition of pregnant women, nursing mothers, and children younger than 2 years, community outreach activities need to be strengthened because these groups were less likely than other people to visit health centres.

	1996–97	1997–98	1998–99	1999–2000
Primary care spending				
Total (billion rupiah)	1988·9	1882·3	1677·3	1656·2
Donor	152·8	113·6	299·3	261·3
Government	1836·1	1768·7	1378·0	1395·9
Per person	10·3	9·6	8·5	8·2
(thousand rupiah)				
Hospital spending				
Total (billion rupiah)	798·9	858·9	915·2	1071·3
Donor	98·9	93·9	278·7	411·8
Government	700·0	765·0	637·5	660·5
Per person	4·1	4·4	4·6	5·3
(thousand rupiah)				

*Amounts used are constant 1993 Indonesian rupiah; US$1=2095 rupiah. Data are from Liberman et al, 2001.[5]

Table 1. Real public expenditure on primary health care and hospital care in Indonesia 1996–2000.

Allocation of health spending: an alternative view

In terms of the linkage between public health spending, access to effective health care, and mortality in Indonesia, several pieces of evidence suggest that the ADB's assessment is overly optimistic and is sometimes inconsistent with other data. The ADB's report to the consultative group of donors focused on the crucial aspect of health financing – ie, how scarce resources are allocated within the Ministry of Health. However, data from other sources do not lend support to the claim that resources allocated to essential health services were maintained at pre-crisis levels. Scrutiny of expenditure on primary care from 1996/97 to 1999/2000 (table 1) shows that there was a 20% reduction in per person spending, and a 25% cut in government spending.

In fact, in August 1999, the World Bank estimated that spending on the routine part of the health-sector budget (i.e., for operation, maintenance, and procurement of medicines and consumables) dropped by 10% in real terms in 1997–98 and 28% in 1998–99; that real expenditure on communicable-disease control fell from 158 billion rupiah (US$16 million) in 1997/98 to 88 billion rupiahs ($11 million) in 1998/99; and that routine spending fell by 28% in real terms.

However, as expenditure in primary healthcare was decreasing, spending on hospital care improved – in fact a 30% rise in hospital spending per person (table 1). This increase seems to have been led by donors: a review of expenditure shows "real donor financing of hospitals in 1998–99 was 3·7 times the 1997–98 levels … it appears that much of this financing came from Japan, Korea, and Australia, and other bilateral donors and took the form of investment in hospital equipment". The misallocation of scarce resources at a time of increased risk of child mortality, especially in marginalised groups, was detrimental to children and to those of the lowest economic status.

The ADB has also stated that priority – i.e., essential or basic – health services were maintained or improved. One critical element of the primary health care package, and a good indicator of the delivery of other basic health care services, is immunisation programmes. In its report to the consultative group, the ADB claims that "health outreach activities have been maintained. The MOH [Ministry of Health] has ensured that a package of essential services including basic curative and preventive services such as immunisation has been available to all ... The continued availability of basic outpatient services through the network of health centres was ensured. Immunisation services for children were maintained."

1993	1994	1995	1996	1997	1998	1999
76·3%	78·7%	77·3%	88·2%	91·0%	92·8%	89·8%

Data are from ADB report, 1999.[7]

Table 2. Immunisation rates in children ages 0–4 years in Indonesia, 1993–99

These statements are consistent with survey data drawn from the ADB's Assessment of Poverty in Indonesia report, which show fairly steady improvements in the proportion of children aged between 0 and 4 years who had received any immunisation between 1993 and 1999 – i.e., an 18% overall increase in coverage (table 2).

	1995	1996	1997	1998	1999
Antigen					
DPT3	92%	91%	90%	65%	64%
Measles	92%	92%	93%	76%	71%
Poliomyelits	97%	89%	87%	77%	74%
BCG	100%	100%	99%	85%	85%

Data are from WHO, 2000.[9]

Table 3. Vaccination coverage rates in Indonesia, 1995–99

However, these data do not correspond with easily accessible WHO data, which provide a fuller picture of the proportion of children fully vaccinated against tuberculosis (with BCG), diphtheria, pertussis, tetanus (DPT), poliomyelitis, and measles in accordance with precise immunisation schedules (table 3). These data show an almost 25% decline in coverage rates between 1995 and 1999, the reduction being most striking in 1997–98. This information in turn, is generally consistent with easily accessible cross-sectional household survey data collected by the demographic and household survey (DHS), a source widely recognised for its quality.

These differences in vaccination rates can be partly explained by the cohorts used to generate data. The ADB study uses a cohort of children aged under 5 years, whereas the demographic and household survey used children aged less than 1 year, yielding a picture of trends in coverage rates that is much less clear than a year-by-year charting of trends. Likewise, use of the category "ever immunised" gives much less precise information than does a disaggregation of vaccine by type. Thus, the ADB did not select the best data available to meet its objective of understanding the effect of the crisis and social safety nets on vaccination coverage rates between 1995 and 1999. Moreover, an even greater drawback is that the ADB did not take into account at all these data from WHO or the demographic and health survey data.

Three key points to be noted are that, first, immunisations by antigens listed in table 3 are an important determinant of childhood survival; second, reversals in coverage rates are widely believed to be related to retraction of services from rural areas and are, therefore, detrimental to the poorest sectors of the community; and third, that these declines point to erosion of other basic services for vulnerable and marginalised populations. This third point is particularly relevant in Indonesia, where outreach services and posyandu (ie, a regular community outreach activity organised by community health volunteers with the support of health-centre staff, which focuses mainly on maternal and child health) are essential for maintenance of basic services to the poor. This reality was noted explicitly and incorporated into the JPS-BK mission statement. Taken together, these three points suggest that the economic crisis might have had a very negative effect on childhood survival in low-income households.

Low economic status and effective health care

Although the ADB reports that outreach services and posyandus for the poor have been maintained, we have seen evidence to the contrary. Table 4 shows a comparison of rates of contact with health workers and visits to modern health facilities for children less than 5 years of age in the poorest economic quintile, with those in the highest quintile. Between 1997 and 1999, the use of health care services by children from poor backgrounds dropped by about 17%, compared with 8% in children from wealthier settings.

	1997	1999	% change
Poorest quintile			
Child contact rate	60·3	51·0	−15·4%
Child visit rate	19·9	16·4	−18%
Wealthiest quintile			
Child contact rate	77·1	69·6	−9·7%
Child visit rate	29·9	27·8	−7%

Data from ADB report.[7]

Table 4. Rates of health worker contact and health centre visits for children aged 0–4 years, 1997–99

When changes in the frequency of visits and contact are calculated for 1995–99 and arranged by descending order of decline, the results suggest a sharp fall-off in use of services by poor households. Table 5 shows that rates of use of services such as posyandu, traditional healers, clinics, and health centres, which are most likely to be used by low-income households fell between 26% and 47%. Visits to hospitals and private providers, where user fees were 10–20 times higher than in the previously described healthcare settings, and thus are more likely to be used by the non-poor, fell between 3% and 13%, probably because of the cost of care.

177

	1995	1997	1998	1999	% change 1995–99
Posyandu	0·19	0·20	0·12	0·10	–47%
Traditional healer	0·73	0·63	0·43	0.40	–45%
Subsidiary health centre	1·69	1·66	1·01	1·01	–40%
Clinic	0·42	0·39	0·34	0·31	–26%
Primary health centre	4·66	4·31	3·25	3·46	–26%
Private doctor	3·01	3·14	2·84	2·63	–13%
Public hospital	0·64	0·60	0·64	0·59	–8%
Paramedical practitioner	2·82	2·93	2·80	2·70	–4%
Private hospital	0·40	0·41	0·40	0·39	–3%

Table 5. Contact rate by type of provider 1995–99

There are some signs that JPS-BK did have a positive effect on access to effective health care. For example, the ADB reports a steady increase in the proportion of women receiving assistance during childbirth: from

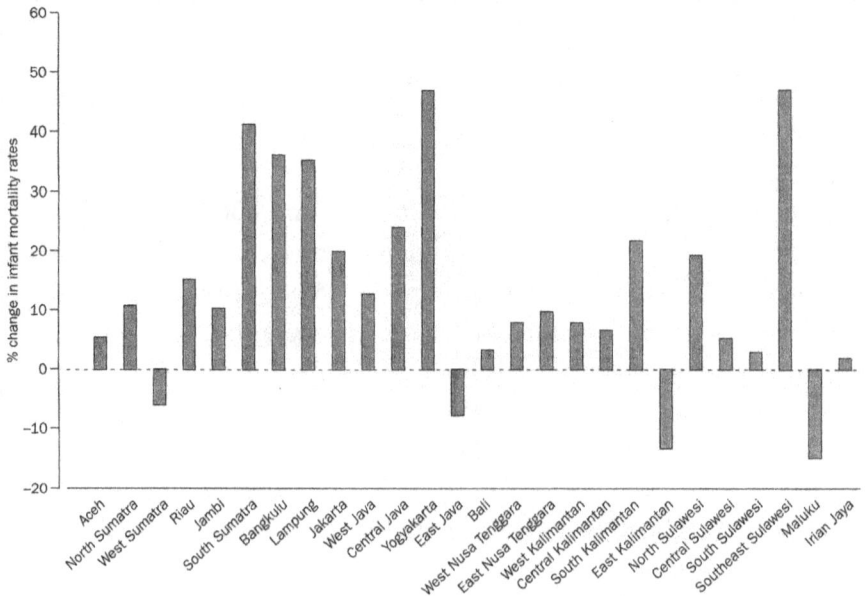

Fig. 6. Change in infant mortality rates in 26 Indonesian provinces, 1996–99

The cost of care

In addition to difficulties in health-service delivery, is the issue of the rising cost of health care during the crisis. Private healthcare expenditure in Indonesia accounts for about two-thirds of total spending, with about 75% of the total being made in cash. Purchase of drugs makes an important contribution to private healthcare expenditure, and cash payments account for about 80% of total spending on pharmaceuticals. Between 1996 and 1999, there was a 25% fall in real spending on drugs that happened in parallel with large price increases of about 170%, resulting from the Indonesian rupiah's massive devaluation during the financial crash. Set against a background of severe economic crisis and falling incomes, these high rates of cash payments obviously put health finance at risk. Although the ADB reports that "targeting and entitlement mechanisms were reviewed to ensure that administrative requirements did not act to prevent access to basic health services by the poor", user fees seem to be an impenetrable barrier for the poor in use of health services, and evidence from around the world shows that exemptions from fees rarely work as intended, especially for the poor and vulnerable. On top of standard outpatient charges, informal costs, such as travel, food, and accommodation, were usually substantial. The World Bank concludes "these extra charges are, of course, a disincentive for the poor".

Rising infant mortality rates

Declining access to effective health care for poor sectors of the community makes the prospect of further improvements in infant mortality rates seem rather remote. However, there were some countervailing policy responses to the crisis that could have had a positive bearing on infant survival. For example, funding from donor agencies in 1998 and 1999, which amounted to billions of dollars, might have had a substantial effect on mortality rates if directed in the right areas: price subsidies for essential foods alone could have had a large effect on income in poor households, and helped to maintain nutritional status. However, in a setting of poor quality health services, low rates of use, expensive health care, the combined effect of rising drug prices, and sharp reductions in essential healthcare services could have been enough to nullify the benefits of health and nutrition investments, especially in low-income households, and to reverse infant mortality rates. The World Bank equivocates on this point, stating that it is "difficult to get a complete and consistent picture of the health impact of the crisis and the effectiveness of policy responses. Some standard barometers suggest catastrophic results were averted. For example, infant mortality rates (IMRs) seemed to have continued a downward trend." The World Bank, usually meticulous in citing data sources, offers no reference to this important statement. In reality, Badan Pusat Statistik (BPS or, the Central Statistics Bureau) data cited in the UN development report show that for the period 1990–96, infant mortality rates improved in all 26 provinces by about 20%; the figure shows that between the years 1996 and 1999, infant mortality increased in 22 of 26 provinces by an average of 14% (figure). Overall, these data suggest that the optimistic assessments were inaccurate, and that the World Bank's claim that a health disaster was averted seems groundless.

Conclusions

The inconsistencies that we report suggest that the ADB's and World Bank's conclusions did not incorporate data that contradicted the notion that the social safety net provided by the JPS-BK had successfully mitigated effects of the economic crisis on the health of Indonesia's poor citizens. Because the donor process was neither transparent nor consultative, the reasons for this optimistic assessment are unclear. Poor attention to important data sources is one factor. Other possible explanations are that, first, the implementation of exit policies from the social safety net were high on the list of international agencies who were eager to convince international investors that the crisis was over. Second, because

JPS-BK was being proposed as the robust framework in the health sector on which to base decentralization, its failure would have been problematic. A debate and reassessment of the effect of the Indonesian economic crisis on key health indicators would be helpful, to provide a fresh starting point for consideration of health and economic policy interventions that enhance equity.

Global Health and Local Poverty: Rich Countries' Responses to Vulnerable Populations[195][196]

Deliberately and Structurally Altering Exposure to Risk This study of 23 OECD countries reveals a correlation between a nation's generosity towards poorer countries, as measured by Overseas Development Assistance (ODA), and the strength of its domestic social safety net. Countries that are less generous internationally tend to have fewer social transfers and greater domestic inequalities. Notably, Scandinavian countries, which report the lowest levels of child poverty, also exhibit the highest levels of ODA. Factors such as ideology, altruism, generosity, and social trust partly explain the variance in social transfer levels. Additionally, a key factor is the degree of identification with the recipients: people are more inclined to support social transfers if they feel a kinship with the recipients. In ethnically homogeneous nations like Norway, the Netherlands, Denmark, and Sweden, robust social programs are more prevalent compared to countries like the US. However, increasing immigration in recent years has fueled the rise of populist political movements even in traditionally homogeneous Scandinavian countries, leading to a decline in support for redistributive policies.

◆

According to the World Health Organization "the world's biggest killer and the greatest cause of ill-health and suffering across the globe" is extreme poverty, listed in the International Classification of Diseases as Z59.5. Efforts to address poverty in developing countries have coalesced around the MDGs – which include the goals to eradicate extreme poverty and hunger, reduce child mortality, and fight HIV, malaria and other major diseases. In high-income countries, efforts to reduce child poverty are rooted in the 1990 United Nations' Convention of the Rights of the Child (CRC) and depend on government, family and other related social transfers. Yet, poverty is widely seen as inevitable and intractable.

In poor countries, issues of good governance and corruption, lack of

[195] Chris Simms and David Persaud
[196] For access to the original article and footnotes, see tiny.cc/LocalPoverty

political will, limited institutional capacities, environmental extremes and political unrest are used to explain persistent poverty, while in high-income countries, personal or generational weaknesses are often cited. In both contexts, governments are provided with a rationale for inaction.

Scholars have long been interested in the relationship between welfare institutions and aid, often focusing on inequalities. This commentary asks what we can learn about poverty by looking at the way rich countries respond to the needs of vulnerable populations both within their own societies and those of low-income countries. Taking advantage of recent efforts by United Nations Children's Fund (Unicef) to redefine child poverty in a way that is consistent with the World Health Organization's Commission on the Social Determinants of Health, three sets of data are reviewed. The first looks at levels of child well-being in 23 rich countries belonging to the Organization of Economic Community Development (OECD). Based on the CRC and supported by 40 outcome indicators that take into account material well-being, health and safety, education, peer and family relationships, behaviors and risks, and children's own subjective sense of well-being, child poverty is defined as the significant lack of the basic needs required for healthy physical, mental, emotional and spiritual development. A drawback to using multiple indicators is that some OECD countries such as Mexico and Turkey are excluded because of lack of data. This study pays particular attention to Canada. The second set of data reports the amount of official development assistance (ODA) that rich (OECD) countries disburse to poorer countries. ODA or foreign aid is disbursed either directly between governments or through multilateral agencies such as the United Nations (UN), with the aim of promoting social and economic development.

In 1969, Lester B. Pearson led a UN expert commission assigned the task of recommending reasonable levels of ODA that ought to be expected from rich countries. Based on Pearson's notion that "it is only right for those who have to share with those who have not", ODA was benchmarked at 0.7% of gross national product (GNP) or, more recently, gross national income (GNI).

Social transfer, according to OECD, is government support to individual households aimed at improving and protecting family security and includes family allowances, disability and sickness benefits, formal day care provision and unemployment insurance. Levels of social transfers are measured as a percentage of GDP.

		Net ODA as % of GNI, 2006	% of Child Population Living in Poverty, 2006	Family and Related Transfers as % of GDP
Countries with ODA/GNI above 0.7%	Sweden	1.03	5.0	12.0
	Norway	.89	8.7	9.5
	Netherlands	.81	4.2	9.5
	Denmark	.80	7.2	13.5
Countries with ODA/GNI between 0.7% and 0.36%	Ireland	.53	10.2	5.6
	UK	.52	18.2	7.0
	Belgium	.50	10.7	10.5
	Austria	.48	13.8	7.0
	France	.47	13.0	9.0
	Finland	.39	7.5	11.5
	Switzerland	.39	8.3	6.5
	Germany	.36	11.2	7.0
Countries with ODA/GNI below 0.36%	Spain	.32	8.0	6.3
	Australia*	.30	14.7	7.3
	Canada	.30	11.8	6.2
	Japan*	.25	14.3	2.1
	Portugal	.21	13.7	5.5
	Italy	.20	10.0	4.0
	USA	.17	18.0	2.3
	Greece	.16	11.8	5.8
	Czech Rep.†	.11	12.5	6.5
	Poland†	.11	12.3	7.8
	Hungary†	.07	14.5	7.5

Table 1. ODA as Percentage of GNI, Percent of Child Population Living in Poverty, and Family and Related Transfers as % of GDP in Selected OECD Countries
* Until 2007, Unicef was using an income-based definition of child poverty which defines a child as poor if the income available to that child is less than half the median income available to other children growing up in that society. † Data or Czech Republic, Poland and Hungary from http://www.oecd.org/dataoecd/52/18/37790990.pdf (Accessed June 9, 2008)

Table 1 (column 2) shows levels of ODA for the selected countries. These levels can be divided into three groups: the first consists of the four donor countries that reach or exceed the UN target of 0.7% of GNI – Sweden (1.03%), Norway (0.89%), the Netherlands (0.81%), and Denmark (0.8%). The second group consists of the countries that achieve more than

0.36% (that is, more than half the recommended ODA contribution) but less than 0.7%. The last group shows the least generous countries, which had ODA flows at less than half the recommended level (that is, less than 0.35%). These countries were ranging from 0.07 to 0.32%; they include some of the world's richest countries, several members of the influential G7, and all of the non-European countries. Rates of ODA contributions made by the United States (0.17%) and Japan (0.24%) – the world's two largest economies – were a fraction of those made by Sweden (1.03%).

Table 1 (column 3) presents data for levels of child well-being in the selected countries. Because data were not available for Japan and Australia, income-based poverty rates were used instead. Column 3 shows that poverty rates range between 4.2% (in the Netherlands) and 18.2% (in the United Kingdom). In the Scandinavian/Nordic countries, child poverty is below 10% while in the 5 non-European countries, Australia, Canada, Japan, and the United States, and most G7 countries, one sees the highest levels of child poverty.

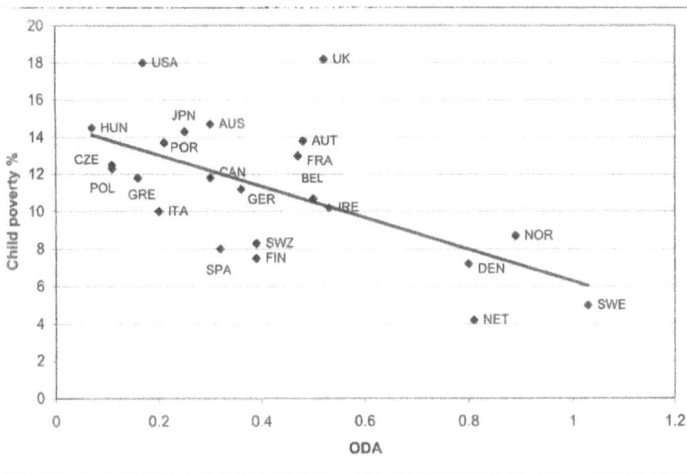

Fig. 1. Relationship between ODA and child poverty in 23 OECD countries Sweden SWE, Norway NOR, Netherlands NET, Denmark DEN, Ireland IRE, United Kingdom UK, Belgium BEL, Austria AUT, France FRA, Finland FIN, Switzerland SWZ, Germany GER, Spain SPA, Australia AUS, Canada CAN, Japan JPN, Portugal POR, Italy ITA, United States of America

USA, Greece GRE, Czech Republic CZE, Poland POL, Hungary HUN

The relationship between levels of ODA and child poverty is shown in Figure 1. It indicates that countries in Northern Europe tend to have lower levels of child poverty and the highest levels of ODA. NonEuropean countries like Australia, Canada, Japan, and the United States, and generally, the G7 countries, are the least generous and have the highest levels of child poverty and lowest levels of ODA. An important exception seems to be the UK, represented in Figure 1 as an outlier: it is generous to developing countries but still has very high child poverty. None of the 4 most generous countries have child poverty above 10%: they contributed on average 0.88% ODA/GNI and had child poverty rates at 6.8%. The average child poverty rate in the least generous countries (which contribute 0.24% ODA) was 13.2%, double that of the most generous countries.

The most obvious explanation for the relationship between levels of child poverty and ODA in the select group of countries is that governments that prioritize the needs of vulnerable populations at home tend to demonstrate concern for the needs of vulnerable populations abroad. Conversely, governments that take a more individualistic and market-based approach to economic development may be prepared to accept higher levels of inequality both domestically and in developing regions of the world. In short, the difference may be ideological, which in turn is expressed in terms of government policies, strategies and programming.

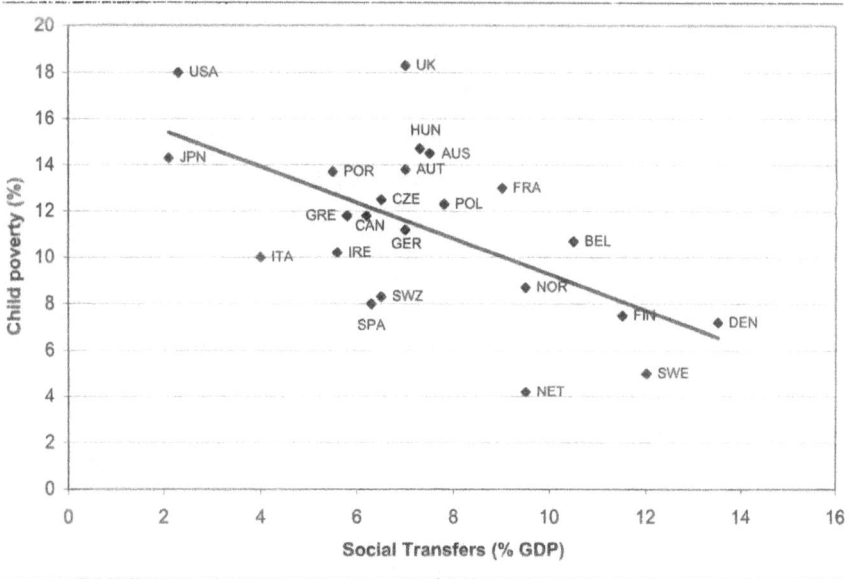

Fig. 2. Relationship between child poverty (%) and social transfers (as % GDP) in OECD countries

UNICEF has examined the actual influence of government policy through social transfers on inequalities. Now using the more robust, 6-dimensional definition of child poverty together with OECD "social transfer" data for the selected 23 OECD countries (Table 1, Column 4), the relationship between the two can be examined. A wide range of government efforts to address poverty become evident, with Sweden allocating 12% of GDP to social transfers and Japan 2.1%. Northern European countries tend to have much higher transfer rates than non-European countries. Figure 2 shows the correlation between levels of child poverty and "family and related transfers" in the selected countries. Direct observation shows that higher government spending on family and social benefits is associated with countries with lower child poverty rates. Countries allocating 10% or more of GDP to family-related social transfers have on average, child poverty rates of 7.5%, whereas countries with poverty rates above 15% allocate just more than 5% on social transfers. Figure 2 indicates that variation in government policy accounts for part of the variation in child poverty between OECD countries and suggests that poverty is neither inevitable nor intractable.

In low-income countries, the influence of resources on levels of poverty is less clear since what keeps poor countries impoverished is not simply inadequate inflow of ODA, but rather non-aid policies including "severe trade barriers, biased migration regimes, lopsided use of natural resources and unfair intellectual property regimes which impose a heavy burden on poor countries". Nevertheless, the '10/90 gap' alone would suggest a very strong relationship between burden of disease in developing countries (93%) and access to global health resources (less than 10%). Furthermore, a robust body of literature shows repeatedly that when the donor community has partnered with governments in well planned and financed interventions, the results can be impressive: recent examples include a 91% reduction in measles mortality in Africa (2000-2006), reduction in rural poverty in Mozambique, reduction of malaria mortality in Kenya, and control of tuberculosis in Asia and adult HIV in East Africa.

The notion that rich countries' responses to the needs of vulnerable populations at home and abroad may be explained in part by ideology is of course not consistent with their claim that they pursue evidence-based policy development or decision-making (EBDM). In Canada, where EBDM is supported and promoted by the relevant bureaucracies (the Department of Human Resources and Social Development, the Canadian International Development Agency and Treasury Board), child poverty has remained unchanged since 1989 and ODA stagnates at a dismal 0.30%. In fact, Unicef is quite critical of Canada which in 1989 declared it would eliminate child poverty at home. Unicef reports that "this target came and went without agreement on what the target means, or how progress towards it is to be measured, or what policies might be necessary to achieve it". For example, with respect to early childcare – one of the four key social transfers cited by Unicef as having a bearing on child well-being, and widely acknowledged as one of the most cost-effective means of reducing child poverty – the Canadian Government's response in 2006 was to cancel the comprehensive early child-care program worked out between the provinces and the previous government. It replaced the program with a paltry monthly cash transfer of CDN$100 – a decision that is not consistent with the Government of Canada's public support for the WHO Commission on Social Determinants of Health. With respect to its levels of foreign aid, the Canadian government cut ODA in its last budgetary cycle and now includes such items as the "training of the Afghanistan army and police" in these reduced allocations. Both of these actions bolster the notion that policy is excessively driven by ideology, making poverty appear as indeed "inevitable".

Although ideology may not prevent governments from publicly supporting altruistic goals such as the MDGs, it appears to hamper their follow-up. Today, failure by rich countries to keep their promises has left the MDGs severely under-funded and off-track while child poverty is rising in 17 of 25 of these same countries – the significance of both being underscored by evidence that poverty is not intractable. The G7 countries, which ostensibly provide political and economic leadership to the rest of the world community, do not fare well in this analysis. In summary, the data show that non-G7 countries are 37% more generous towards developing countries and 53% more generous in their allocation towards child poverty at home. Child poverty is 35% higher in G7 countries, leading to questions as to what sort of leadership they are providing and for whom. In Canada, all of this provides fresh evidence that often those "who have" literally avert their gaze from the face of poverty on the streets while figuratively turning their backs on the vulnerable abroad.

Health and Human Rights in Canada: A Global Concern[197]

Social Murder: "This is not the Canada I know" During the runup to the 2015 Federal Election, Stephen Harper enlisted Lynton Crosby, known for his "dog-whistle politics," to help with his re-election campaign, which played on racial and ethnic divides. Toward the campaign's end, Harper used the term "old-stock Canadians" in a nationally televised debate—a phrase that symbolized divisive us-them politics and was widely rejected by Canadians. On October 19, 2015, Justin Trudeau defeated Stephen Harper. During his decade-long tenure, Harper implemented various policies that curtailed human rights and freedoms. A member of the UN Committee on Human Rights remarked, "This is not the Canada I know."

◆

A new report by the UN Committee on Human Rights (UNCOHR) is sharply critical of Canada's worsening human rights record. The first such assessment in 10 years (a period coinciding with a decade of conservative government), it describes policies that undermine human rights including the ability of civil society to lawfully protest such policies. Most issues cited relate to public health and safety and I illustrate some of them here ahead of Canada's federal election next week.

The report is particularly concerned about the rights of out-groups (such as prisoners, people with mental illnesses, and refugees) and vulnerable populations. For instance, cuts to basic health services for refugees led Canadian doctors and lawyers to petition the federal courts to restore services; in doing so, the courts described government policy as "cruel and unusual". Indeed, with a large parliamentary majority, it is often left to the courts to provide a check on government power. For example, the federal courts reversed attempts to close harm-reduction services for drug users and legislation that threatened the health and safety

---

[197] For access to the original article and footnotes, see tiny.cc/HealthHumanRights

of prostitutes, and repeatedly stepped in to protect aboriginal land rights.

The report is especially concerned about the passage of Bill 51 which gives government greater power to undertake domestic surveillance on groups and individuals such a environmentalists, aboriginal people, or simply any that disagree with government policy – with little or no oversight. One member of the UN committee noted "This is not the Canada that I know".

As Canadians queue to vote in the federal election next week, some will be uncomfortable knowing that the new Fair Elections Act that requires an official photo identification will overwhelmingly discriminate against those who are least likely to produce it – the very groups cited by UNCOHR. Many Canadians perhaps already uncomfortable with Canada's tepid response to the Syrian refugee crisis will have been further dismayed to learn this past week that it was Harper's interference with the refugee claimant process that shut the doors; as they cast their ballot, some will recall a different era when Canada welcomed tens of thousands of refugees from Vietnam and Kosovo. But no Canadian will recall anything to compare with the recent descent into identity politics in which the Prime Minister referred to "old-stock"[198] Canadians (as distinct from those born abroad) on national television – the stratification of society to which Michael Marmot so often refers. And because many do not recognize it as Canadian or the context in which it nests, they will reject it – some with anger, others with hope.

---

[198] In Ken Burns' award-winning PBS documentary, "The US and the Holocaust" (2022), the phrase "old stock" is described as being associated with deep hatred and antipathy towards immigrants.

Indigenous Health and the Rise of Racism in Canada
Lancet, April 13 2015[199]

Crimes against Humanity This term refers to acts committed by or on behalf of a state that grossly violate human rights, causing significant pain and suffering, and are widespread or systematic. Evidence suggests that during his administration, Stephen Harper sought to undermine four key strategies used by First Nations to reduce discrimination: enhancing public information, addressing inequalities, building coalitions, and initiating collective action. He reportedly utilized law enforcement agencies such as the RCMP, CSIS, and the Canada Revenue Agency (CRA) to suppress Indigenous peoples and their advocates. These collective actions may be considered as crimes against humanity due to their intent and impact on human rights.

◆

Are Canada's 1.3 million Aboriginal people being deliberately or inadvertently discriminated against by a government overly concerned about its resource development strategy? However, counter-intuitive the question is of a nation widely seen as tolerant (and that ranks 7th of 132 countries on the Social Progress Index), it's being asked by Aboriginal people wary of more policies that exclude and control.

Recent studies show a rise in discrimination against Aboriginal people such that Canada may have a worse race problem than the USA; racism pervades the health system and is highly correlated with poor outcomes. Indeed, astonishing public health images of First Nations communities confirm health outcomes on par with many poorer countries, worsened by epidemic levels of depressive and behavioral disorders. These are associated with the intergenerational impact of an abusive assimilation program known as the Indian Residential School (IRS) system (1880-1996) in which 150,000 children were taken from their families and forced to attend the schools ten months of every year.

In 2006, new reasons for discrimination emerged. A newly elected

---

[199] For access to the original article and footnotes, see tiny.cc/HealthRacism

Conservative government launched a $600 billion development plan for the oil, gas, mining, and pipeline industries with many of its initiatives on, or near, aboriginal traditional lands. In a departure from the past, aboriginals began to fight back with increasing success by accessing the courts, holding public demonstrations and forming alliances with non-Aboriginal interest groups.

Government responses to First Nations' initiatives have been swift and harsh. Carried out by a worrisome combination of those who make the laws and those that enforce them, this approach portrays Aboriginal people as the main barrier to Canada's resource development and its future prosperity. Especially striking is that these responses constitute the opposite of common discrimination-reducing strategies – tackling inequalities, increasing public information, building coalitions, and collective action – and therefore seem systematic and purposive.

Four strategies thwarted

One means of marginalizing (and promoting racist views) is "victim-blaming", that is, making victims appear responsible for the circumstances in which they find themselves. The federal government has managed information so that data that would help explain antisocial behavior and disparities are repressed while data that bolster the stereotypes (violence, alcohol abuse and so forth) are left to flourish. For example, Prime Minister Stephen Harper's government has fought hard to withhold IRS documents showing government sponsored medical and nutritional experiments on the children, the use of electric shocks on the recalcitrant, and an astonishing 3,000 onsite child deaths at the residential schools. Despite pleadings from First Nations leadership, Canadian Archivist and the Commissioner of Truth and Reconciliation Commission (TRC), the government has stymied full access to IRS documents; when 40,000 IRS abuse victims finally gave recorded testimony to the TRC, the government turned to the Courts for permission to destroy this very evidence.

Similarly, pleadings by Canadian and international scientists for data on existing and new disparities (particularly those related to the oil sands) have been ignored by the Harper government. As to inequalities themselves and the notion of creating a more level playing field, the government has been stone-faced, responding instead by cancelling a 5-billion-dollar Federal Accord and, over recent years, cutting most Aboriginal-led health programming meant to address the sequelae of the IRS.

Another discrimination-reducing strategy, extension of group boundaries, was embraced by First Nations who began to form high-profile alliances with a host of well-respected environmental non-governmental organizations (NGOs). Among its responses, the government publically engaged the Canada Revenue Agency (CRA) to conduct extensive audits on their records based on the notion that they were too political. The Minister of Finance unabashedly warned, that if he were one of these groups "I would be cautious". What he did not say was that the CRA – which will launch an investigation in response to public complaints – received formal filings from Ethical Oil (an online activists group working in defense of the oil-sands development) whose founder, is currently the director of issues management in the Prime Minister's Office.

Aboriginals also took collective action as an obvious discrimination-reducing option. The First Nations and Family Caring Society (headed by Cindy Blackstock) filed legal claims against the government for failing to provide adequate healthcare to Aboriginal children; the government had the Royal Canadian Mounted Police (RCMP) and Canadian Security Intelligence Service (CSIS) place her under surveillance, gathering a 400 page file on her in the process. The Federal Privacy Commissioner condemned these actions, ordered the agencies to cease and desist and destroy the files. Similarly, reports released this month show that these two agencies are proactively monitoring aboriginal peaceful protest groups in expectation of demonstrations against resource extraction projects.

Indeed, critics are questioning the professionalism, non-partisanship, and closeness of these agencies to industry that is so detrimental to aboriginal well-being. They ask of CSIS "why are they producing these "intelligence reports" on protest activity they acknowledge is legitimate and outside their mandate?[200] Revelations of a 44-page RCMP memo this month identifying Aboriginal protesters as the political fringe while extolling the virtues and inevitability of the oil sands and repeatedly casting doubt on global warming. Past revelations that these agencies are sharing information with industry and that the watchdog overseeing them was led by industry lobbyists lent credence to these worries.

An evolving polity points the way forward

As to a way forward, the government may wish to take a step back now that the oil market has partially collapsed, towards a more balanced and less frenetic approach to economic development. The polity is evolving. While ordinary Canadians may not yet perceive the plight of Aboriginal people as a top priority, they are nonetheless uncomfortable with the persistence of the Indian Act of 1886 (the only race-based legislation in a Western democracy), the requirement that Aboriginal people have an identity card and their disenfranchisement by the so-called Fair Elections Act (having only gained the vote in 1960). They are embarrassed by the quality of public discourse: by Mr. Harper's assertion to the G20 that "Every nation wants to be Canada … We also have no colonial history";[201] by a former acting Minister for Indian and Northern Affairs claim that it isn't the government's job to make sure children have full bellies – then asking "Is it my job to feed my neighbour's child? I don't think so".[202] In contrast, provincial and territorial governments have signaled a desire to tackle at least some of the inequalities related to First Nations grievances. The courts have increasingly handed First Nations victories related to resource development, suggesting consultation and dialogue are the way forward for

[200] https://www.broadbentinstitute.ca/en/post/james-scrooge-moore-talks-child-poverty
[201] https://www.reuters.com/article/columns-us-g20-canada-advantages-idUS-TRE58P05Z20090926
[202] https://www.ctvnews.ca/politics/moore-apologizes-for-insensitive-comment-about-child-poverty-1.1595811

the federal government. It ought to realign its strategic planning and management with core Canadian values; better lean than mean.

Deracination: Canada's Aboriginal Suicides
BMJ, April 29 2016[203]

Evidence of great human suffering, physical and mental Suicide is the leading cause of death among Indigenous youth, with their suicide rates being three to fourtimes higher than those of non-Indigenous populations. This article explores the cumulative intergenerational impacts of historic and ongoing human rights abuses inflicted on Indigenous peoples by the Canadian government and its agents. It highlights a youth suicide epidemic in the Attawapiskat community, including video evidence that illustrates the profound despair experienced by youth living in deplorable conditions and lacking hope. Additionally, the article presents audio evidence of a longstanding governmental trend of prioritizing resource allocation over human rights, spanningvarious political ideologies. Former Liberal Minister and Prime Minister Jean Chretien (1993-2003), despite being seen as a progressive agent for change, frequently prioritized the interests of resource industries over the fundamental needs of Indigenouscommunities. He implemented contradictory policies of assimilation and marginalization of Indigenous peoples during his tenure as head of the Department of Indian Affairs and Northern Development.

◆

Four aboriginal boys, two aged 8 and two aged 9, bolted midday from their school, half-clad, mid-winter, to make the 12 mile trek to their families in Nautley Reserve. When they were found the next day in the slush-ice on Lake Fraser less than a mile from home – arms wrapped around one another in a frozen embrace – few could have guessed the circumstances.

When, 80 years later, the community of Attawapiskat (population 2000) declared a state of emergency on 9 April 2016, reporting 11 attempted suicides in one day (and 100 attempts over the winter), Canadians may have been shocked, yet few would have been surprised. Several pieces of evidence including audio and video clips explain why.

---

[203]   For access to the original article and footnotes, see tiny.cc/Deracination

Both events trace back to the federal government's paradoxical policies of marginalization and assimilation. The most pernicious of the marginalization policies was the forcible removal of aboriginals from their homeland. Recent award winning research details the clearing of the Canadian Plains – one of many land grabs designed to make way for white Europeans through the deliberate starvation and pacification of aboriginals.

The most pernicious of the assimilation policies was the Indian Residential Schools (IRS), a program (1880-1996) that led to the forcible removal of 150 000 children from their families for 10 months of each school year. Its explicit aim was "to kill the Indian in the child." Associated with pervasive physical, emotional, and sexual abuse of children, it led to 40 000 survivors eventually receiving robust compensation. The unearthing of new evidence of medical and then nutritional experiments, torture by use of a makeshift electric chair, and records showing an estimated 6000 on-site deaths has unsettled Canadians.

Horrific as the implementation of these two policies was, it was only the beginning. Once removed (and often confined) to reservations, aboriginals were largely ignored. For example, there were no attempts to secure basic public health amenities for aboriginal populations and they were excluded from Canada's generous social safety net that emerged after the second world war.

A disquieting 10-minute video[204] (November 2011) of Attawapiskat reveals an environment that may have helped give rise to the suicide epidemic. It shows a community without water, without electricity, and – with no sewage system – buckets for toilets. Many families are seen living in tents and sheds with walls covered in black mould, while 90 families are living in work trailers abandoned by DeBeers from a nearby diamond mine.

The First Nations Child and Family Caring Society has successfully sued the federal government for failure to provide adequate healthcare

---

[204]   https://www.youtube.com/watch?v=6abZ0LFT5CQ

for aboriginal children; in January 2016, in a legally binding decision, the Canadian Human Rights Tribunal ordered the government to "cease the discriminatory practice" that underfunds child health on reserves.

Several features of the Attawapiskat suicides are revealing: (1) the suicide epidemic is similar to many others in First Nations across Canada in which the idea of suicide is the contagion; (2) it overlays other "epidemics" such as addition, depression, violence, and fetal alcohol syndrome (and alcohol related birth defects); (3) crises are intergenerational; (4) they are cumulative; and (5) they are steadily worsening. For example, statistics show a steady rise in the percentage of aboriginals in custody, with aboriginals representing 44% of girls in youth custody. While the natural behavior of epidemics is to rise, fall, and stabilize, demographic show a large pool of young people at risk (the mean age of the aboriginal population being 28 compared with 41 in the general population) and that this epidemic is on an ascending limb with no end in sight.

Ongoing marginalization and assimilation policies are seen by First Nations as a continuing effort by the government to access rich natural resources abundant on traditional lands and territories.

The response to the Attawapiskat suicide crisis by former Liberal Prime Minister Jean Chretien (1993-2003), a lobbyist for resource industries, is revealing. On 13 April 2016, he told a large gathering of Ottawa media that "people have to move sometimes" – articulating the assimilationist view that the solution to these crises is in the hands of First Nations who should consider leaving the North.[205] It would also, of course, relieve the federal government of the burden of providing health and social services while furthering the possibility of accessing valuable land. He was broadly criticized inside and outside of the House of Commons – the grand chief of First Nations said "We are not bison."[206] Indeed, as former minister of Indian affairs and northern development

---

[205] https://www.cbc.ca/news/politics/chretien-attawapiskat-1.3533331
[206] https://nationalpost.com/news/canada/were-not-bison-grand-chief-says-to-suggestion-first-nations-people-leave-afflicted-reserves-like-attawapiskat

(1968-74), Mr. Chretien's department produced the "White Paper" in 1969 on "Indian Policy," seen by First Nations as "a thinly disguised program of extermination through assimilation." It would have abolished the special status of indigenous people while failing to deal with aboriginal title and treaty rights. However, it failed to pass into law, and actually prompted the Supreme Court to step in and recognize aboriginal title in Canadian law in 1973. The liberal party apologized for the initiative in 2014.

Audio recordings archived by the CBC capture the twin (and of ten conflicting) priorities of the Department of Indian Affairs and Northern Development and the response of the minister (Chretien) to them. For example, when a group of children from Cold Lake Reserve (perhaps not dissimilar to those of Attawapiskat) came to his office in 1971 to ask him to come and look at the terrible conditions on their reserve he refused.[207] In 1974 when he was asked by CBC if he would recognize the land claims of the Inuit and Dene Nations who objected to the Mackenzie Valley pipeline, he said "we cannot stop development because of Indian claims."

One means to gain an insight into the underlying reasons the four aboriginal boys bolted from their school 80 years ago, or why so many young aboriginal give up in despair, is by considering the term "deracinate." It means to extirpate, remove, or separate from a native environment or culture. It seems applicable to the removal of the individual from community, from family, and, in fact, from self.

It does not suggest the relatively benign term "transplanting" or "uprooting" since both imply "roots and all." Rather, it evokes just the opposite: the cutting away of the roots through the destruction of language, culture, and ties to family and community – indeed, "the killing of the Indian in the Indian." The four boys were running from an abusive school and back to home and family; eight decades on, perhaps the Attawapiskat youth felt like running, yet had nowhere to go.

---

[207] https://www.cbc.ca/player/play/1735334000

Canada at 150:
The Racialization of Healthcare
BMJ, June 30 2017[208]

Social Murder: sharing only with those who look like us A growing body of evidence indicates that healthcare systems across Canada discriminate against racial minorities. This article, released during Canada's 150th anniversary celebrations, portrays Canadians as proud of their Medicare system, which they believe reflects core national values of mutual concern, tolerance, and diversity. However, this pride may be somewhat misplaced. Historically, Canada was primarily settled by white Europeans who shared a common identity, facilitating the establishment of a welfare state and the adoption of universal healthcare. Yet, this majority did not easily identify with First Nations, Métis, and Inuit populations, leading to their marginalization from comprehensive social safety nets. The First Nations, comprising 600 tribes spread across remote and peripheral regions of the country, have been limited in their ability to influence national policy and have often been overlooked. In this context, Canada's shortcomings are particularly stark compared to those of the United States, given that Canada purports to uphold values of equity and fair play. As such, the discrepancy between Canada's professed values and its practices is especially disappointing.

———————◆———————

Canadians tend to look south of the border to the US to help define who they are and who they are not, often citing differences between the two healthcare systems – a tendency that has markedly increased since the rise of Trump.

It seems poignant that as Canada celebrates its 150 years since Confederation (1 July 1867), the US Senate seeks to replace Obamacare with Trumpcare – "a plan" that is predicted to make Medicaid spending about 35% lower by 2036 (mostly hitting poor and older people) while benefitting the very rich with tax cuts of $250 000 (according to the Tax Policy Center).

Canada's Medicare, modeled on the British Beveridge system (and usually described as single payer), covers about 70% of healthcare costs

---

[208] For access to the original article and footnotes, see tiny.cc/Canada150

(excluding important costs such as prescription drugs and dental care) and is administered by the 10 provinces and three territories. The federal government is responsible for First Nations and Inuit peoples, the armed forces, Royal Canadian Mounted Police officers, federal prisons, and some primary prevention activities.

Canadians are fiercely proud of Medicare, perceiving it to be reflective of their core values: concern for the welfare of one another, tolerance, and diversity. It is seen as an important part of the national social safety net and one of the reasons Canada's quality of life ranks at the top or near the top globally. Furthermore, this same generosity is evident on the international stage, typified, perhaps, by Prime Minister Justin Trudeau's welcome of 25,000 Syrian refugees – the same population disparaged and banned by Trump.

However, this is only part of the story and the remainder deserves attention. The influential Commonwealth Fund Survey (CWS 2016) shows that in a group of 11 countries, Canada performed "below average and bottom of the pack" on most measures of timely access to care, including emergency services; after hours and weekends services; and same day or following day appointments with family doctor GP services. The average number of physicians per 1000 population for 11 countries was 3.5 while in Canada it was 2.5. More worrisome still – given that reasonable and equitable access to healthcare services is the principal objective of our universal healthcare system – are data from a recent study showing that socioeconomic status affects waiting times.

Despite these poor outcomes, Medicare has traditionally received overwhelming support from Canadians and survey data show that around 60% of Canadians want the healthcare system expanded and are willing to pay more personal income tax to make that happen.

This public perception is explained in part by Canadians' "gratitude" that the country does not have a US market based system; the fact that

Donald Trump describes Canada's Medicare as "catastrophic" perhaps provides further reassurance. A second reason for the strong support is that once patients access the system they tend to be very satisfied with the quality of healthcare. A third reason above) is that those with higher socioeconomic status (the opinion makers) have better access than those who are poor and without a voice.

A fourth reason is that Canada's most disadvantaged group, 1.4 million First Nations and Inuit peoples, are not covered by Medicare; therefore their very poor health status, health service, and outcomes are excluded from any theoretical or actual evaluation of Medicare. This allows politicians and policy makers to talk about Medicare, as opposed to the national healthcare system, and explains why many Canadians tend to have a more sanguine view of their healthcare than is actually deserved.

Canada claims superiority to the racialized welfare system in the US, where a recent report (from the Urban Institute) suggested that white people are less willing to support redistribution (such as Medicare) if it benefits those different from themselves i.e. from different ethnicities. Data show that states with a larger population of black people have the weakest social safety nets. For example, in Louisiana (where 32% of the population are black) only four out of 100 families living in poverty received cash assistance compared to 78 in Vermont (where 1% of the population are black).

In reality, Canada hasn't performed much better. It has had an easier path: the country was settled mainly by white Europeans who generally could identify with one another, which perhaps made it easier to build a welfare state after the Second World War and adopt universal healthcare. Those with whom it could not identify (First Nations) have mostly been excluded from its social safety net. First Nations were made up of 600 tribes scattered across the country, mainly in the north and at the periphery – virtually powerless, without a voice, and easily ignored. In a sense, our failure is worse than the US's because our core values were based on equity and fair play – we should have known better.

Against this dismal background, Trudeau represents a bright light. For one thing, he is not Stephen Harper who diminished Canada's international reputation over a 10 year period (and for another, he is not Donald Trump, who's doing the same for the US in a fraction of the time). He has reached a "health accord" with provinces, an important first step to meeting some of the country's health delivery challenges; and he has begun to invest in the social determinants of health in First Nations communities along the lines suggested by Michael Marmot – community development, education, water and sanitation, and healthcare services. His ministers too have begun to address the horrors of the thousands of murdered and missing Aboriginal women and girls and the legacy of the residential school system. However, whether he meets his commitments and delivers on promises will need to be carefully monitored.

The Global Risk Report 2016: Who Listened?
BMJ, January 5 2017[209]

Social Murder: the scene of the crimes This article delves into the phenomena of social murder and societal unrest, presenting compelling evidence of deepening North-South inequalities and growing intergenerational divides in the UK. It draws on studies exploring the geography of despair and unemployment, which illustrate the expansion and intensification of disparities—a phenomenon that has contributed to the rise of populism and Brexit's success. The evidence further suggests that since 2012, national leaders have strategically exploited these divisions for political gain. Notably-,the Grenfell Tower fire occurred six months after this article's publication, epitomizing the nation's inequalities and the harmful consequences of deregulation. This tragedy highlighted the dangerous outcomes of policies like David Cameron's push for "a bonfire of regulations" and Boris Johnson's controversial assertion in his "greed is-good" speech, which proclaimed that "some measure of inequality is essential for the spirit of envy and keeping up with the Joneses," describing it as a catalyst for economic activity.

———————◆———————

What has the global community learnt from the World Economic Forum's annual global Risk Report released last January? The evidence suggests it has not learnt enough to prioritize and take effective steps to mediate risk and, instead, over the past 12 months we have seemed transfixed and bewildered by an onslaught of world events. As a new year begins, we're confronted by what many are calling "a new world order."

The 29 interconnected global risks (divided into five categories: economic, societal, geopolitical, environmental, and technological) cited by the report are portrayed in Figure 1[i] of the report and include (to name a few) food crises, interstate conflict, and extreme weather events. Its authors warned that these risks are becoming more potent, more frequent, more probable, and more interconnected than ever before.

[209] For access to the original article and footnotes, see tiny.cc/GlobalHealthReport

Most risks have a direct bearing on the health and wellbeing of ordinary people – and are therefore relevant to healthcare providers and researchers. Indeed, few professions know more about inequalities, natural disasters, migration, violence, spread of infectious diseases, and pandemics. They are well placed "to know" the levels and trends of wellbeing at the household and community level.

The report warned that two core features of risks are their complexity and interconnectedness, which can create unexpected consequences. It focused on North Africa, the Caribbean, and Latin America as key regions where global stability is threatened by the disempowered citizen feeling disconnected from existing government structures; it said that social instability and unemployment (or underemployment) are the most interconnected risks this year.

Yet high levels of social instability were underestimated in the US and Europe, where a sense of disenfranchisement, disconnectedness, and distrust of government is predominant. Rising income and wealth inequalities, the collapse of manufacturing industries, the onset of the knowledge economy, shrinking social safety nets, and New Public Management policies have been central to explaining widespread public resentment.

In contrast to the report, a robust body of work by health researchers and clinicians working at the grassroots level in England depicts a pervasive and increasing sense of loss and disenfranchisement, which is replicated in many western countries. This research would not have predicted either Brexit or the election of Trump, yet it has identified the shift in values that underlies both events and the risk of not attending to related social and economic inequalities. This research shows, for example, a steep social gradient in access to effective healthcare, which leads to increased morbidity and decreased life expectancy; North-South inequalities increasing over four decades; and progressive intergenerational divisions adding to social instability.

Research into the geography of despair and geography of

unemployment both in Europe and the US shows a deepening and widening of a less secure strata of society ("low waged unskilled workers, the long term unemployed, households dependent on shrinking social benefits, residents of public housing, single parent families, and poorer white populations") – a strata that will eventually need to make its voice heard.

The World Economic Forum states that we are now entering the fourth industrial revolution in which we will see a "fusion of technologies that blur the lines between physical, digital, and biological spheres"; it will create a level of change humanity has never seen before, affecting economies, countries, and people (especially the health sector). This revolution depends upon the collaboration and cooperation of business, science, civil society, academia, and policy makers.

However, the events of the past 12 months suggest a global community at odds with itself; the rise of inequalities, distrust, self-interest, populism, and nationalism exacerbates already high levels of global risk and threatens to undermine the potential for the creation of substantive public good. We are obviously not prepared to meet the challenges of a "new world order" or the fourth industrial revolution.

The media and many observers have had, by their own account, difficulty reporting on a year that changed the world. Leading world dictionaries inform us that the "word of the year" includes post-truth, paranoid, surreal, chaos, and anxiety – most of which seem relevant to today's reality. In normal circumstances these challenges would be met with a call for leadership, but, of course, it is the leadership that is part of the problem. Therefore, it will have to be a call for moral leadership in the hope that it is both strong and influential.

The Measure of America: American Human Development Report 2008-2009[210]

New England Journal of Medicine, March 19 2009[211]

Social Murder: acts of omission or commission. Large segments of the US population, delineated by race and ethnicity, face a structurally high risk of foreseeable and avoidable premature death. This series of readings delves into inequalities and human rights in the United States. The first piece is a book review of *The Measure of America* (2008), notable for being the first application of the United Nations Development Program (UNDP) methodology—typically used to assess wellbeing and inequalities in poorer nations—to a wealthy country. Esteemed by scholars Amartya Sen and Jeffrey Sachs as a ground breaking analysis, this publication reveals that certain areas in theUS are comparable to some of the world's most impoverished regions, underscoring the rationale for its application. Subsequent readings explore the inequalities President Obama faced when initiating health reform. Another article discusses his efforts to mitigate these disparities through the Affordable Care Act and the subsequent impact this struggle had on American politics, racial tensions, the rise of populism, and ultimately, the election of Trump. It further reviews Trump's policies 100 days into his term when he declared that "Obamacare will explode."

———————◆———————

Progress in the United States is traditionally measured in terms of economic growth, trade, and investment, and that makes *The Measure of America* a welcome book. Its editors introduce the American Human Development Index, which is a single measure of well-being for all Americans that is based on three factors: life expectancy, access to knowledge, and income. Data in this index are disaggregated by state and by congressional district, as well as by race, ethnic group, and sex. Modeled on the United Nations Development Program's Human Development Report, this is the first time the Human Development Index has been

---
[210] Edited by Sarah Burd-Sharps, Kristen Lewis, and Eduardo Borges Martins. 246 pp., illustrated. New York, Social Science Research Council/Columbia University Press, 2008
[211] For access to the original article and footnotes, see tiny.cc/MeasureAmerica

applied to an industrialized nation.

The book is meant to answer the question: How are people in the United States doing? It is a good question, asked at the right time; the United States, the world's richest nation, is spending an average of three times more on health care than other wealthy nations are spending, and yet it is achieving only mediocre results in terms of human development. This discrepancy is due in part to huge inequalities. US rates of infant mortality, for example, have not improved during the past 8 years and are on par with the rates in Cuba, Croatia, Poland, and Estonia. The book is accompanied by a truly impressive Website[212] that offers free access to a set of interactive maps that show information about more than 60 different indicators, disaggregated by state.

Race is dealt with effectively in the discussions of health, education, and income, but analysis of these three factors by race is lacking in the maps within the book and on the Web site. This oversight should be addressed in the next edition of the book, and in the interim, analysis by race should be included in the maps that are available online.

This book is strongly recommended for those who want to know how people are doing in the United States. This question seems especially relevant now because the effect of the financial crisis on Americans is being felt through rising levels of unemployment, increased household debt, and reduced personal assets, as well as lost health insurance – a drama that is likely to broaden and deepen existing inequalities.

---

[212] http://measureofamerica.org

Inequalities in the American Healthcare System

Lancet, April 11, 2009[213]

Reducing risk of foreseeable and avoidable death The societal architecture that supports the large inequalities in access to health care by race, income, class, sex, and geography in the USA seems poised for change. The new administration has proposed a US$634 billion down-payment on a $1 trillion healthcare reform package aimed at achieving universal health care. Congress has been assigned the task of working out the details of this proposal in the coming months. Given the severity of the economic crisis, mounting and unpredictable deficits, powerful interest lobbies, and other competing social agendas, success will not come easily.

———————◆———————

Of the many inequalities that distort access to health care in the USA, perhaps the most striking are, historically, those defined by race and place of residence. For example, research showing that African Americans with vascular disease or diabetes are four times more likely to have a leg amputated than are white people also reveals enormous inequalities between regions and states for evidence-based services such as screening mammography and testing for diabetes. Routinely collected data show that infant mortality rates (IMRs) among African Americans are more than twice, and in some southern states three times higher than the national average. Nine states share the worst levels of health and human development, and these are in the south (Mississippi, West Virginia, Louisiana, Arkansas, Alabama, Oklahoma, Tennessee, Kentucky, and South Carolina) where African-American populations are 70% larger than the national average.

Inequalities seem certain to worsen without substantial investments. Medicaid, the state-federal health programme intended to deal directly with these very disparities, has been cut in 19 states this fiscal year and

[213] For access to the original article and footnotes, see tiny.cc/USHealthcare

more and larger cuts are scheduled for the coming year. IMRs, which have stagnated nationally since 2000, have registered small increases in many states. In Mississippi a significant rise in IMR was reported: from 14·2 to 17·0 for blacks and 6·1 to 6·6 for whites.

The inefficiency and inequity of a system that spends 17% of gross domestic product on health care yet leaves 48 million uninsured and the nation uncompetitive in a global economy is less palatable to the American public than ever before. The new administration and congress need to take advantage of the brief "policy window" while health reform is at the top of the public agenda, goodwill abounds, the healthcare industry is somewhat on the defensive, and the potential costs seem to pale compared with the overall stimulus package, to design an acceptable piece of legislation that will lead to universal health care.

Trump Versus Obamacare:100 Days in

BMJ, May 3 2017[214]

Crime Scene: a divided house: Donald Trump continues to threaten to pull the trigger and scrap the Affordable Care Act (ACA). The day after his failed attempt to repeal and replace the ACA on 24 March, he tweeted, "Obamacare will explode ... Do not worry." Then, in mid-April, one way this might happen was put forward: by cutting costs sharing reduction (CSR) payments to seven million lower income ACA enrollees. These subsidy payments reduce out of pocket costs for lower income families by reducing or eliminating deductibles.

◆

More recently, over the past two weeks the administration has sought to appeal to hardline conservatives: firstly, by giving more power to individual states on how to move forward on reform, and secondly, by removing safeguards for people with pre-existing conditions. Both proposed changes have been met with fierce resistance this week by moderate Republicans. But with the recent promise to inject an additional $8bn spending into Trump's reform package, the outcome hangs by a thread.

Obamacare Obama sought to make good on his commitment to create a level playing field for all Americans, especially in healthcare. Yet although he began his presidency with the "promise of change, unity, and bipartisanship" (and indeed, 80% of the public described themselves as optimistic about the new president), he soon hit a brick wall with his proposed healthcare bill. According to a recent documentary series *The Divided States of America*,[215] as he embarked upon health reform he "quickly collided with political realities, including unified Republican opposition to his agenda and racially charged resistance." After a year of intense

---

[214] For access to the original article and footnotes, see tiny.cc/TrumpVObama
[215] https://www.pbs.org/wgbh/frontline/article/watch-how-obamacare-became-a-symbol-of-americas-divide

struggle, Obamacare passed the House of Representatives on 21 March 2010 by a vote of 219 to 210, but without a single Republican vote. A general theme of the PBS report was that Obamacare "contributed to years of polarization and a wave of anti-establishment sentiment that helped fuel Trump's road to victory" (see transcripts online[46]). Drawing from dozens of experts and Congressional leaders, the documentary reported that "Obamacare came to symbolize the divisions in America." It claimed that "what happened after it was passed, and because of the way it was passed, it became the symbol of the divide, and the reality of it in many ways." This portrayal of Obamacare as a bill forced through amid discord was a view that Trump successfully exploited on his campaign trail.

The documentary concluded that the future of Obamacare is uncertain since it is unclear "whether or when the country might finally accept what he has done" (by passing the ACA). Trump's efforts to repeal and replace Obamacare are also based on the notion that most Americans do not accept Obamacare. Yet these assessments do not seem consistent with the evidence, or at least are no longer consistent with the latest evidence.

For example, a Kaiser tracking poll done in early April and then a Washington Post-ABC News poll done at the end of April contradict this conclusion. Kaiser showed that 64% of the American public thought it was a good thing that Trump's American Health Care Act failed to pass. Seventy-five per cent of the public think that Trump and his administration "should do what they can to make the current law work." The Washington-Post-ABC News poll found that 61% of the public thought Trump should keep and improve Obamacare. Other noteworthy findings are that 70% of the public (including a majority of Republicans) want a nationwide mandate for pre-existing conditions rather than Trump's notion of leaving it up to the states to decide – as was under consideration last week and this week.

One explanation for the mismatch between the PBS assessment (and indeed, Trump's misreading of the public) and the results of these two polls is that the tone and quality of leadership and decision making of the past 100 days may have disenchanted many Americans. The executive orders aimed at deregulation – especially of the finance and banking sectors – and the proposed enormous tax cuts appear to benefit the privileged 1%. Consistent with this is a Kaiser poll finding that the percentage of Americans who believed that Trump could deliver better and cheaper healthcare dropped from 47% before the election to 37% three months later.

Behind these poll results may also be a growing perception that Obamacare is actually a populist law and that Trumpcare is anti-populist. The fact that this was not taken on board before the election perhaps confirms the adage that left wing economics can never satisfy right wing populism.

Trump may not be returning America back to greatness, but he is certainly committed to returning it to the direction from whence it came – a time of greater inequality and variation in access to healthcare.

Explaining Trumpcare: The Appalling Appeal

Lancet, June 2 2017 [216]

Social murder and its enablers Kaiser Family Foundation polls consistently indicate that opinions on Obamacare are sharply divided along party lines and racial identities. This article, written early in Trump's presidency when he prioritized repealing Obamacare, highlights the profound divisions within the nation, which appear poised to deepen. It offers insights into why the US lacks a universal healthcare system, possesses the weakest social safety nets among its peers, and why a significant segment of the electorate seems prepared to act against its own best interests by opposing redistributive policies that could benefit them. The article suggests that support for redistribution is contingent upon voters believing their tax dollars will benefit individuals with whom they can empathize. Specifically, it mentions that white voters are reluctant to fund programs perceived to primarily benefit Black or Hispanic communities.

———————◆———————

On May 5th, 2017 the US House of Representatives voted to repeal the Affordable Care Act (Obamacare) and replace it with H.R. 1628, the American Heath Care Act (Trumpcare) by a count of 217 to 213 (all Democrats and 25 moderate Republicans opposed the bill; all supporters were Republican).

Under Obamacare, 13 million Americans gained health insurance through marketplace programmes and another 20 million were added to insurance or expanded Medicaid role. This feat was achieved by increasing taxes of the richest 2% of the population.

A new Kaiser tracking poll (May 31st), consistent with the findings from three previous polls (a Kaiser tracking poll April 4th, Washington Post-ABC News poll April 25th, and a Politico/Harvard Poll April 25th, 2017) shows that 60-65% of the public want Obamacare left in place and improved upon. The question arises as to why Republican legislators

---

[216] For access to the original article and footnotes, see tiny.cc/Trumpcare

would ignore the wishes of most citizens and risk their wrath in the 2018 mid-term elections.

Part of the answer is that on May 5th these legislators wanted to avoid dispiriting the political base by a defeat of Trumpcare; passing the bill was also seen as crucial to passing tax reform; and some legislators may have been influenced by private sector interests. For example, the Koch brothers promised millions to Republican campaigns in the midterm if they voted to repeal Obamacare.

At another level however, the answer is more complex and is one that might help answer other important questions (such as why the US is the only industrialised nation without a universal health care system, why it has the weakest social safety net of its peers, why a large portion of the US electorate is fully prepared to act against its own best interests (rather than support beneficial distributive initiatives) and, why perhaps, Trump was elected in the first place?) These questions are relevant as some version of Trumpcare will go before the Senate in the near future. The following paragraphs look at some contributing factors.

First, recent analysis shows working class (especially white) males have felt increasingly disempowered and disenfranchised by globalisation and neoliberal policies. In the US, while the wealthy have become wealthier, the real incomes of ordinary people have stagnated or declined. Even as they became increasingly marginalised, they were expected to accept cultural values that were not theirs – for example, those related to the environment, gender and racial equality, and LGBT persons. Economic loss and cultural backlash contributed to their "rage against the machine".

Second, prospect theory tells us that those who feel they have not participated in the benefits of global trends or have lost benefits may be willing to take risks in making their political choices – they feel they have nothing to lose. This theory is rooted in economics and psychology and addresses the behavioral underpinnings of choice in the face of uncertainty. It recognises, for example, that people with poor prospects are more likely to take risks and make irrational choices by disregarding low probabilities.

Third, recent data from the Per Research Center shows that partisan animosity has increased to record levels in the US. It is core to explaining why, for example, working class Americans continue to support Trump despite his "Cabinet of billionaires", deregulation that will hit ordinary people, and in particular, a health bill that is explicitly against their self-interests. For example, the (non-partisan) Congressional Budget Office (CBO) estimated in a May 24th report that Trumpcare would lead to an additional 23 million uninsured Americans. Partisanship (as "tribal self-expression") is a way of expressing multiple identities; party loyalty is bigger than any single policy. These identities are less about class or rich versus poor than "racial identity, professional identity, religious identity, even geographical identity". Abandoning Trump would constitute a betrayal of these tribal allegiances.

Fourth, evidence suggests that left-wing economics is not the answer to right-wing populism. Trump (and his policies such as Trumpcare) appeals directly to those who see themselves living in the "domain of losses". Yet the May 31st Kaiser Poll shows that only 15 percent of those questioned felt that Trumpcare would actually fulfill all or most of his promises – for example, "insurance for everybody". In reality, within the US support for liberal distribution policies is greatly complicated by racial and cultural identities. "People are only willing to support redistribution if they believe their tax dollars are going to people they can sympathise with. White voters, in other words, don't want to spend their tax dollars on programs that they think will benefit black or Hispanic people".[47] A PBS documentary *The Divided States of America* concurs and reports that the "racially charged resistance" to Obamacare came to symbolise this division in America and now Trumpcare.[217]

These factors not only help explain the House vote to replace

---

[217] https://www.pbs.org/wgbh/frontline/article/watch-how-obamacare-became-a-symbol-of-americas-divide/

Obamacare with Trumpcare and set the stage for a Senate vote, but also explain the lack of a robust social safety net to protect all Americans.

One week after the repeal of Obamacare in the House, conservative senators began making plans to drop millions of adults from Medicaid; indeed, the release of Trump's budget (May 23rd) reveals plans for massive cuts in the range of 25-45% over 10 years. Eight years on and perhaps eight years hence, the Trump promise is one of leading the US in circles and they seem to be part of a spiral..

Voice: The Importance of Diversity in Healthcare

International Journal of Clinical Practice, May 2013[218]

Race and diversity This article emphasizes the significance of diversity and inclusion across all sectors of the economy and throughout society at large, not just in healthcare. It argues that increasing representation from underrepresented groups (URGs) enhances advocacy, communication, decision-making, outcomes, client satisfaction, and leadership diversity, ultimately providing more effective role models. Most organizations now implement diversity and inclusion strategies primarily because these approaches contribute to better business outcomes, rather than solely for altruistic reasons. These strategies are akin to the arguments for reducing national social inequalities, such as achieving greater efficiencies, enhanced competitiveness, and increased prosperity. Additionally, the article examines a specific community that has struggled to effectively address racial issues and promote diversity within its healthcare system and explores the broader societal context in which this community operates.

———————◆———————

We know that 'voice' matters in healthcare. We undertake patient opinion surveys for humanistic and medical reasons, as measures of outcome and quality improvement, as well as efficiency and even for marketing purposes. At our hospitals and health authorities we seek public engagement and participation because it helps inform decision-making and provides legitimacy, credibility, transparency, accountability to the process and promotes partnership and trust. We also expect our leadership to reflect this ethos of good governance through consultation and collaborative eff orts. For example, we know that when confronted with difficult resource allocation or disinvestment decisions, broad participation from managers and clinicians at all levels is often the most effective approach.

But what of those who are intended to listen directly to 'voice' and

---

[218]   For access to the original article and footnotes, see tiny.cc/DiversityHealthcare

then interpret and transmit information? Are the right people in place?

For example, although most observers would agree that the ability to cre ate and maintain an effective, efficient and motivated workforce is central to good outcomes, not all would assign equal value to a diverse healthcare workforce. For some organizations diversity means in-groups and outgroups, stereotyping, polarization, conflict and performance loss and, in reality, a challenge to be dealt with the best way possible while for many others, putting in place a well-thought out diversity strategy that seeks to develop a workforce that is reflective of the communities they serve, is one way to achieve better outputs, outcomes and ultimately, to improve population health.

These improvements might be realized through multiple pathways. First, minority healthcare workers are more likely than other healthcare workers to reach out to provide services to minorities in the community and to advocate on their behalf; second, where there is commonality between patient and practitioner communications, decision-making and adherence improve; third, improving the diversity of the workforce also augments the pool of medically trained personnel that can take leadership positions; and fourth, a diverse healthcare workforce provides role models for young people in minority communities.

The most important of these pathways as well as the most relevant to clinicians is racial, ethnic, and language concordance. Increasing the under-represented minorities (URM) helps improve the probability that minority patients will see a clinician from their own racial or ethnic group or who speaks their primary language. Concordance 'may improve the quality of communication, comfort level, or trust in patient-practitioner relationships and thereby improve partnership and decision making. This may in turn increase adherence to effective programs or regimens, ultimately resulting in improved health outcomes'. Evidence also suggests that racial concordance may influence disparities in health and mortality.

For similar types of reasons, many argue that where taxpayer dol-lars are involved, health authority or hospital boards ought to reflect the diversity of the communities they serve – to offer voice for those groups that might otherwise be overlooked, to articulate their needs and desires, strengthen the relationship between public and provider, to educate and be educated and to authenticate diversity and plurality in the community.

Participation, engagement and inclusion imply a redistribution of power. It is for this reason that most organizations stress the business case for a 'diversity and inclusion' strategy rather than a humanistic reason. For example, the Institute of Medicine's diversity document In the Nation's Compelling Interest: Ensuring Diversity in the Health Care Workforce strikes a similar chord to its position paper on global health entitled 'America's Vital Interest in Global Health: Protecting Our people, Enhancing Our Economy and Advancing Our International Interests' in that the emphasis is on self-interest – perhaps a more a dependable motivator and more likely to achieve stakeholder 'buy in' than the more volatile humanistic approach. Yet, organizations using this approach alone run the risk of appearing shallow if it is somehow implied that an injustice would be overlooked or let stand if the business case could not be made.

What is perhaps more striking than the evidence that diversity and inclusion strategies lead to better outcomes, is the evidence showing that failure to implement or to implement in a half-hearted manner usually has an accumulative and detrimental effect on institutional legitimacy, credibility and morale. In instances where this failure occurs without apparent consequences may actually suggest total occlusion and suppression of underrepresented groups. The following paragraphs look briefly at a local example of this, the black diaspora in Nova Scotia, the largest and most troubled in Canada.

Black Nova Scotians, descended from African American former slaves or freemen, first arrived in the province in the 18th and 19th centuries and settled in separate and distinct communities, at the geographic, economic and social margins of society. One indicator of this marginalization is that about half of blacks come from families who live or have lived within 5 km of landfill projects. Although the last geographically segregated school was closed in 1983, ghettoization still defines the in digenous black community and for most, particularly young people, prospects are dismal. Research shows that blacks have higher morbidity and mortality rates than the general population; one study reports that the incidence rate ratios for blacks were significantly elevated for the three diseases: circulatory disease (1.19, 95% CI 1.08–1.29), diabetes (1.43, 95% CI 1.21–1.64) and psychiatric disorders (1.13, 95% CI 1.06– 1.20). A core theme in a multitude of equity studies is that black Nova Scotians 'have limited access to appropriate social, economic, and health services; and they are under-represented in healthcare delivery, in health research, and in the design and implementation of health policies'. Although we have universal health care, black Nova Scotians are often disinclined to access services, programs or facilities that they perceive as culturally incompetent.

Although one would expect some sort of accumulation of black Nova Scotians in the healthcare workforce, there is little evidence of this – perhaps one physician. The local medical school which has a fine international reputation yet has only produced one physician from the local black community in its 100 year history. Furthermore, there is no representation of blacks on hospitals boards which tend to be made up of influential professionals from affluent neighborhoods. As might be imagined, the story does not end there. Anger and frustration turn to drugs and violence and some of those disinclined to utilize health facilities often find their way by ambulance or police escort. Unhappily, other sectors of civil society that are mandated with creating and applying laws are sometimes perceived as weakened by institutionalized racism.,

Most local health institutions have in place some sort of cultural competence training initiative based on the government's all-inclusive version of what constitutes diversity. Yet, consistent with the literature, these training initiatives have yielded few measurable results. Instead what is called for is a more direct approach – increased concordance between clinician and patient. This unfortunately, requires actually acknowledging the severity of the problem and the will and resources to do something about it. Political leadership at both the provincial and local level seems to lack the metacognitive ability to recognize existing failures and oversights; leaders not only don't know what it is they ought to be doing, they don't know that they don't know. This of course is consistent with the view of black Nova Scotians – that it's not simply that they have not been listened to but rather they have no voice to be heard.

A few bright lights are showing a way forward: for example, consistent with research that suggests that the best means to improve levels of URM in the health sector is to start early, the School of Nursing has been running annual summer camps to reach out to junior and senior high school students with mentorship and some financial aid to help bring then into the health professions. Key decision-makers, who are otherwise well-intentioned and competent, could learn from the grit and determination of the handful of students now enrolled in nursing; it's time to deal with this shameful situation that is the black diaspora in Nova Scotia and give voice to those who yearn for it.

The Precarity of Being Indigenous: The Case of Canada

Lancet, Global Health, 2017[219]

Systematic and Widespread Crimes against humanity involve acts committed by or on behalf of the state that grossly violate human rights, causing significant pain and suffering, and are either widespread or systematic. From the perspective of Indigenous peoples, these violations are both systematic and pervasive. This article discusses how, although Trudeau has taken measures to address historical injustices such as the residential school system and the forced removal of Indigenous children from their homes ("the scoop"), these efforts have been undermined by systemic racism within federal institutions, notably the Department of Justice. The government has vigorously contested Indigenous claims for compensation and deliberately underfunded Indigenous child health services. For years, Ottawa attempted to conceal, manipulate, or destroy records related to residential schools through various bureaucratic, judicial, and law enforcement channels. The Department of Justice has recently recognized these shortcomings and initiated a comprehensive campaign to eradicate anti-Indigenous and anti-Black racism within its ranks.

———————◆———————

Canadian Prime Minister Justin Trudeau's Sept 21 speech to the UN General Assembly focused on "Canada's shame" in dealing with First Nations, Metis, and Inuit populations. Although his address drew global attention, it would have resonated in particular with the 370 million Indigenous people around the world.

Trudeau cited the intergenerational health impact on Indigenous people of residential schools, child removals, and failure to provide basic services, describing their experience as being "mostly one of humiliation, neglect and abuse". Indeed, the record bears him out; for example, a recent scoping review of 61 studies shows increased rates of chronic and infectious disease among school "survivors" as well as depression,

---

[219]   For access to the original article and footnotes, see tiny.cc/BeingIndigenous

anxiety, addictive behaviour, stress, and suicidal behaviour.

Trudeau was contrite and adamant that he was addressing these injustices, yet the speech itself and ensuing federal decisions in the weeks following had the opposite effect, stoking the distrust felt by Indigenous people towards government.

For example, 15 days after the speech, the Canadian Government announced that it would compensate the approximately 16,00020,000 survivors of the so-called "sixties scoop" – the programme by which children were forcibly taken from their families and placed in non-indigenous care (in "white homes") as far away Scotland, New Zealand, California, and Alabama (1965-84). The finding of the Ontario Superior Court – which formed the rationale for the settlement – was that Canada had breached its "duty of care" and ignored the damaging psychological effects of the programme. Although the Government lauded the compensation package (Cdn$800 million), in reality it had fought survivors' claims "tooth and nail" in a bitter 8-year court battle. Justice Murray Sinclair, who headed up the Truth and Reconciliation Commission on residential school abuse, said it was "unconscionable" for the Government to acknowledge the genocidal aspects of the removals but then claim in court that "it had no legal obligation to prevent it".

Another decision announced in October was by the Supreme Court of Canada (SCC) which concerned the records of 38,000 survivors of the Indian Residential Schools – narratives which described their physical, sexual, and emotional abuse. The Government had sought to retain control of these records. In a unanimous decision, the SCC sided with the survivors, stating that indigenous people should decide the fate of the records; it said that sharing the stories was meant to be a "private process" and claimants had relied on the "confidentiality assurance". According to Judges Brown and Rowe, Ottawa retaining control "is plainly not what the parties bargained for". Reneging on this agreement with school survivors (who as children, the Government put in harm's way in the first place) evoked long-standing resentment of school survivors against Ottawa which has over the decades repeatedly sought to hide, control, or destroy residential school records through the bureaucracies, courts, or law enforcement agencies.

Trudeau's UN address itself raised questions of trust. His claim that the Government was a "full supporter" of the UN Declaration on the Rights of Indigenous Peoples was inconsistent with his Minister of Justice's stated view that it is an unworkable document and his own failure to adopt and implement the Declaration. He also claimed to have prioritized social inequalities of First Nations children when in fact he has ignored the findings of the Canadian Human Rights Tribunal that Ottawa was discriminating against indigenous children by underfunding their health care. Recent documents reveal that Ottawa had the data that showed indigenous "children faced a massive gap in health services compared with what was available provincially". Rather than following the Tribunal's recommendations, the Government chose instead to respond through the courts, once again initiating an acrimonious legal battle.

In reality, Trudeau's UN speech is widely seen as part of a larger agenda to secure a seat on the UN Security Council. Using one agenda to advance another may suggest lack of sincerity and lack of commitment. However, in describing the needs of Canada's First Nations, Metis, and Inuit populations he evoked the UN's Sustainable Development Goals (6, 4, 5, and 11 – safe water and sanitation, education, gender equality, and sustainable communities). Trudeau will need to deliver on his promises. Early in his mandate he claimed that he inherited the distrust Indigenous people feel towards Ottawa from previous governments, yet the past months suggest that his Government earned some of this distrust itself. Taking effective steps to deliver on his promises may help address the precarity of being Indigenous in Canada and the view that federal authorities typically say one thing and mean another.

Human Rights at the World Bank: Inside Out

Lancet, December 1 2015[220]

Deliberately and structurally exposing the vulnerable to high risk A report by the UN Special Rapporteur on Human Rights sharply criticizes the World Bank's (WB) approach to human rights, labeling it as a "human rights free zone" at the operational level. The World Bank defends itself by citing its "political prohibition" clause, which it claims bars it from intervening in the political affairs of client nations, including matters related to potential human rights abuses. However, this UN report aligns with numerous other sources in this collection that illustrate the World Bank's consistent neglect of human rights concerns. This includes its policies during structural adjustments, health reform initiatives, responses to the HIV/AIDS crisis, and the forced displacement of vulnerable communities from areas affected by World Bank-funded projects. These actions have been linked to social murder and crimes against humanity.

———————◆———————

Few organisations know more about human rights, inequalities, and diversity than the World Bank; indeed, its website and e-library are replete with information on how each of these relate to the health and wellbeing of individuals and populations. Yet a recent report from the UN Special Rapporteur on Human Rights adds to claims that, internally and externally, the bank does not practise what it preaches and that it often seems incapable of learning from past failures.

The report states that the Bank ignores human rights and treats them "more like a disease than universal values and obligations"; operationally its approach is "incoherent, counterproductive and unsustainable".

Jim Yong Kim addressed the issue earlier this year, blaming the political prohibition clause that prevents it from involving itself in the political affairs and thus the human rights of any country. However, the UN Global Health and Social Murder rapporteur calls this "misplaced

---

[220] For access to the original article and footnotes, see tiny.cc/WorldBankHumanRights

legalism" and says that, together with institutional culture, a lack of transparency, and a host of other factors, the Bank's response on human rights is anachronistic and, for most purposes, the institution "is a human rights-free zone".

Interestingly, these same factors also help explain the Bank's failure to address internal human rights abuses. Especially striking is the lack of response to studies (many undertaken by the Bank itself) showing a culture of systemic discrimination against African-Americans at senior bank levels. Again, because of a legalism, the Bank (as a UN agency headquartered in the USA) is not required to collect race-based data nor provide independent arms-length assessment of claims of discrimination – so it does neither. A recently released survey taken by 10,000 Bank employees shows that (among other important findings) only 43% of respondents said managers are held to account when actions or behaviour are contrary to the institution's values on diversity and inclusion.

A Way Forward

To close the gap between knowing and doing, Bank leadership ought to listen to the independent evaluators whose advice it seeks and for which it pays. Their reports describe worsening trends in performance, mainly driven by poor quality of work before implementation – i.e., not "getting things right from the outset". Special attention is drawn to poor risk assessment and risk management. Indeed, recent investigators into Bank projects reveal a doubling of projects graded highest risk for "irreversible or unprecedented" social or environmental impacts and that, over the last 10 years, "projects funded by the World Bank have physically or economically displaced an estimated 3.4 million people".

The UN report says the Bank is reducing the probability of success by delinking what is inextricably linked – health and human rights. It says human rights need to be integrated from the outset and that therefore the Bank should adopt an approach that is above all "principled, compelling and transparent", making use of "the universally accepted human rights framework".

Similarly, diversity frameworks commonly used in the public and private sectors are acknowledged to lead to better process and outcomes. The Bank might take into account two key functions performed by its neighbour in Washington, DC – the Equal Employment Opportunity Commission (EEOC) which enforces discrimination in employment laws in the USA. First, it requires businesses to report their diversity data; second, it provides independent assessment of claims of discrimination. Critics claim that the Bank's internal Administrative Tribunal (whose members work for the Bank) has yet to find a single case of discrimination against African-Americans.

Calls for the Bank to address human rights come at a time when its leadership and strategic direction are in question by two-thirds of its employees. At issue are reform efforts: first to shift from a country-centred structure to one that is sector-based, and second to create knowledge-based departments. Critics worry that the sector-wide approach will reduce human rights social safeguards by placing the onus to protect them on country governments, which may not have the required resources or inclination to do so. The goal to become a "knowledge-based organization" seems improbable since, by its own account, it has yet to become a "learning organization" – one that sees learning as more than an "optional extra".

There is a disquieting symmetry between discrimination in the executive suites at World Bank headquarters in downtown Washington and human rights abuses in the field that affect millions – both the consequence of "misplaced legalism". It is also worrisome that only 26% of Bank staff believes they work in climate of "openness and trust"; worrisome too is Kim's observation that "I've done this before in other organizations and what I've found is that if you know a change has to be made, just do it as quickly as you can, and get it done". None of this is indicative of a learning organisation, one that is going to close to the gap between what it practises and what it preaches, one that will lead by example. The

UN rapporteur is right – what is needed is transparent dialogue that will generate an "informed and nuanced policy" on human rights.

PART FOUR
Lessons

Lessons

This book presents *prima facie* evidence that, over decades, acts of "social murder" and "crimes against humanity" have contributed to or resulted from the polycrisis that now seems to have us careening toward an abyss. We have defined the polycrisis as "the causal entanglement of crises in multiple global systems in ways that significantly degrade humanity's prospects." The crises themselves exhibit distinct structures, functions, histories, patterns, an architecture of sorts. Above all, they are exquisitely opportunistic and flourish in environments of weak leadership deep inequalities.

In prescribing a way forward, systems thinking is essential, one that entails a thorough understanding of the dynamic interactions among complex economic, environmental, and social systems.

A comprehensive approach is needed since the crises are densely entangled with one another. Attention should be directed towards the interactions between crises, the points of entanglements rather than on a single threat – which typically happens when decision-makers are caught reacting or "putting out fires".

A systematic and integrated assessment is needed since intervention to resolve one crisis may worsen or create new crises. Conversely, however, an integrated approach may enable decision-makers to take advantage of the interconnectivity, so interventions have a multiplier effect on a range of crises. In other words, the aim is to reverse the dynamic where one crisis begets, so that one "solution" begets many others vis a vis co-benefits - either simultaneously or sequentially For example, mitigation initiatives aimed at reducing large inequalities and inequities may address social justice, fairness, and social cohesion concerns as well as economic efficiencies and global competitiveness.

Just as the crises exhibit distinct structures, functions, histories, and patterns, the polycrisis itself has an architecture. Policy-makers should seek, where possible, to alter the structures that convey hazards rather than solely reacting to events. They should aim to either eliminate pathways or insert firewalls and guardrails. However, in this collection, we have seen decisions heading in the opposite direction. For example, in 1998, unregulated financial derivatives contributed to the 2008 Great Recession. At the time, the Commodities Futures Trading Commission's Brooksley Born warned of disaster and strongly recommended regulatory safeguards. She was rebuffed and subsequently resigned. The drive for deregulation across many economic sectors has led to numerous crises, including those related to the environment, food security, social order, and good governance.

An important path forward is to take advantage of "high-leverage intervention points." We have seen how the CDC pursued this approach in China by making relatively modest investments in well-placed preventive measures—these "smoke-detector-type" efforts can have a significant impact. They epitomize Dr. Larry Brilliant's observation: "Outbreaks are inevitable, pandemics are optional."

The application of global and planetary health values offers a means to improve decision-making and tackle barriers that might impede it. A shift from 'go-it-alone' policies to global cooperation and collaboration, from bilateralism to multilateralism, from single-country interventions to targeting transnational determinants of health, seems mandatory. Even though globalization as we have known it has come to an end, these values offer better outcomes and may help address the erosion of trust in multilateralism, encouraging the collective action needed to prepare for, prevent, and mitigate cross-border risks. Given that most regional or global risks (environmental, societal, geopolitical, economic, and technological) can only be addressed effectively by nations working together, the rationale for cooperative and collaborative action is clear. Better decisions and outcomes are more likely when multiple disciplines are consulted, including those from social and behavioral sciences, law, economics, history, engineering, and biomedical and environmental sciences. One way that multidisciplinarity is examined in this section is through the lens of "consilience," which imagines the sciences working together with the humanities in the future.

There is a pathway to a more stable and equitable world. Yet this requires collective, decisive action. It means addressing issues that have thus far been avoided. It means acknowledging errors, which most actors seem loath to do; it means accountability needs to come to the fore and, in some cases, restitution, compensation, and a pathway to reconciliation. Critically, it means closing the gap between what science deems necessary and what is politically feasible and preparing for the future with a longterm perspective. The polycrisis is bigger on the inside than the outside, so we will need to find the space that enables us to bring greater conscience to the problem than we did in creating it.

Global Health and Brexit: Choosing When Anxious
BMJ Opinion, 2016[221]

Social Murder: perpetrators and their victims This reading explores the dangers associated with anxiety-driven decision-making, short-term thinking, and the failure to plan ahead. Individuals and groups within highly dynamic and interconnected systems, such as public health, must recognize how crises can escalate and breed further crises, often tempting leaders into making suboptimal or convenient choices. Decision-makers who understand the importance of evidence-based collaborative action also need to be cautious of the risks of proceeding without it. This article highlights prospect-theory, which suggests that individuals in the domain of losses, feeling they have nothing to lose, may make irrational choices. They are particularly vulnerable to manipulation by political or economic elites who, recognizing this susceptibility, may exploit it to their own benefit. This dynamic can help explain events like Brexit, the election of Donald Trump, the January 6th insurrection at the US Capitol, and the support for stolen election and replacement theories.

◆

Recent research shows that anxiety not only fails to produce good decisions but seems "exquisitely designed" to produce bad ones. In local and global health, where anxiety often thwarts good decision making, efforts to improve how choices are made have focused on collaboration and the use of scientific evidence. These efforts may have some relevance to an anxious public deciding this week whether the United Kingdom remains in the European Union.

Patient centered care envisions collaboration and shared decision making. One recommended way to improve medical decision making is through the application of prospect theory. This theory is rooted in economics and psychology and addresses the behavioural underpinnings of choice in the face of uncertainty.

---

[221] For access to the original article and footnotes, see tiny.cc/GlobalHealthBrexit

It recognizes, for example, that patients with poor prospects are more likely to take risks and make irrational choices by disregarding low probabilities. While this may mean that they are more willing to undergo treatment with less probability of success, it may also explain their embrace of dubious or pseudoscientific interventions to recoup their losses. The goal of prospect theory as applied to healthcare is to augment *Choosing Wisely* guidelines by addressing the patient's tendency of thinking in relative rather than absolute terms and the natural tendency of some patients to engage in risk averse or risk seeking behaviour.

In global health, achieving stated goals has been thwarted by unwise policy choices by anxious decision makers – fearful perhaps of upcoming elections, appearing weak to the public, or failing to satisfy powerful vested interests. These choices typically share three features: they tend to be dismissive of (scientific) evidence, dismissive of the opinion of peers, and dismissive of victim impact.

Among the more striking examples is the former President of South Africa Thabo Mbeki's questioning of the link between HIV and AIDS; he told the *Washington Post*: "Personally, I don't know anybody who has died of AIDS." The South African government's failure to provide an antiretroviral treatment program from 2000-05 has, in fact, been estimated to have contributed to at least 330,000 deaths in the country.

Similarly, Canadian Prime Minister Stephen Harper's support of asbestos mining and export dumbfounded his peers when he promised "this government will not put Canadian [asbestos] industry in a position where it is discriminated against in a market where it is permitted." Recent assertions by Donald Trump, potential future leader of the US, that global warming is a hoax even as CO_2 levels reach new milestones this past week are a reminder of this irrationality.

Policy outliers are becoming less acceptable. Indeed, 750 experts contributing to the Global Risk Report 2016 confirm that catastrophic events (such as profound large scale involuntary migration, epidemics, close to home terrorism, and "natural disasters") are becoming more common-place, more impactful, more immanent, more reflective of real time experience, and more anxiety producing. These experts insist that only collaborative action based on scientific evidence will yield an effective and efficient response. Most industrial countries have developed global health strategies; developments in global health diplomacy, global health security, and international relations reflect this trend.

Set against this background, the desire to leave the European Union seems to be, conceptually and practically, a move in the opposite direction. While countries from South America to the Far East are widening and deepening European style regional unions, Brexit would suggest a negation of the benefits of aggregation.

Prospect theory tells us that those who feel they have not participated in the benefits of EU membership or have lost benefits may want to take the risk of exiting – feeling, perhaps, that they have nothing to lose and perhaps something to gain or regain. Prospect theory tells us that we don't need to cite xenophobia, anti-immigrationism, or racism to explain this support for Brexit; it may result from ordinary people acting in ways anticipated by behavioral economics.

The decision of whether the United Kingdom ought to stay in the European Union casts many shadows – some long, some dark – yet the most regrettable shadow is how fear-mongering by both camps has diminished the process.

We Need to Prioritize Cyber Security in this Age of Global Risks

BMJ, May 16, 2017, [222]

Social Murder is Easier with AI Geoffrey Hinton, often referred to as the "godfather of AI," left Google to join a group of experts who are raising alarms about the societal risks posed by the rapid deployment of generative AI products, warning that these could lead to catastrophic outcomes. One of the most critical risks identified is an increase in cyberattacks. The ability to generate functional malicious code through precise prompts is leading to more frequent, larger, and increasingly diverse cyberattacks. The cyber world also serves as a fertile ground for spreading doubt, fake news, half-truths, and alternative facts, all of which can stoke fear and anger, and dangerously reframe critical issues. This platform is particularly effective in reaching vulnerable audiences, especially those who feel they have nothing to lose, thereby eroding social cohesion. A focal point of this discussion, which includes an examination of a cyber-attack on the NHS, is the urgent need to recognize the potential downsides of AI and to make cybersecurity a priority.

———————◆———————

Earlier this year when the World Economic Forum launched its annual 2017 Global Risks Report, an obvious question was whether the global community had learnt from the previous 2016 Global Risk Report. The evidence suggested that it had not, or at least not enough to have prioritised and taken effective steps to mediate risk and avoid chaos. This was particularly notable in the technological sector, where cyber attacks have dominated national elections and international relations.

The report warned that the failure to understand and address the risks of cyber attacks could have far reaching consequences. No sector has been harder hit by cyber attacks than the healthcare industry, where health records contain large amounts of personal information. A 2016 analysis shows that the leading sector for cyber attacks was the

[222]   For access to the original article and footnotes, see tiny.cc/CyberSecurityRisk

healthcare industry (more so than financial services and manufacturing), where more than 100 million health records were compromised.

In Britain, these warnings were repeated over the past year. In July the NHS regulator, the Care Quality Commission, and the national data guardian, Dame Fiona Caldicott, warned that not only do cyber attacks threaten to "put patient information at risk of loss or compromise … [they] also jeopardise access to critical patient record systems by clinicians."

Set against this context and the events over the past few days, several points made by the 2017 Risks Report seem relevant to the WannaCry cyber attack that began last Friday and its impact on the NHS.

Firstly, it seems that the NHS was caught in the net of a non-targeted cyber attack. The health sector is large and crosscuts many other sectors; it is inevitably vulnerable to global risks of multiple sorts. Indeed, most of the risks cited by the Global Risks Report have a direct bearing on the health and wellbeing of ordinary people – and are therefore relevant to healthcare providers and health organisations. Few professions and institutions know more about inequalities, natural disasters, migration, violence, environmental disease, pandemics, and, indeed, cyber attacks than those related to health.

Secondly, as the interconnectedness of the world increases, so too do global risks. For example, while the NHS's plans for a full roll-out of electronic records by 2020 reflects a desire to improve efficiencies and provide better healthcare for the patient, it also brings with it greater risks since it increases the (electronic) interconnectedness with other networks over which it has no control. The 2017 report warned that these risks are becoming more potent, more frequent, and more probable than ever before.

Thirdly, in making its recommendations, the Risks Report's main message was to deal with risks and hazards before they turn into crises. This can be done through a culture of prevention, a thorough understanding of risk, by ongoing review of policies and priorities, and by good governance in support of collaboration and partnership. Yet an early review of the cyber attack on the NHS suggests a striking imbalance between the proactive and reactive, between strategic plans and operational plans. For example, when NHS Providers' director of policy and strategy spoke with the BBC it was explained that trusts:

"will have business continuity plans in place, which will mean that they will declare an internal incident. They will go into what's called Silver Command and they will mandate a Silver Commander who will be absolutely responsible for sorting it out operationally and they won't stop until it is sorted out … And this is the same approach that hospitals take to any outbreak, so if they had an outbreak of a physical illness, or a contagious illness, they would take a similar approach. They are very practiced in dealing with this."

While this suggests a strong (and ultimately successful) operational plan to deal with the "outbreak," there is inadequate evidence that it is matched by a strong prevention strategy, one that was commensurate with the overall investment in technology. For example, *Personalized health and care 2020: a framework for action* describes the government's plan to embrace the electronic revolution to improve health and care, but it does not highlight cyber security – it is mentioned just once in the last sentence of the last paragraph in a section entitled "Build and Sustain Public Trust." In contrast, the literature describing the strategies, programmes, and projects needed to implement electronic data systems in healthcare systems without exception cite the need to make cyber security a top priority.

Of course, the NHS's struggle with cyber security is nested in a national political context. Government critics claim that the NHS had been left exposed by cuts to its budget and that "infrastructure budgets have been raided, have been cut back, which has meant hospital trusts have not been able to upgrade their IT systems." Dr. David Wrigley (deputy chair of the British Medical Association), who was on a panel that drew up guidelines on cybersecurity, said "it's disappointing that funding hasn't been given to upgrade the system. It needs urgent action by politicians … I don't think it's acceptable for politicians to say, 'It's all down to local NHS and management.' They have got a duty to ensure everything is up to date."

As the rest of the global community is learning this week, addressing the risk of cyber attacks is a shared responsibility, and as Krishna Chinthapalli warned last week in *The BMJ* many hospitals are running on "ancient operating systems" and obsolete protection. Both the government and managers need to prioritise cyber security in this age of global risks.

International Health to Global Health:
How Africa'sHIV/AIDS Crisis Influenced the Rise of Global Health
Medicus Mundi Schweiz, March 2012 [223]

Reducing exposure to risk and premature death This reading delves into how the HIV/AIDS crisis influenced the evolution from international health to global health, set against the backdrop of millions of foreseeable and avoidable deaths. It explores the transition from isolationist policies to a framework of global cooperation and collaboration, highlighting the shift from bilateral to multilateral approaches, and from modest to robust interdisciplinarity. The narrative emphasizes the importance of addressing transnational determinants of health and prioritizing equity both within and between countries. The foundational values driving these shifts are crucial for the global community's response to widespread risks, particularly the climate crisis. Additionally, the reading suggests that the lessons learned from the pandemic present a policy window that should be utilized to embed these values firmly within our decision-making processes, enhancing our collective ability to manage global health challenges effectively.

———————◆———————

Over the last dozen years 'global health' has been replacing 'international health' in public health discourse and the transition from one to the other is seen to represent an important paradigm shift. Among different factors the HIV/AIDS crisis played a key role, explains Chris Simms.

Among the factors explaining the paradigm shift from international to global health are globalization itself, terrorism, and the fear of newly emerging infectious diseases. Several pieces of evidence suggest however, that the donor community's abject failure to respond to the HIV/AIDS crisis in the 1990s, particularly in Sub-Saharan Africa (SSA) was

---

[223] For access to the original article and footnotes, see tiny.cc/GlobalHealth

central to the decline of international health and the shaping of global health. The following paragraphs briefly explore this evidence using a simple matrix developed by the Consortium of Universities for Global Health Executive Board that describes global and international health according to five basic categories (see Table 1).

		Global Health	International Health
1.	Geographical Reach	Focuses on issues that directly or indirectly affect health but that can transcend national boundaries	Focuses on health issues of countries other than one's own, especially those of low-income and middle-income
2.	Level of Co-operation	Development and implementation of solutions often requires global cooperation	Development and implementation of solutions often requires bi-national cooperation
3.	Individuals or Population	Embraces both prevention in populations and clinical care of individuals	Embraces both prevention in populations and clinical care of individuals
4.	Range of Disciplines	Highly interdisciplinary and multidisciplinary within and beyond health sciences	Embraces a few disciplines but has not emphasized multidisciplinarity
5.	Access to Health	Health equity among nations and for all people is a major objective	Seeks to help people in other countries

Table 1. Comparison of global and international health Source adopted from Lancet 2009 (JP Kaplan and TC Bond, 2009)

First, the most obvious feature of global health distinguishing it from international health is its 'geographic reach'; this represents a shift in focus from poor countries to encompass all countries and all populations. AIDS, the first disease to become global in our time, was unlike other diseases that typically beset Africa; it first came to light in the United States of America (USA) in 1980. This was important in the long run since influential western AIDS activists, advocacy groups (such as Act Up) and the World Health Organization's (WHO) Global Program on AIDS (GPA) took the view that tackling AIDS was a burden to be shared. They helped cast this first post-modern epidemic as truly global.

Formation of global partnerships

Second, the AIDS crisis prompted a new way of funding and delivering development aid that led to the formation of global partnerships and cooperative action. Before 2000, most donor aid was delivered mainly through bilateral relationships. The GPA began to change this by reaching out for the first time in the WHO's history to nongovernmental organizations (NGOs). (UNAIDS, 2008) When UNAIDS replaced GPA in 1996, one of the main rationales for its creation was to establish more cooperation and partnership among the UN agencies. The novel UNAIDS structure, originally made up of six, later 10 UN agencies represented a radical restructuring of global architecture towards cooperation and partnership, now a hallmark of global health action.

Third, HIV/AIDS elicited levels of multidisciplinary action not previously seen. Although international health was nominally multidisciplinary, donors placed little emphasis on the determinants of health that lie outside the medical care system. The nature of the HIV/AIDS crisis changed this in several well-known ways: its enormity soon made it clear this was not only a health crisis but an economic and development crisis as well; it seemed to reveal the essence of many cross-cutting issues such as poverty, gender inequalities and human rights; it changed traditional disciplines such as demography and epidemiology forever while at the same time introduced many to newer ideas such as complexity science and social networks and; without an AIDS cure, intersectoral behavioral change strategies drew upon many new disciplines. A key driver of the creation of UNAIDS was to develop truly multisectoral responses that included support for public-health interventions as well as structural determinants. (Merson / O'Malley et al., 2008)

The new goal of equity

Fourth, while international health embraced both prevention in populations and clinical care of individuals, the HIV crisis led to an increased emphasis on curative, rehabilitative, and other aspects of clinical medicine and basic sciences. Part of this stems from the heavy burden placed on African health systems by HIV and other related illnesses and the need for ongoing home care and social support. Ultimately though, it was the introduction of antiretroviral drugs (ARVs) in the late 1990s that eventually led to enormous investments in curative care. Total per capital spending on health in SSA in the 1990s that tended to average about US$10-15 per person annually, is in sharp contrast to today's spending on ARVs that range about US$900 per infected person. (Rosen / Long, 2010)

Fifth, Africa's HIV/AIDS crisis made international health's access goal, "seeks to help people in other countries", irrelevant and it was replaced by the goal of equity. The world community, long-accustomed to the extreme inequalities between North and South, was unprepared for the inequalities associated with the pandemic: the 30 million Africans dead or dying from HIV; the fizzling out of donor aid to US$3 per infected individual by 1998; and, the exclusion of all but a few thousand Africans from access to ARVs while the North contemplated universal access. The results left the world community appalled and the donor community certain of its own failure.

Conclusion

The reasons for the rise of global health are not necessarily the same as those that explain the decline in international health, yet the features of each seem explain the trajectory of both. Until this first post-modern epidemic hit SSA, the effectiveness of the donor community had never been fully and publicly tested. The vacuum created by donors' failure to respond effectively and appropriately with a robust, equitable, multidisciplinary, team effort led to a reconfiguration of the aid architecture, pouring in of fresh resources, new ideas, new standards and an insistence on better accountability.

"Canada Needs a Global Health Strategy"

Border Crossing, the Diplomat Magazine, the Hague, Netherlands, April 2016 [224]

Reducing exposure to risk by collaboration Published four years before COVID-19, this reading builds on the previous discussion by emphasizing our susceptibility to newly emerging infectious diseases (EIDs), which can arise naturally, accidentally, or deliberately. It highlights the urgent need for Canada to develop and implement a comprehensive global health strategy—a goal that remains unfulfilled. In the context of the polycrisis, the rationale for Canada to adopt such a strategy is equally pertinent to the global community's need to engage in robust collaborative efforts to address global risks, particularly the climate crisis. The devastating Canadian wildfires of 2023 and 2024, serve as stark reminders that crises can transcend borders and species with ease.

If "self-interest" is indeed the motivating force behind this Government's actions, it then ought to consider designing and implementing a global health strategy as many of its closest partners have done. The rationale for this undertaking is generally self-evident and tends to mirror the evolution of events that led to the displacement of 'international health' by 'global health'. Among the reasons for adopting a strategy is globalisation itself, terrorism and bioterrorism, the fear of newly emerging infectious disease (EIDs) – that may occur naturally, accidently, or deliberately (including HIV, West Nile virus, SARS, BSE and H1N1) and concerns about food and product safety standards. Also included are past failures to deal with priority diseases in poor countries. Most high-income countries have taken the view that a less unequal world will be safer and more prosperous; many of these have developed a global health strategy that envisions the world cast in a net of interconnectivity

---

[224] For access to the original article and footnotes, see tiny.cc/CanadaHealthStrategy

– where disease knows no borders, where mobility is easy and where experience shows that much more is achieved by acting in partnership than going it alone. Evidence suggests that it helps set priorities, guides decision-making, and creates efficiency and cooperation. A global health strategy ought to prompt greater fairness and, with less to hide, greater transparency.

The very process of developing a strategic plan is useful. It should help clarify mandates, our particular competencies as well short-comings and relate these to global threats and opportunities. The process helps identify local partners (including the academic and research communities, civil society groups, philanthropic organizations and the private sector) as well as their counterparts throughout the global health and donor communities. Most importantly though, the process ought to help Canada "to know" who our global partners are and how they measure success.

Review of the global health field over the last 10 years shows what can be achieved when nations work together with a focus on populations, on interdisciplinary approaches, systems and structures and on the scope of problems not their location. The global health strategy fosters an understanding that in global health we are dealing with complex transactions between societies and that bilateral relationships will not suffice. Reductionist and linear thinking which have typified relationships between rich and poor countries, donors and recipients, policy-makers and policy-takers have faltered and given way to the realisation that health is global and that we are part of a whole. As we replace the Millennium Development Goals (MDGs) with Sustainable Development Goals (SDGs), scientists are now turning their attention to how and why the parts fit together and to the rules that govern interconnections and coherence.

Whether it's embraced now or later, the need for a global strategy will only increase as will the cost of ignoring it. Perhaps what is particularly interesting is that countries that have implemented a global health strategy and are embracing the new SDGs are taking the opportunity to examine their own health outcomes indicators and systems performance. A global health strategy will not only help prevent morbidity and mortality in Canada but may reprioritize the importance of equal access to effective health care and social inequalities and the social determinants of health – perhaps reversing current trends.

Global Risks and Consilience: Mapping a Way Forward
Lancet, July 2016 225

Social Murder: reducing exposure to risk by multidisciplinarity This reading explores the concept of consilience, which involves integrating multiple disciplines, including both the sciences and the humanities, to achieve a more comprehensive understanding of complex issues. Dr. John Snow, often regarded as the father of modern epidemiology and one of the first modern consilient thinkers, exemplifies this approach. During the 1854 London cholera epidemic, Snow utilized his knowledge across bacteriology, medicine, and statistics, and incorporated local insights to map cholera cases and pinpoint the source of the outbreak—a neighborhood water pump. The principles of using local knowledge, contact tracing, and multidisciplinary approaches are highly relevant today, particularly in the context of COVID-19. In response to current global challenges, there is a growing recognition of the need for greater collaboration and cooperation across different fields of expertise, encompassing both public and private sectors.

---◆---

Along with good intentions, fear and anxiety pervade the agendas of recent world community gatherings such as the World Humanitarian Summit that took place in May 2016, the High-Level Signing Ceremony of the Paris Agreement on Climate Change in April of the same year, the High Level Conference on Global Health Security in March 2016, and the World Economic Forum in January. World leaders as well as ordinary people are increasingly worried about rising numbers of catastrophic events, including those related to climate change, migration global health security, and social instability.

Concurrently, there is a broadening and deepening of public awareness of conspicuous inequalities, plummeting social trust, and failure by the global community to mitigate and adapt to risks even as they cascade into one another. Over the last two decades, the global community has

225 For access to the original article and footnotes, see tiny.cc/RiskConsilience

sought to address risk, for example, by reducing relative and absolute poverty. The evolution of international health into global health, and its introduction into foreign affairs, diplomacy and international relations are part of this trend.

However, with global warming, terrorism and migration now at the fore, other efforts to understand and deal with new and existing risks have emerged. For example, public and private sectors (as well as academics) are turning to so-called superforecasters to predict near-term social and political events. With a record of consistently outperforming the experts, superforecasters use statistics and systematic analysis to synthesize material from diverse fields of investigation; although they make predictions with precision, they keep an open mind and are prepared to adjust and readjust their predictions as they learn from mistakes and take into account new data. Other efforts have built on research into social networks (which suggest that we are led by people around us) that may help predict major events such as epidemics. Elsewhere, there is a focus on connectography which claims that connectivity not geography will map out destiny and integration and globality will be our new morality.

Another means of understanding anxiety-producing global risk is by looking at historical events and the maps that described them. For example, the public health and epidemiological factors underlying the Black Death in 14th Century England that killed more than one third of the population are today well understood. Recent research and mapping of the epidemic reveal a country living "in constant fear of God's wrath and the end of the world". This is captured in what today might pass for a blog post or a tweet: scratched into the stone of St. Mary's Church (north wall of the nave) in Ashwell, Hertfordshire in 1361 is the following – "There was a plague 1000, three times 100, five times 10, a pitiable, fierce violent [plague departed]; a wretched populace survives".

In contrast, when cholera hit a district of London known as "the Golden Square" centuries on (1854), it elicited a different response; this time maps were not drawn retrospectively by historians but rather by a local physician, Dr. John Snow. He is described as a consilient thinker, that is, he drew on different disciplines (including bacteriology, medicine, statistics and what would be, epidemiology) to plot out cholera cases and a map of the epidemic. With the help of a clergyman who provided local knowledge he identified the neighbourhood water pump as the source of the outbreak and then acted as an advocate to persuade authorities to close the pump, thus ending the epidemic.

This notion of consilience (a term resurrected by E. O. Wilson) is discernible in the Global Risk Report's interconnected maps, global health (as defined by the Consortium of Universities for Global Health), super-forecasting, and connectography all of which draw on many disciplines. Global health bolsters its consilient profile by drawing on knowledge and experience from developed and developing countries, by using quantitative, qualitative, perception data (from ordinary people as well as specialists) and, by stressing partnerships and collaboration to bring these worlds together. If "consilience" evokes the notion of reform of global learning in order to tackle global risk, it is relevant to this discussion.

However, despite E.O. Wilson's "noble and unifying vision" of consilience and its embrace by parts of the global community, the community itself is not unified. Many observers are disconcerted by the great divide between the development and humanitarian communities as well as between the global health and humanitarian communities. For example, the scheduling conflict between the World Humanitarian Summit and the World Health Assembly (in May 2016), and the notable absence from the Summit of high-level support, Ministers of Health and other stakeholders seem to underscore this divide – one which makes any significant decisions less likely, especially as they relate to resource allocation – leaving ordinary people vulnerable to catastrophic events still vulnerable.

In a recent BBC interview, Peter Piot reached back 20 years ago to when, as Executive Director of UNAIDS, he witnessed up-close a fractured global community as it sought to deny antiretroviral therapy (ARVs) to Africans – when the science and opportunity existed to save lives. He was surprised and angered by this ignoble undertaking. Yet it's unclear how much has changed over the last two decades. Despite the science and mapped predictions, the global community has failed to deal effectively with climate change. With consilience as a backdrop, perhaps the way forward is to examine the fracture itself and the handful of stakeholders that direct it through opaque negotiations and decisions typically unmoved by science, peers, or victims. In the meantime, it appears that the global community has not yet the capacity to deal with the overarching paradox – that while we are more hyperconnected than ever, we are increasingly fractured.

An Overlooked WWI Legacy: Maternal and Child Health in Sub-Saharan Africa

Lancet, November 11 2014[226]

Finding a Way Forward This article examines initiatives aimed at preventing the foreseeable and avoidable premature deaths of vulnerable groups by deliberately and structurally reducing their exposure to high risk more than 100 years ago. It details significant investments in maternal and child health (MCH) in England during World War I (1914-1918), which not only led to sustainable improvements in childhood survival rates but also addressed several societal needs. These included addressing plummeting birth rates, replenishing a depleted workforce, and enhancing the country's defense capabilities. For similar reasons, these health reforms were "exported" to England's colonial administrations in Sub-Saharan Africa (SSA), where they also resulted in significant improvements in maternal and child health, creating a "win-win" outcome. This historical analysis underscores the multifaceted benefits of targeted health interventions, both domestically and internationally.

◆

An important legacy of World War I was the rise of maternal and child health care in many European centres; a related yet overlooked legacy is the simultaneous transfer of these services to their colonial possessions during the years of conflict and those immediately following.

In England, the surge of maternal and child health care was prompted by humanitarianism and concerns about the loss of lives, plummeting birth rates, a depleted workforce, and the ability of the Empire to defend itself. Women's groups, medical associations, religious charities, and other parts of civil society contributed to the development of services. Th e provision of antenatal care, delivery assistance at birth, and health education in the areas of hygiene and nutrition – together with a better standard of living – led to improved health outcomes: infant mortality rates

---

[226] For access to the original article and footnotes, see tiny.cc/WWILegacy

which declined by 7% from 1905 to 1913 fell by 20% during the period 1914-18. In some industrialised centres with little evidence of wage increases or water and sanitation improvements, infant mortality rates still fell significantly; in Wigan, England, it declined from 179 deaths to 117 (per 1000 livebirths) between 1913 and 1919.

Colonial administrators expressed similar concerns in sub-Saharan Africa during the war years about very high levels of infant mortality and the viability of the local workforce. The Imperialist rhetoric at the time was to introduce "modern and civilizing ideas" to the colonial possessions; the introduction of maternal and infant health in particular, "was designed to improve the colonial labor supply, pacify indigenous populations and promote modernization". The rise of humanitarianism and volunteerism seen in England spilled over into the colonies through volunteerism and provided the means to deliver maternal and child health services to Africans, mainly by medical missionaries.

Although reliable household survey data show that maternal and child health care has a large impact on childhood mortality (which is typically 50-100% higher for women who receive no antenatal care or delivery assistance at birth than for women who receive both) and medical missions provided 25-50% of maternal and child health care in sub-Saharan Africa throughout most of the 20th century, "little scholarship addresses their influence on African health care and health status" and a vast mission archive remains almost completely unexplored. This neglect is partially explained by the justifiable view that traditional missionaries (as distinct from the new breed of independent evangelists) were a colonial construct used to justify the actions of imperialist powers, and generally an embarrassment to academics.

Yet from the medical or public health point of view, evidence from Tanzania, Zambia, and many other parts of sub-Saharan Africa would suggest that traditional medical missions have been professionally staffed and managed – at least since the 1960s independence era. Indeed, studies suggest that, rather than being a source of embarrassment, medical missions have shown what can be achieved when health initiatives are planned and implemented as if ordinary people mattered. Delivered mainly by women working at the grassroots level, often incorporating local knowledge and sometimes reproducing "aspects of indigenous models of the healer", they provided, in essence, family-centred health care.

Furthermore, medical missions often protected the communities they served from some of the most egregious policies implemented by the international community. For example, over the past 30 years or so – an era of deregulation, free flow of capital, and proliferation of other neoliberal policies – the IFIs and donor aid agencies (by their own account) implemented adjustment operations and health-sector reforms without paying attention to their impact on the most vulnerable. Their austerity measures typically led to a 50% cut in healthcare expenditures in sub-Saharan Africa, a collapse of healthcare systems, and a reversal of child survival trends.

In Zambia, where maternal and child health care fell into disarray and infant mortality rates skyrocketed, the World Bank (without a trace of irony) reported that "the people have nowhere to turn for help. Those (rural) buildings which have been historically PHC centers or district hospitals are empty shells. Many institutions are losing qualified health personnel, are utterly devoid of basic health materials". Yet in districts where medical missionaries delivered basic services to Zambians, quality and access by the poor were generally maintained by staying focused on the careful allocation of scarce resources to cost-effective care that targeted the most vulnerable. Although their catchment areas were more geographically remote, had higher levels of poverty and childhood malnutrition, more female-headed households, less food security, and were more vulnerable to drought, they provided 75% more assisted deliveries per head than non-mission districts and had childhood mortality rates that were 12% lower. In fact, so striking were the differences that statistical analysis of district data showed that neither poverty nor malnutrition but rather access to maternal and child health services explained variation in child survival.

As HIV gripped Africa in the 1990s, mission health facilities with strong community care networks were well placed to tackle the crisis at the local and household level and typically responded a full 10-12 years before the international donor community and national governments took substantive action. By 1988, mission facilities in Mbeya, Tanzania, for instance, had already launched robust programming that included a sweeping condom distribution initiative, voluntary counselling and testing, community education programming, home-support programmes, and eventually prevention of mother-to-child transmission programmes. In contrast, the World Bank, the lead donor in Africa's health sector, repeatedly eschewed involvement in the pandemic in favour of its health reform package. It warned in 1992 that, "an expanded role of the Bank in AIDS should not be allowed to overtake the critical agenda for strengthening health systems". It was only by 2000 that the donor community began to invest in the prevention and control of HIV, by which time 30 million Africans were dead or dying.

Negative sentiments towards missionaries have been bolstered in recent years by some Christian fundamentalists who have sought abstinence-only approaches to HIV prevention and by the appalling rhetoric of mission fringe groups that has encouraged the criminalization of homosexuality in parts of sub-Saharan Africa – neither of which have a bearing on the traditional medical missionaries under discussion. Th e risk, however, of dismissing missionaries as an embarrassment, too "intimately tied up with colonialism and exploitation" is that a one-sided view of events persists unchallenged (that of the military and bureaucracy); it means missing the opportunity to obtain a bottom-up view of colonial and post-colonial history, one that incorporates the voice of ordinary people (the so-called subalterns). Ironically this is the type of information that most national aid agencies now insist on when taking a "livelihoods approach" to development.

It also implies that lessons-to-be-learned are neither identified, nor acted upon, and that past mistakes will be repeated. For some, of course, failure to design and implement development strategies as if ordinary people mattered would help explain repeated policy miscues and the rise in inequalities in sub-Saharan Africa over the past 30 years. The simultaneous rise of maternal and child health care in sub-Saharan Africa and England is interesting because both were driven by the practical and the altruistic – a good combination when enduring social policy is the objective.

Brexit: Acknowledging Error

Medicus Mundi, 2018²²⁷

Admitting Guilt This reading explores how to move forward and overcome barriers that hinder sound, evidence-based decision-making. It highlights the importance of addressing past errors and the necessity for leaders and decision-makers to have a space of psychological safety where they can admit mistakes, alter courses, and avoid the pitfalls of confirmation bias and doubling down on failed policies. The reading particularly focuses on Brexit and the failures of British leadership, themes that recur throughout this collection. Despite the consensus among economists regarding the detrimental impact of Brexit on the 2023 cost of living crisis and the British economy at large, three successive British Prime Ministers have failed to acknowledge this reality or offer any apologies. In a similar vein, at the 2023 COVID-19 inquiry, David Cameron refused to recognize or apologize for the impact of years of austerity measures on the NHS and public health, which significantly hampered the government's ability to respond effectively to the pandemic. This analysis emphasizes the broader implications of failing to confront and learn from past mistakes, not just in the context of British politics, but as a general principle in leadership and governance.

———————◆———————

Britain is scheduled to formally separate from the European Union March 29, 2019.

Many high-profile studies indicate that Brexit will have serious social and economic consequences. In the health sector it will lead to cuts in expenditure, availability of skilled workers, and reduced access to effective healthcare and, poorer outcomes; globally, it will undermine the UK's (and EU's) capacity to influence and contribute to sustainable development goals. For many commentators, Brexit represents a tragedy of errors.

About the duty to admit errors in the health sector

What can public health and medicine tell us about acknowledging a

---

²²⁷ For access to the original article and footnotes, see tiny.cc/Error

mistaken set of beliefs, an ill-chosen path or, individual or collective error – in particular, the dangers of doubling down, escalation of commitment, confirmation bias, saving face or, with courage failing, denying a disaster and walking away? Whether it's personal, professional or institutional, research shows that admitting error often means modifying sense of self and loss of self-esteem. The history of global health (with its beginnings in public health) shows that acknowledging erroneous beliefs does not come easily or quickly. Its record is sometimes one of mistaken theories and practices, often confusing correlation with cause, eventually being displaced by evidence-based interventions leading to better outcomes. For example, in Victorian London, Chadwick and his board of health refused for 30 years to accept that cholera was a waterborne disease – despite robust evidence. A century later, acceptance of Marshall's discovery that bacterium Helicobacter pylori caused stomach ulcers (and not correlated factors such as untreated stress and lifestyle) was slow; the CDC reported that despite the available evidence in 1982, only 5% of cases in 1995 were treated with antibiotic.

As to acknowledging errors in practice, physicians and other health providers across the globe have a duty of candor, a burden eased by concepts such as taxonomy of error and safety science; efforts to establish a "no blame" culture and sense of "psychological safety" help providers acknowledge and learn from errors. These approaches help distinguish between system and individual errors. In multilateral and bilateral agencies, struggles to acknowledge and learn from mistakes (typically system errors) are well-known – the Ebola crisis and response to the Haiti earthquake being among recent examples. Leading development charities are now confronting the results of failing to acknowledge their mishandling of serious allegations in the workplace – at home and abroad.

The mantra in politics: "never apologize and never explain"

In the political realm of course, the culture works against being forthright, the mantra being "never apologize and never explain". Perhaps it ﬁgﬁ

would be naïve to expect otherwise – yet when historic decisions are being made, failure to admit errors or take into account new information, wide-spread doubts, saving face seems negligent.

Wrong assumptions fueled the crisis

Yet, as it stands, Britain is headed in the opposite direction with key decisions in the hands of a beleaguered and weakened few who seem transfixed by administrative matters and vexed by a crisis of their own making – in the eyes of many, an implausible desire to return to the vanishing past. A key issue (yet not the only issue) at the heart of the crisis is the mistaken notion that uncontrolled immigration rather than globalization is the cause of the disempowerment and disenfranchisement felt by many who voted for Brexit. This notion has been promoted by Brexit politicians together with parts of the media. The crisis has been fueled by evocative images of migrants on the move, of the Calais Jungle together with what IPSO describes as "nasty" commentary. Even more striking than phrases that describe migrants as "unwanted invaders" or "swarm" are those describing parts of England "like being in a foreign land" and that harken back to pre-1973 Britain. Not surprisingly data (obtained through Freedom of Information Act) show that race and religious hate crimes soared to record highs in the 11 months following the referendum.

Inequality will increase

For many frustrated leavers living in the domain of losses, their vote was a call for fairness. Recent government figures show that over the last five years vulnerable and disadvantaged populations have borne the brunt of NHS cuts; they have also seen rising infant mortality rates and worsening health outcomes. Yet it is this group that will be hit hardest by Brexit – further increasing their inequalities. Among those who led Brexit there is the disquieting notion that "some measure of inequality is essential for the spirit of envy ... that is like greed, a valuable spur for economic activity".

The cluster of revelations related to the Windrush generation, the creation of a "hostile environment", the "go home van" and deportation targets of illegals ought to be seen as an agenda nested within a larger agenda – that is Brexit. And as with Brexit, political response to the Windrush scandal began (November 28, 2017) with failure to acknowledge mistakes, followed on by doubling down even as "evidence" slowly accumulated – eventually ending in an apology and a stand-down. With Brexit of course, an apology will be too little and a stand-down, too late. Historical review of the 19th century miasmaists' refusal to consider the evidence led to a call for a new discipline – sociology of error. That it seems applicable to Brexit (and Windrush) must be source of sadness and shame. Those in the position to do so are encouraged to provide decision-makers a "safe space" to separate out facts from beliefs, the rational from the irrational – this would represent leadership leading in the right direction.

Undoing the Undoing of Canada as a Global Health Citizen

Lancet, February 26 2016[228]

Reducing exposure to risk and premature death This reading scrutinizes Justin Trudeau's premiership, particularly focusing on the initial months of his administration. It highlights how Trudeau's policy agenda starkly contrasted with that of this predecessor, Stephen Harper, and many contemporary global leaders. Trudeau is portrayed as having embraced policies that championed immigration, diversity, and inclusiveness, positioning himself as an internationalist, environmentalist, humanitarian, and progressive leader. However, as explored in other readings, over time, certain flaws in his leadership and decision-making emerged that somewhat tarnished his reputation.

———————◆———————

When Canada's new Prime Minister, Justin Trudeau addressed the World Economic Forum (WEF) at Davos last month, restoring trust in Canada as a global citizen was at the top of his agenda. Th e previous government's 10-year record of "multilateralism as a weak-nation policy" and the just-released WEF 2016 Global Risk Report helped provide the encouragement needed to change the policies that were the previous administration's downfall.

Former conservative Prime Minister Stephen Harper (2006-2015) made resource development the centerpiece of his administration without fully taking into account its environmental impact, aboriginal rights, scientific evidence or the opinion of the global community.

While Canada's reputation as global citizen declined internationally, democratic values and social trust were threatened domestically by a clamp-down on legitimate and peaceful protest, access to government information, the muzzling of government scientists and intimidation of

---

[228]   For access to the original article and footnotes, see tiny.cc/GlobalHealthCitizen

civil society groups – most notably by agencies meant to enforce the law.

As to the troubling WEF Report (reflecting the opinion of more than 750 experts), it warned that global threats (such as catastrophic climate events, large-scale involuntary migration and global health insecurity) are now more interconnected, more likely, more impactful, and more imminent than ever before. For the global community, creating trust within and between nations is seen by WEF as the main challenge and solution to global risks

Mr. Trudeau seems committed to building trust. He promised open and accountable government, close cooperation with the global community, re-engagement with the United Nations and multilateral institutions and, a policy of inclusivity and diversity. Having already chosen for his cabinet of 30 ministers, 15 women and 2 aboriginals, he was inclined to cite "diversity" 12 times in his Davos speech – describing it as a source of strength and resilience for Canada.

Detailed and transparent (online) mandate letters to each cabinet member on what is to be done and how have led to a cascade of policy changes directed at reversing the Harper legacy –, many coming into immediate effect, most notably in the area of public health. For example, to restore the flow of information expected of a pluralistic, democratic society, Canada's 6000 federal scientists have been de-muzzled allowing them to share their findings on the health and safety of Canadians as they see fit; the long-form census, an important source of data on vulnerable groups has been reinstated. As to information from civil society to government – the Canadian Revenue Agency was ordered to end its harassment of environmental NGOs critical of the oil sands and the Minister of Justice has been instructed to amend controversial Bill 51 that portrays environmentalists and First Nations activists as terrorists.

A fundamental resetting of relations with First Nations, the indigenous Canadian population, has begun under Mr. Trudeau. Action on long-ignored inequalities is promised including robust social sector investment, full implementation of the 94 Truth and Reconciliation Commission recommendations (meant to deal with the on-going suffering associated with the Indian Residential System); a national inquiry into "murdered and missing aboriginal women and girls"; and the immediate end of long-term solitary confinement in federal prisons (that affects mainly aboriginals). This shift in tone has perhaps emboldened other agencies: the Human Rights Commissioner has now ruled that the federal government indeed discriminates against aboriginal women and children in providing health care and; the Commissioner of the Royal Canadian Mounted Police (RCMP), an institution that First Nations deeply distrust, has acknowledged on national television that racism exits within its ranks and promised to rectify it.

An unshackled Department of Foreign Affairs has swiftly reversed a policy known as "sovereign self-interest" that saw trade and commerce suborn human rights, international development and humanitarian assistance. For example, 50,000 Syrian refugees have been welcomed to Canada (25,000 by the end of February 2016); aid for maternal, newborn and child health has been refocused to include reproductive rights. Commitments made at the Paris Climate Talks have led to actions at home: strengthening of the oil and gas industry to include upstream greenhouse emissions. Perhaps emboldened as well, the Commissioner of the Environment reported that audit of the National Energy Board (NEB) shows it failed to track compliance by pipeline industry and that nearly half requested files were missing or outdated.

Although these policies suggest good governance begets good governance, they are drawn from a diminishing supply of "low-hanging fruit" and subject to the criticism of being reactive, linked more to campaign promises than an overall plan; they represent practically and conceptually a fraction of what is needed to confront an increasingly complex and dangerous world. Perhaps acknowledging this, superforecasting expertise has been introduced into Prime Minister's Office to help guide decision-making. Yet what is more obviously needed (and more transparent) is a global health strategy to help set priorities, guide choices, and create efficiency and cooperation; the very process of developing such a framework would help identify local and global partners and how they measure success. In contrast to recent years where such a strategy would have exposed abject failure, it would highlight and enhance efforts to confront global risks through trust and partnerships.

Canada's First Nations: The Social and Political Determinants of Health

BMJ Opinion, April 1 2016 [229]

Social Murder and the Harper Government This reading opens with Sir Michael Marmot drawing on Aldous Huxley's dystopian narrative in "Brave New World" to discuss societal stratification. Marmot argues that although society does not deliberately aim to stratify itself, it nonetheless tolerates significant social injustices with minimal uproar for change. In contrast, Prime Minister Stephen Harper took explicit and measurable steps to deepen these divisions, particularly targeting Indigenous communities in ways that jeopardized their health and well-being.

———————◆———————

To what extent are the social determinants of health (SDH) political determinants, and which of these are the most amenable to policy reversals that will increase or decrease inequalities? Reviewing the actions of the conservative government under Prime Minister Stephen Harper (2006-15), together with early initiatives taken by the just elected Prime Minister Justin Trudeau, may help answer these questions.

The Harper government: The rise in inequalities among Canada's 1.4 million aboriginals during the conservative decade may surprise some SDH experts. At the last World Medical Association meeting its president and leading SDH expert, Sir Michael Marmot, cited Aldous Huxley's dystopic *Brave New World* to help describe the effects of social stratification on inequalities. He said that while society may not take deliberate steps to stratify, it nevertheless tolerates this social injustice "with seemingly little clamour for change."

Yet under the conservative administration, the stratification of Canadian aboriginals was not only tolerated but often seemed intentional.

---

[229] For access to the original article and footnotes, see tiny.cc/CanadaFirstNations

In pursuit of its resource development strategy, the government sought access to important natural resources on First Nations' traditional lands. Aboriginals objected to projects without their prior consent, and, with some success, they petitioned the courts and held peaceful protest demonstrations across the country. Their resistance was met by a series of government responses that harkened back to colonial relationships of the 18th or 19th centuries. In the process, impoverished aboriginals were portrayed as masters of their own making, undeserving stewards, and a threat to Canada's future prosperity.

Firstly, the government appeared to deny aboriginals their history – 150 years of discrimination; the prime minister told the G20 summit in Pittsburgh that "every country wants to be Canada; we have no colonial past." This, despite a well documented record of genocide, starvation, theft of land, and an abusive Indian residential school system – the essence of a colonial relationship and the very inequities that Marmot says matter most.

Secondly, even with their SDH in question, the government still canceled billions of dollars in public programs in education and health explicitly designed to address these inequalities – cuts described by the most restrained of observers as a "travesty of public policy."

Thirdly, as new inequalities were added to old ones, the government reduced access to much needed data to describe these worsening trends by abolishing the First Nations Statistical Institute, canceling the long-form census (needed to describe vulnerable populations), axing a host of environmental monitoring agencies, and by muzzling federal scientists.

Fourthly, it created fear and apprehension among First Nations activists protesting their own poverty and the environmental degradation of their communities by engaging the Royal Canadian Mounted Police (RCMP) and Canadian Security Intelligence Service (CSIS) infiltrate and monitor their activities. Revelations that these two agencies subsequently shared this information with industry stakeholders startled many observers; when it was revealed that the watchdog body mandated to oversee these two agencies is led by lobbyists for the resource industries it led to immediate resignations.

The Trudeau government: Many of these dystopic policies ended abruptly with the election of Prime Minister Justin Trudeau (October 2015). With explicit online mandate letters to the ministers responsible, he restored the long-form census, de-muzzled 6000 government scientists, ended the harassment of aboriginal activists and their advocates, and committed to reversing injustices stemming from what he called "one of the darkest chapters in Canadian history" – the Indian residential schools.

In support of these reversals and a range of aboriginal social and public health issues, he earmarked $8.4 billion in his federal budget (22 March 2016) – all of which were framed in terms of the SDH. These investments would essentially reverse 10 years of budgetary cuts. With 10 aboriginals elected as members of parliament, and two selected for cabinet (out of 30 positions, 15 of which are filled by women), these undertakings seem consistent with Mr. Trudeau's assertion that "no relationship is more important to me and to Canada than the one with First Nations."

A recent editorial in *The BMJ* reminds us, however, that "health is a political choice." Citing the final report from the Commission on the Social Determinants of Health, it warns that health is ultimately shaped by such factors as "the distribution of money, power, and resources," and in Canada, resource extraction industries remain key economic drivers.

In this context two concerns have arisen: when Mr. Trudeau was given the opportunity to endorse his key promise to support First Nations having a veto on resource development he appeared to back away. Secondly, a review of his budget shows that most of the promised $8.4 billion is budgeted for after the next election. These items represent important political determinants of health for which the new government will need to be held accountable by all Canadians.

Confederates and Canadian Colonialists: Imprisoned by the Past

BMJ Opinion, 2017 [230]

Torture This article discusses the ongoing global efforts to dismantle symbols of past colonialism and racist policies, a movement that contrasts sharply with the increasing racial and ethnic tensions in many countries. In Canada, the government has initiated the removal of monuments and the renaming of streets and buildings linked to Indian Residential Schools (IRS) and other racist policies. However, to Indigenous leaders, these efforts seem superficial and merely symbolic. The enduring legacy of these schools and policies not only persists but is intensifying. Notably, Indigenous women now constitute half of the female population in federal prisons, marking a historic and concerning milestone. The United Nations Mandela Rules stipulate that holding an individual in solitary confinement for more than 15 consecutive days is considered torture, classified as a crime against humanity. Despite this, these rules are frequently disregarded in Canadian prisons. Alarmingly, two-thirds of Indigenous prisoners have been subjected to solitary confinement, and they consistently make up 50% of the population in solitary at any given time. This disproportionate representation highlights a severe systemic issue that necessitates urgent attention and corrective action.[231]

◆

Canada's experience is not the Confederates' in Charlottesville, yet it's also in the process of renaming buildings and removing monuments across the country that evoke its colonial past and the abrogation of Aboriginal people's human rights. Mainly at issue are Canadian government policies that established the Indian Reserves and abusive residential school systems. Among the statues and memorials targeted for dismantlement or renaming are those that memorialise the architects of the school system, a governor that issued a bounty for the scalps of Aboriginal people, a so called "hanging judge," and others that wantonly

---

[230] For access to the original article and footnotes, see tiny.cc/Confederates

[231] https://policyoptions.irpp.org/magazines/january-2022/the-use-of-solitary-confinement-continues-in-canada/

and egregiously altered the life course of the country's first peoples.

Global Health and Social Murder

From a clinical and public health point of view, these two events ought to resonate since the most striking feature of these policies (which paradoxically marginalised and tried to assimilate people at the same time) is that their health effects (physical, emotional, behavioural) are now seen to be (1) intergenerational, (2) cumulative, and (3) becoming progressively worse in relative and absolute terms.

Recent research in the BMJ *Journal of Epidemiology and Community Health*, for example, shows that familial attendance at a residential school directly affects "health and mental health outcomes, and is associated with lower self-perceived health and mental health, and a higher risk for distress and suicidal behaviours." A scoping review published this year of 61 studies details the impact of residential schools on health and wellbeing, including increased rates of chronic and infectious disease, and increased risk of anxiety, depression, and addictive and suicidal behaviour.

Common demographic indicators also suggest growing disparities. A population based study shows a rise in infant mortality among Aboriginal people between 1996 and 2010, but "more worrisomely, the widening disparities in infant mortality comparing Inuit vs. non-Aboriginal infants, and in postneonatal mortality comparing First Nations or Inuit vs. non-Aboriginal infants suggest worsening infant health inequalities over the recent decade." A report on the health of people in Alberta found that the life expectancy of First Nations people is 12 years lower than the general population; although little trend data are available, life expectancy for First Nations people in Alberta is the worst it has been in five years.

A recent study (2017) shows that among off-reserve Aboriginal Canadians, income related inequalities in health increased by 23% from 2001 to 2012. In terms of access to healthcare, the Wellesley Institute concluded that racism against Aboriginal people is key to explaining their poor health and wellbeing; a 2014 report form the United Nations (UN) concurs. It concludes that the quality of Canada's relationship with its Indigenous peoples has deteriorated and that "human rights problems faced by Indigenous peoples in Canada … have reached crisis proportions in many respects."

All of this ought to trigger an immediate policy response. Instead Canadians have witnessed just the opposite (at least until recently) – with cuts to social programming specifically aimed at Indigenous Canadians by the Conservative government (2006-2015) and a "law and order" agenda that also looks like it was aimed at Aboriginal people.

As in the United States, Canada's "tough on crime" stance (penal populism) often seemed to target racial minorities. Observers have commented that "Canada's justice system is set against Indigenous people" and that its prisons "are the new residential schools." Data from the Office of the Correctional Investigator (OCI) show that between 2005 and 2015, the number of Indigenous Canadians in prison increased by 50% compared to an overall offender growth rate of 10%, and that Aboriginal people form 25% of the total inmate population despite only making up 4.3% of the Canadian population. Between 2001-02 and 2011-12 the number of Aboriginal women in prison grew by 109% and account for 33% of the female federal population (in provincial institutions this figure rises to 41%).

A recent case that captures the inappropriateness of a "tough on crime" approach when a mental health intervention is warranted relates to a 29 year old man from Yellowknife, who discharged a firearm in attempting suicide while intoxicated. Based on the previous government's "mandatory minimum sentence" laws, the Crown is pressing for a four year sentence while defence lawyers claim four years is disproportionate and a "cruel and unusual punishment" – unlawful under the Canadian Charter of Rights and Freedoms.

Yet there is more evidence to suggest that corrections facilities in

Canada often represent places of "cruel and unusual punishment" – especially for Aboriginal people. An OCI report (2015) showed that 55.9% of the Aboriginal inmate population had spent time in solitary confinement. Suicide attempts and self-harm in prison have tripled over the past decade; in 2016-17 Aboriginal inmates accounted for 61.7%[i] of self-inflicted injuries. Many self-harm incidents are taking place in solitary confinement.

Indeed, cases of solitary confinement leading to the suicides of Aboriginal people have dominated the media over the past year – with the UN pointing out that solitary confinement is torture not punishment.

Canada does not have 1500 Confederate statues and memorials or political leadership that would defend their presence. Yet it does have a persistently bleak relationship with Aboriginal people – and a growing body of research showing the nature and extent of related health issues as they evolve. Prime Minister Justin Trudeau seems to acknowledge the challenge and has sought to reverse unjust law and order legislation, curtail or eliminate solitary confinement, and deal with the health and mental health of Aboriginal people in and out of their communities. Yet although his current investments in the social determinants of health are encouraging, they are but a fraction of what is needed. As for most black Americans, statues and memorials would not matter quite so much to Aboriginal people and their advocates if there were fewer inequalities, yet the outsized statues seem to loom larger as more detail is learnt of past injustices and their ongoing repercussions.

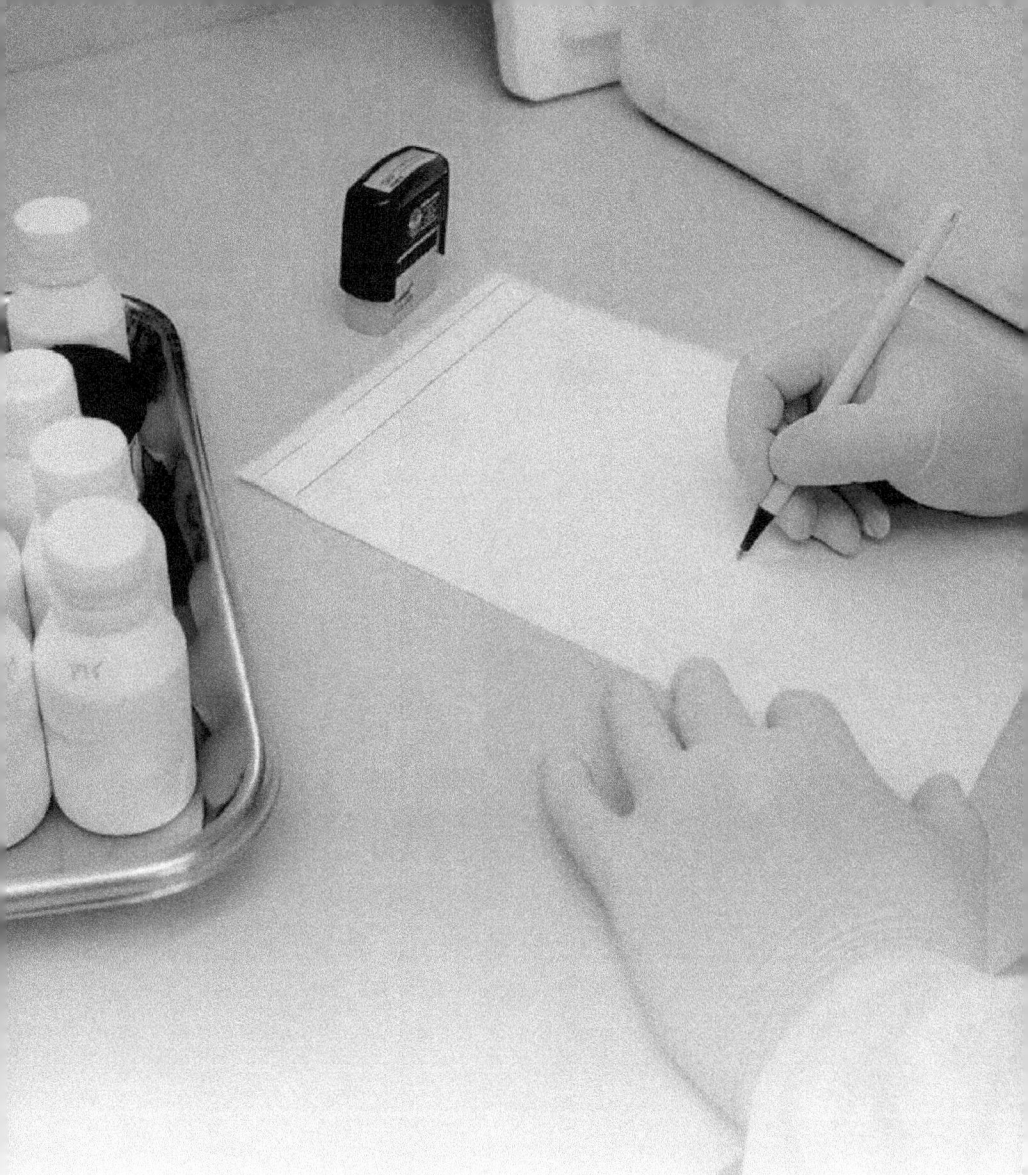

PART FIVE
Social Murder:
Eyewitness Reports

Spearheading Reform

———————◆———————

When selecting articles for this compilation, a young, insightful professor at my university noted that few students in social or political science would be interested in the historical impact of World Bank or IMF policies on Africa's impoverished populations, despite their significant consequences. However, in 2025, these same students show keen intertest in topics like Trump's dismantling of USAID, US withdrawal from the World Health Organization, cuts to global health investments and research, and the rise of Robert Kennedy Jr.

Part Five focuses on perception data—capturing the "voices" of the international donor community (expatriates) I interviewed and consulted while working in countries such Tanzania, Zambia, Kenya, Madagascar, and Senegal.

The goal is to provide insights into the often-conflicting thoughts, words, and actions of individuals tasked with implementing policies they may not necessarily endorse. Some expressed indifference to the losses suffered by vulnerable groups, aligning with the perceived injustices of these policies. Others were clearly disturbed by the policies they enforced and were often unguarded in their criticism.

In 2025, the relevance of these perception data lies in how they reflect current public discourse on topics such as science versus politics, public health versus economic stability, individualism versus the greater good, and ongoing tensions between the powerful and the powerless.

These voices support the *prima facie* evidence that the WB, IMF, and other donors have directly contributed to the foreseeable and preventable deaths of vulnerable populations by systematically exposing them to high risks. The policies discussed include structural adjustments and health reforms—specifically austerity, deregulation, cost recovery, privatization, and decentralization.

Before moving forward, it is crucial to underscore two significant points: Firstly, the World Bank often placed poor countries in a compromised position, compelling them to accept policies that were ostensibly recommended but essentially imposed. Illustratively, a senior World Bank economist imprudently admitted to the British Medical Journal that: *policy-based lending is where the Bank really has power— I mean brute force. When countries really have their backs to the wall, they can be pushed into reforming things at a broad policy level that normally, in the context of policies, they can't.*[207]

Second, it was inappropriate that the World Bank was the lead donor in SSA's health sector since, as a "bank", it was principally interested in making loans, not improving health outcomes. To the chagrin of WB leadership, it's own Operations Evaluation Department (1999) reached the horrific conclusion that the institution's *core business processes and incentives remained focused on lending money rather than achieving impact ... Forums for staff to discuss and review progress towards development objectives or recognize and reward evidence of HNP development impact are lacking. Staff still perceived that rewards were linked primarily to project approval and disbursement.*[232]

The following material is extracted from a Save the Children (SCF) report on collapsing health systems if Sub-Saharan Africa [209] [233] and from an Institute of Development Studies (IDS) *Working Paper.*[234] Both documents utilize perception data collected through hundreds of interviews

[232]   http://documents.worldbank.org/curated/en/687751468137983175/Investing-in-health-development-effectiveness-in-the-health-nutrition-and-population-sector
[209]   Chris Simms et al (2001) The Bitterest Pill of All: The Collapse of Africa's Health Systems Save the Children Fund
[233]   For access to the original paper, see: https://www.equinetafrica.org/sites/default/files/ uploads/documents/SIMehs.pdf
[234]   Chris Simms (2000) "Health Reformers' Response to Zambia's Childhood Mortality", IDS Working Paper 121 For access to the original paper, see tiny.cc/HealthReformersResponse

and consultations I conducted with representatives of the international donor community between 1988 and 2002.

Eyewitnesses to Cost Recovery

———————◆———————

The implementation of cost recovery, or user fees, was a key component of the World Bank's health sector reform. The intent behind these fees was to make the health sector more sustainable and to reduce frivolous use of services. The policy was designed to include an exemption system to protect the most vulnerable, but the World Bank admitted to failing in creating administratively feasible methods to apply these exemptions effectively.

I gained insight into the detrimental impact of user fees on ordinary people through discussions with Dr. Loes Schelamkamp, Medical Officer-in-Charge at the Mukumi Health Centre in Tanzania. She detailed how user fees have adversely affected child health outcomes. Dr. Schelamkamp explains:

Things are in a real mess at the under-five clinic. If you look at the re-attendance figures for 1996, 1997 and 1998 for our catchment area you see a decline from 14,000 to 11,000. This is due partly to the rain and partly user fees; user fees are quite high

We don't get the poorest people here; we have very poor we know, but overall, they don't come to the Centre...even though our fees are Ts300 versus Ts500 in government facilities. We did a small (utilisation) study which showed travels costs are Ts600 one-way. We reviewed 380 records of which only 88 were children; you can see mothers are not bringing their children when they are sick. They wait until they are very sick and then they come. About 23% of total are under-fives.

Then you look at percentage of children who were ill (50%). We aren't getting the very poor. In the first 24 hours 33% die and in first 48 hours, 53% die.

She reports that the number of children seriously ill, simply exhausted, is very alarming; they are dying from malaria and anaemia.

I did this study because I was worried about the number of blood transfusions. The number of blood transfusion goes up since 1996. I've tested all children for haemoglobin at end of December and early January. The distribution shows that nearly all (samples) are below 10. We give transfusions below 5. We have already had 500 blood transfusions. It's been going up and up. They come in gasping for air. We don't have an official blood bank.

One donor in Kenya said of user fees:

We know that ours is the right policy. We see that districts are not getting support from government. They don't put up the dollars. We need contribution from beneficiaries. If you use services, you must pay. Health services must be sustainable and generate income.

Another donor states:

We want to raise user fees. We have done an important study which shows women can afford the pill. Under the category "discretionary spending": they spend money on hairdresser, clothes, lottery, harambe etc. It is an important study because we want to raise fees and it shows they can pay for it without too much trouble, even the poorest. They can go to the hairdresser every 6 months rather than every 3 months.

Many health systems appear dependent upon beneficiary contributions to finance healthcare, especially in Franco-phone Africa. One UN agency official states:

In Senegal you have to pay for health services. If we eliminated user fees the social cost would be even greater because the health service delivery system depends on these fees – services would decline. There is nothing to discuss – it's a fait accompli.

However, other donors expressed deep concern about user fees' impact on vulnerable populations, children, the poor and geographically isolated. A UN country representative in Madagascar states that "I was shocked by user fees. Here, people in Antananarivo are told straight to their face that if they cannot pay, they must be refused treatment. These rules are strictly applied".

In Zambia, implementation of user fees in 1993 when there was 90% poverty was inappropriate. A senior donor official in Lusaka says:

To some extent, some of the policies in the early 1990s were ill-conceived, not just in the health sector but across the board. Any new government is going to make mistakes. Its possible that the application immediately of user fees could be seen retrospectively as a mistake – but that doesn't deny the validity of the theory on which they were based – that you cannot depend on government for free care.

Although donors considered user fees as a fundamental part of re-form with established policy guidelines and exemptions, field research shows that charges were improperly applied to OPD emergencies, deliveries, antenatal care, under-five treatment and STD clinics. Milimo found for example, "access to health services is often determined by one's ability to pay for them … Expectant mothers in Chadiza complained of the K500 they have to pay to the antenatal clinic. Those who do not have the money are denied access to the clinic."

A senior health policy advisor to Central Board of Health did not know but should have known that fees were being charged for services for pregnant women and children despite the exemptions. He stated:

As long as I have been working in Zambia since 1994, I never heard that user fee exemptions were an issue. There were always exemptions for children under-five and pregnant women. I thought there were always exemptions for children under-five. I hadn't realised that they were not applied. That's insane, that's crazy, that's a policy failure.

Another senior donor official in Lusaka says:

I think we have made a series of mistakes which have been absolutely disastrous. There were exemptions for user fees, but districts don't know what they are. Some districts are asking for money, and some are not. But it's all because the districts don't know the exemptions. They were so strapped for cash last year that if you wanted services, you would be charged.

Donors typically did not go into the field and indeed, seemed unaware of the difficulties entailed by the levy of service fees. There was for example, the widely-held view that Zambians are willing and capable of paying tuition and user fees and that they apportion their budget accordingly. However, Wisdom Kanganga, a community worker in Kabanana Township states:

In rural and peri-urban Lusaka there are many health facilities, but you have to pay. For the under-five clinics, ANC and delivery assistance, you have to pay. Of course. How do the very poor pay? They do anything, collect garbage, collect papers and sell them again, crush stone. It's a question of survival. Some use their children. Imagine sending your children at night to sell themselves in the bars. The security guards control them, and they bring back the profits to their parents. Children ages 11, 12, 13 and 14. They get pregnant and there's HIV.

Eyewitnesses to "Cut and Run"

———————◆———————

In the early 1990s, the World Bank's health sector reform project mandated reductions in the size of the public sector and the transfer of key donor-funded basic programs to governmental control. The stated aim was to integrate and decentralize services. However, these changes were implemented with poor planning and minimal consultation with those affected. Client governments were known to be ill-prepared, lacking the necessary financial resources and expertise.

The fate of the Expanded Program on Immunization (EPI) exemplifies the detrimental impact of these reforms on essential services. EPI had previously achieved very high coverage rates in Sub-Saharan Africa (SSA), thanks in part to sustained support from UNICEF. The hasty transition to government management resulted in chaos and significantly reduced coverage rates. For some donors, this outcome was both predictable and acceptable. A leading donor in Senegal remarked:

We have been to the moon, and we can't go the moon every year. We know we can reach ambitious immunisation targets through concentrated activity. What we had earlier was artificial improvement. It's a question of true development. I was in charge of EPI 1987-90 in eight countries in Africa. We had a large amount of money for EPI. We used to have resources, training and supervision and vaccines were free. It was artificial. Today we have realistic results reflecting the level of development of the countries.

On the other hand, some donors found not find these reversals necessary or acceptable. They argued rather that they reflected widespread donor negligence in efforts to integrate and decentralise EPI and handover to MOH. A donor in Kenya says:

We handed over EPI to Government of Kenya. They took it over but didn't come through and meet their responsibility. The result was neither an integrated nor vertical programme. The management functions to decide rational use of resources were not in place. I would call the result confusion. There was never a plan, or strategy. Maybe the pace, maybe the suddenness was too much. This is our fault. I strongly suspect that recurrent cost and availability of funds for supervisory systems were the first to be cut. They were the nerve centres, and they were destroyed. We were naive. We should have expected this would happen. We should have known. Our eyes were closed, and we went straight into it. Let's be frank, we didn't even have a follow-up to see what they did.

Another donor in Tanzania said the integration of immunisation with other basic health care services was poorly conceived. He said:

There was no thinking in terms of transition strategies by the reformers. They thought they could do things over night like switching a key. Inside EPI people were very concerned. They could see what was happening and where integration was going to lead. There was insufficient money and attention devoted to the integrated system. Indicators were affected. What about appropriate levels of transport, information systems, training, maintenance programmes and supervision? They are under-funded and of poor quality. They didn't put real dollars and attention to get that system off the ground.

Another key donor said:

We made a critical error with integration. In terms of resources, it has to be additive support. We cannot piggyback one programme on top of another. Each program has to come with its own money. We say integration is a means to improve cost effectiveness (but) the approach was wrong; who was going to pay? We need additional money. We want to combine EPI with other programmes but without twice as much money. It's absolutely ludicrous.

Eyewitnesses to Zambia's Reform

———◆———

Between 1980 and 1991, the proportion of Zambian children who died before reaching five years of age increased from 15% to 19%, a mortality rate that continued to worsen throughout the 1990s. The actions and inactions of the World Bank, the International Monetary Fund (IMF), and other donors are central to understanding this remarkable policy-induced reversal in mortality rates.

Zambia was the World Bank's flagship project for health sector reform, with donors investing hundreds of millions of dollars into the initiative. Significant investments were made in developing integrated information and accounting systems. However, the actual delivery of healthcare services was largely neglected. A senior donor official in Lusaka comments:

There were pilot studies and that took a long time to happen. As to the actual services themselves, training never happened. Nursing and institutional jobs have never been really addressed. CBOH did not have the capacity to provide technical assistance to districts. Guidelines have not been forthcoming; policy development has taken two or three years to develop in certain areas including family planning. In 1995-96, the family planning policy, which was widely disseminated, was not actually finished. The policy which was developed was not put in practice, so all we have is a strengthening of our central office.

In 1999, it is generally recognised that greater efforts should have been made to improve basic health care services. Another senior donor official in Lusaka says:

Something has gone terribly wrong…we spent our money on management capacities and what has it produced? A lot of workshops, courses and FHANIS.[235]

Another senior donor official in Lusaka says:

The claim that the focus of health reform was mistakenly on building district management capacities rather than improving services is a very valid issue. The reforms focused on management and financial capacity building for districts and there was no focus on technical issues and service delivery.

Still another senior donor official in Lusaka says:

I think you could safely say that if we had done things differently over the last years, we could have perhaps made some kind of difference … What a lot of people are saying just now is that while health sector reform is a good concept, there is quite a strong feeling that we put too much time for too long on trying to strengthen the capacities themselves in finance and administration. What's suffered as a result is the delivery of basic health care services. What's being said is that we should have done this hand in hand, together.

---

235   Food, Health and Nutrition Information System

The World Bank's Neoliberalism versus the World Health Organization's Public Health Values

———————◆———————

This concluding section of Part Five aims to illustrate the differences and conflicts between the values of the World Bank and the World Health Organization by examining a pivotal moment in Zambia's health sector reform.

However, to fully understand this context, we must first introduce or (re)introduce Dr. Halfdan Mahler. Dr. Mahler served three consecutive terms as the Director-General of the WHO from 1973 to 1988. For him, "social justice" were pivotal watchwords. In 1976, he introduced the slogan "Health for all by the year 2000" at the World Health Assembly and was instrumental in advancing the principles of "primary health care" (PHC) as outlined in the Alma Ata Declaration of 1978. This declaration promoted appropriate, community-based healthcare that considered the social determinants of health (SDH). Along with Dr. David Tejada-deRivero, the Assistant Director-General of WHO, who organized the conference, Mahler spearheaded a groundbreaking advancement in international health that had enduring impacts into subsequent decades.

However, the Declaration was criticized by influential figures as being expensive, logistically impractical, and politically unfeasible—broadly considered naive. In 1979, the Rockefeller Foundation convened a select conference in Bellagio, Italy, attended by notable figures including David E. Bell, executive vice-president of the Ford Foundation, Maurice Strong of CIDA, and Robert McNamara, president of the World Bank.

The conference centered around a paper by Julia Walsh and Ken Warren entitled "Selective Primary Health Care (SPHC), an Interim Strategy for Disease Control in Developing Countries." This approach rejected Mahler's comprehensive vision of PHC and its underlying values, proposing instead a minimalist approach consisting of "cost-effective" interventions: growth monitoring, oral rehydration, breastfeeding, and immunization—collectively known as GOBI. This alternative was favored by donors as it was economical, measurable, and goal-oriented. For academic, public health researchers, and practitioners and those working in the field, SPHC was a parsimonious response to just need; it was about the global community doing as little as possible and getting away with it.

Julia Walsh's personal note on her NYU Grossman School of Medicine profile captures the essence of these sentiments. She recounts an interaction with the professor who led her master's program at the London School of Tropical Medicine: "How can you, a graduate of our program, write this paper? Comprehensive primary health care is what you should be pushing," he challenged. Dr. Walsh recalls her response: "Well, that's very nice, but we can't afford it." [236] This phrase, echoed throughout this reader, reflects the prevailing attitude of the advantaged towards the disadvantaged, both internationally and domestically.

Back to Zambia's story: Between 1993 and 1995, the Zambian Ministry of Health and its donors were so enthusiastic about the health reform process that they requested an external review to assess its progress. Dr. Mahler led an expert team for this evaluation. A senior donor official recalled, "The government requested the review expecting to receive unmitigated praise. While there was some commendation, they also faced stinging criticism." The Mahler Report (1996, p. 6) revealed::

emphasis seems to have been given to management of service delivery, while less attention was given to quality of care and the technical support for the peripheral staff in their efforts to raise the health of the population ... (I)t needs to be redressed

236   https://grapevine.mydigitalpublication.com/articles/profile-julia-walsh-70

The Mahler Report (1997: 5) went on to state:

We exhort the reformers to listen carefully to the 'noise' (turbulence?) produced by the implementation practices at various levels within the system in order not to lose touch with the reality on the ground.

GRZ and the donors were furious both with this criticism and the way it was presented. The donors did not accept the Report. A senior donor official in Lusaka says:

The Report was straight-away not accepted. There were donors who wanted a success so badly for health reform and decentralisation in 1996 and 1997 – including the World Bank. The first draft was embargoed. I was very upset. 'Hey, we discussed this in the open in 1993 and 1994. If you embargo it everyone will jump on it.'

The Report concluded that the reform process was off-track and had to consolidate and focus on delivery of basic health care services. The response of the donors to this warning was to ignore the Report and push ahead with reform. The World Bank simply took the Report out of the public domain, and it disappeared. A senior donor official in Lusaka says:

I complained because it took one and a half years before the Mahler Report was out officially by the World Bank. I wrote to the World Bank. I said 'What is this? Do you accept this? Is this the way you do business? Is this the way you deal with Government?' But we never had an official discussion. Every time I raised it I was given silence. 'Hey, don't be too critical, this is past.' Well, it's not past. Most of the issues are still there.

During the period of 1997-98, following the suppression of the Mahler Report, health reform in Zambia persisted along its previous trajectory despite mounting evidence of deteriorating healthcare quality; the Zambia Demographic and Health Survey (ZDHS) of 1996 indicated a continued increase in childhood mortality. Reform advocates believed that the only way to achieve decentralization was to aggressively push forward, fearing that any hesitation might derail the process entirely. A DANIDA official interviewed in 1997 starkly dismissed the significance of the Mahler Report, stating, 'We do not consider the Mahler Report a working document.' Compounding this, another senior donor official in Lusaka remarked:

The donors made a big mistake. It was the time for the donors to say 'Stop! Put on the brakes. Let's see it as a new start.' I have never understood why the donors never used the opportunity. I asked myself 'Should I shout "Stop! Put on the brake" after the Mahler Report?' You asked for a review, and you got a good group of people out. Use it as a new start.

Still another senior official in Lusaka states in retrospect that:

The other donors thought some of the decisions we made were a bit hasty and we had not consulted them. I am aware that in 1996 we pushed full steam ahead and were not listening. That's a problem we have discussed here at the Embassy – that we shouldn't push forward, we should not develop new things, that we should consolidate rather than come up with new ideas and try to build on that. I think that's the general view. I am aware that there are bad feelings.

In April 1998, a new Minister of Health took office. She contended that since the health reform process had yielded few tangible results, it needed to be paused and reassessed. By 1999, the health reform initiative was in disarray. Donors were at odds both among themselves and with the new minister. Some expressed grave concerns, stating, "the children are worse off than ever before; they are not obtaining the needed health care." A senior donor official in Lusaka commented:

The health sector has deteriorated considerably. Certainly, at district level the services are of a poorer quality, less reliable, no drugs. Nothing! A total mess! There's no procurement plan to ensure there's no stoppage in essential drugs. We don't have a TB programme. There's been a complete collapse. The National AIDS Programme shut down in 1997. There's not been a TB programme for two years. All of the last year there was no one at CBOH to head the secretariat so effectively there has been no manager of the HIV directorate. So none of the last mid-term plans for 1996, '97, '98 has been implemented so that means TB has suffered. So we don't have a TB Programme and we don't have TB drugs.

Another senior UN official in Lusaka said:

Over the last 18 months there has been a breakdown. A couple of the big do-nors are going to walk away. There's a breakdown in confidence and trust in the health sector. On the delivery side, there are no TB drugs whatsoever. People are trying but the structure is clearly not working. The donors themselves, some of them are so committed to their idea of reform — their concept of reform, not the government's — that we have got a completely polarised community.

I would say that in the last few years we've seen a massive acceleration in the so-cial crisis. 50-60 per cent of the donors' money is going on palliative care and at the moment there is little money for anything else — almost no preventive health care. We have measles, cholera, anthrax and so on. Nobody realises that this government cannot project a way that it can deliver any services even if it had the money

By the end of the decade, Zambia's health system was in collapse. Although progress had been made in financial and health information systems, the reformers had neglected the delivery of basic services. These reversals were emblematic of broader trends in Sub-Saharan Africa (SSA) in the 1990s, and the moniker "the Lost Decade" was fitting.

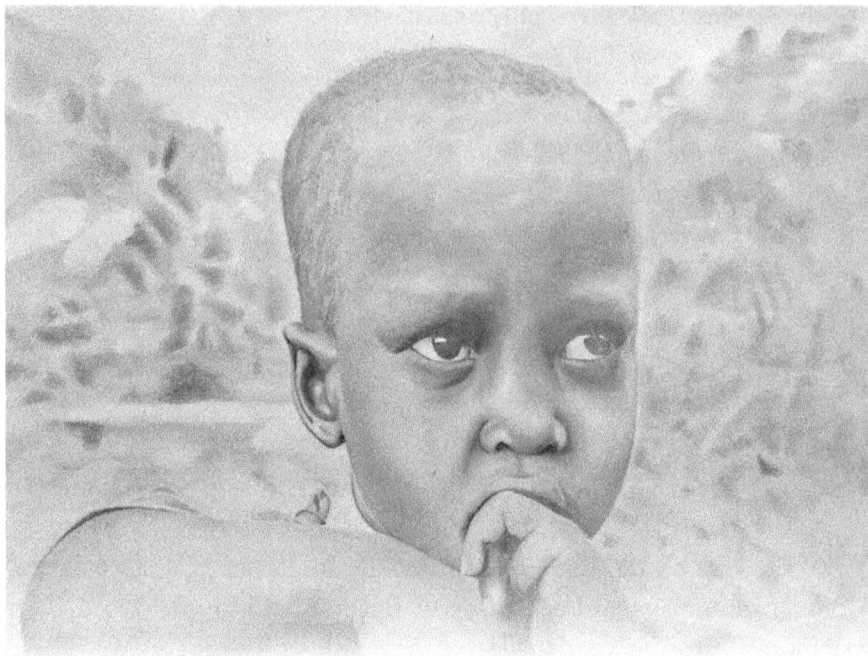

Zambian Child. Illustration: Samantha Simms, 2019.

Afterword

"Events are in the saddle and ride mankind"
- **Ralph Waldo Emerson**

It's late 2025, nearly 40 years since I first observed the HIV/AIDS pandemic sweeping across Africa, and 20 years before rich countries did much of anything—by which time 30 million people were dead or dying. Helen Epstein noted in *The New York Review of Books* a 2001 poll showing that only 7 percent of American evangelicals would contribute to a Christian organization to help AIDS orphans. This situation was redeemed in 2003 by George W. Bush's PEPFAR initiative. The ensuing work of USAID and its African partners saved the lives of more than 25 million people. And now in 2025 you have returned to the state I first found you (and for the same reasons) - this time shutting down UNAIDS, upending its people and programs, and with the full knowledge that the lives of millions are at stake. When Elon Musk said, "I could have gone to a party, but instead we spent the weekend putting USAID in the woodchipper," he exemplified the dehumanization that serves as a mental loophole, allowing you to ignore those you committed to help.

Today, the the greater danger is that NRx ideas are spreading around the world like a contagion, and this is to the detriment of global and planetary health. For example, in August 2025, EPA Director Lee Zeldin announcement that the EPA would revoke its own ability to combat the climate crisis by abandoning the "endangerment principle" – the landmark scientific finding that empowers government to regulate greenhouse gas emissions. He claimed that the costs of addressing the climate crisis outweigh the benefits. This decision is significant blow to global efforts to tackle the climate crisis, and other countries are now following suit.

This collection is about "social murder" and crimes against humanity. To many scientists around the world Zeldin's actions constitute "ecocide" - defined as "unlawful or wanton acts committed with knowledge that there is a substantial likelihood of severe and widespread or long-term damage to the environment being caused by those acts". Many argue that such acts should be classified as "crimes against humanity". Though not yet recognized as a crime, these actions may ultimately lead to legitimate accusations of social murder.

I conclude this collection by returning to the words of Barbara Tuchman in *The March of Folly*, where she observed—and warned- that "a phenomenon noticeable throughout history regardless of place or period is the pursuit by governments of policies contrary to their own interests." The worry is that, just as US democracy is too weak to stop Trump, democracies around the world may be too weak to stop the United States.

About The Author

Dr. Chris Simms has taught at Dalhousie University, Faculty of Health, School of Health Administration since 2006. He has lived and worked in many countries including the Philippines, Indonesia, Sri Lanka, Senegal, Tanzania, Zambia, Kenya, South Africa, Madagascar and Peru. He has studied at Dalhousie University, the Johns Hopkins School of Public Health, Harvard School of Public Health and the University of Sussex. He has contributed to international health on various boards including the International Journal of Clinical Practice.

He has two children and lives in Halifax, Nova Scotia.

Appendix 1

To: Christopher Simms
Thu 11/30/2006 5:05 PM

Dear Christopher,

After reading the report "Mortality after the 2003 invasion of Iraq: a cross-sectional cluster sample survey" by Burnham et al., I have the following comments.

The survey, the analysis and the report seem to be well done, except for some points. First, the sampling procedure used could lead to some bias, in some areas to overestimate and others to underestimate mortality. In particular, the random selection of residential streets off of a selected main road and of dwellings along that street is done at the same time as the interviewing and by the same team. On the one hand, it is possible that the interviewers would not want to venture too far from the main road, and dwellings nearer main roads may be more likely to suffer violence-related mortality. On the other hand, areas where violence continues and thought to be dangerous may be omitted leading to an undercount. Moreover, dwellings may be vacant if all members perished or have migrated outside Iraq, also leading to an undercount since there is no one left to report the deaths. It is understandable, however, that it may have been too dangerous to list all dwellings in the administrative units selected in the second stage, select the dwellings to be interviewed (not necessarily adjacent to one another), and return to the area to interview the selected dwellings. Of course, there may also be response bias if households are reluctant to report a death if the person was involved in the insurgency or may report deaths to relatives but who did not live in the household during the time period (leading to a potential for double counting). Since a death certificate was available for most of the deaths, the double counting is less likely to have occurred.

A second point has to do with the sample size. Indeed only 47 clusters with 1849 households were interviewed. The confidence intervals are quite large due to the small sample size and give estimates that can vary by 100% between the top and bottom of the interval. Indeed, the confidence intervals overlap for the periods May 04 –May 05 and June 05June 06, which means that one cannot conclude that there was a change in mortality between the two periods. Because of the small number of clusters, I think the analysis by province should not have been presented (only Baghdad has enough to present).

I do not find much fault with the analysis. Using the report's figures for deaths and exposure, I estimate just about the same number of deaths and confidence intervals. Indeed the estimate that I produce using UN projections is slightly higher.

Technical Director
ORC Macro
11785 Beltsville Drive
Calverton, MD 20705

Gilbert M. Burnham <gburnha1@jhu.edu>
Mon 2023-03-20 9:57 PM

Dear Chris,

Thanks for your note, which catches me on the road, without my written notes. The memory is a bit vague on some areas. Here some points from the memory:

We accepted that sampling would be potentially a problem. Many areas had some reasonable local estimates of population, but not all, and population movement impact was based on local knowledge and estimates. Iraq's last national census was 1987. In each area we engaged a local colleague familiar with the area to help in the sampling. Known to the community he or she also gave the teams a sense of security and help in negotiations for access where needed. In all unstable areas (including Afghanistan, Yemen and Syria) our policy is to finish one cluster in one day, and never to come back. Returning to the same area on a second day runs personal risks up to a level unacceptable to the interview teams. We realize this may introduce some bias. To lessen potential biases on residential street, we first counted all the houses on that street, and selected a random house to start. There was an erroneous belief that most death were from bombs or explosions, which gave rise to some people believing that there was more violence close to main streets. Gunshots turned out to be the most common causes of death. In a subsequent study we found that on average deaths occurred 1.7km from the place of residence. We kept an informal tally of destroyed or empty houses, which in most places was not high. It was a big problem in a couple of places, especially in Fallujah. Anticipating this, we oversampled Fallujah, and in one of the three clusters the teams estimated that one third of households were destroyed or damaged to the point that they were vacant. For our analysis we randomly chose one of the 3 Fallujah clusters, which turned out to be the lowest mortality cluster. Our statistician colleagues criticized use later saying we should have averaged numbers—never through away data was their moto. In our Mosul study we kept careful tally of the destroyed or empty houses, but never used the data in analysis for Mosul, as no one could estimate to the nearest million the number of people in the city at the time of the survey. In Mosul we used GPS geolocations, with their own biases.

We accept that some HHs may have not reported deaths related to insurgent activities, and indeed listed that as a study limitation. That would have in any case biased the deaths downward.

Since the violence would come and go in some areas, we found that we could return to some selected clusters later that had been originally redlined as unsafe. We always let the field teams decide on safety issues. My goal had been 100 clusters, but in extensive negotiations with the data collectors, 47 clusters was the maximum number they would accept for personal safety reasons—so that's where the number came from, and we recognized that this would give wide confidence intervals. The distribution of deaths among governates was widely confirmed by Iraqis conversant with the conflict. So although statistical comparisons were not that strong, it was consistent with local opinion.

Communication during the study and analysis was difficult, and there were some procedures on the ground that should have been tightened up...The interview team did an amazing job, some spending nights in jail and being threatened for their life while doing the data collection. Afterwards, of course there were many threats and accusations against all of us. My Iraqi colleague had threats against his life and dropped out of sight for a while. His teenage son was involved in some mysterious setup event that resulted in him spending a year in prison. My colleague had to sell his mother's house and use the proceeds to buy off a longer sentence.

Writing the paper was in itself a challenge, with the analysis being done in Baltimore, input difficult through poor phone connections from Iraq, and I was trying to do much of the writing while in Afghanistan. Would we have the courage to do this again? Not really sure.

Best wishes,

Gilbert

www.ingramcontent.com/pod-product-compliance
Lightning Source LLC
Chambersburg PA
CBHW031140020426
42333CB00013B/458